THE CHARM OF WISE HESITANCY

Talmudic Stories in Contemporary Israeli Culture

ACADEMIC STUDIES PRESS

THE CHARM OF WISE HESITANCY

Talmudic Stories in Contemporary Israeli Culture

DAVID C. JACOBSON

Library of Congress Cataloging-in-Publication Data

Names: Jacobson, David C., 1947- author.

Title: The charm of wise hesitancy: Talmudic stories in contemporary Israeli culture / David C. Jacobson.

Description: Brighton, MA: Academic Studies Press, 2017.

Series: Israel: Society, Culture and History

Identifiers: LCCN 2016042036 (print) | LCCN 2016042919 (ebook) | ISBN 9781618115546 (hardcover) | ISBN 9781618115553 (e-book)

Subjects: LCSH: Aggada. | Secularism—Israel. | Orthodox Judaism—Israel—Relations—Nontraditional Jews.

Classification: LCC BM516.5 .J335 2017 (print) | LCC BM516.5 (ebook) | DDC 296.1/9—dc23

LC record available at https://lccn.loc.gov/2016042036

ISBN 978-1-61811-788-5 (paperback)
ISBN 978-1-61811-555-3 (electronic)

Book design by Kryon Publishing
www.kryonpublishing.com

On the cover: "Walk along the Ancient Safed," by Shimon Bar/Sutterstock
Cover design by Jen Stacey

Published by Academic Studies Press in 2017, paperback 2018.
28 Montfern Avenue
Brighton, MA 02135, USA
press@academicstudiespress.com
www.academicstudiespress.com

In memory of my good friends
Bob Liberles and Josh Stein

CONTENTS

A NOTE ON TRANSLATION AND TRANSLITERATION

Unless otherwise indicated, all translations from Hebrew and Aramaic are mine. In preparing the translations of biblical and rabbinic texts, I have consulted published translations of these texts and translations of them quoted in books and articles by writers to whom I refer throughout the book.

The transliteration of Hebrew and Aramaic is based on the "general" transliteration style for Hebrew of *Encyclopaedia Judaica*, 2nd Edition, edited by Michael Berenbaum and Fred Skolnik (Detroit: Macmillan Reference USA, 2007), with some modifications. Some words are spelled according to common usage in English, even when the spelling differs from the *Encyclopaedia Judaica* transliteration style.

PREFACE

Political revolutions and movements of cultural renewal are often guided by a master narrative according to which the problems of the present can be solved by returning to the lost vitality of a golden age. According to the Zionist narrative embraced by the movement's secular majority, rabbinic Judaism, which had dominated Diaspora Jewish life for nearly two thousand years, played a central role in the problematic existence of Jews in their day. Secular Zionists viewed the Talmud and other rabbinic texts, including collections of Midrash and codes of Jewish law, as the source of the negative qualities of Diaspora existence that needed to be removed from Jewish life. To a large extent, Zionists looked to the Bible, which so vividly captured the glorious national past of the Jews, as a source of inspiration from their cultural heritage. The Zionist dream envisioned the physical return of Jews to their ancient homeland, the Land of Israel, and their reconnection with the vitality of their biblical past in that Land. Given the negative view of rabbinic Judaism held by secular Zionists, it is not surprising that from the period of Zionist settlement in the Land of Israel through the first decades following the establishment of the State of Israel in 1948, the voluminous post-biblical literature produced by rabbis, while not completely ignored, played a relatively marginal role in the curriculum of secular schools attended by most Jewish children as well as in broader cultural discourse.

Ideologies based on a rejection of one's contemporary existence and the yearning for a radical renewal of a glorious past do not always survive over time. Once the rejected features of existence have been defeated, it is not uncommon for members of later generations to wonder why their parents or grandparents were so adamant in turning against what had once been viewed as valid. This is what began to happen in Israel in the 1960s, following the fulfillment of the Zionist dream when the State of Israel was established. At this time, some members of the new generation of secular Israelis found the Zionist narrative of rebellion against rabbinic Judaism and a return to the Bible to be inadequate and sought to reconsider rabbinic literature and other post-biblical traditional Jewish texts as possible resources to guide them in their lives.

This newly emergent dissatisfaction with the anti-rabbinic bias of the Zionist narrative had a number of causes. It can be explained in part by the natural tendency of a new generation to question the ideology of their parents. Such questioning can be particularly acute when the younger generation's historical circumstances differ radically from those of the older generation. In this case, those who questioned the anti-rabbinic bias of Zionism largely belonged to the first generation of Jews born in the Land of Israel. Having lived only in the Land of Israel, they did not have the need felt by the previous generation to actively rebel against a Diaspora existence dominated by rabbinic Judaism, and they therefore could afford to develop a more open-minded attitude toward the rabbis. Furthermore, this new generation had grown into adulthood during a period in which Israel was continuously under existential threat from the Arab countries that surrounded it and had witnessed a tremendous loss of life in wars fought with its Arab enemies. The anxieties and tensions this generation had experienced in living through this period inevitably called into question the secure national rebirth that Zionism had purported to deliver to the Jewish people. The experience of feeling existentially vulnerable opened up members of this generation to an appreciation of how rabbinic Judaism had dealt with the political uncertainties of Jewish life after the destruction of the Second Temple in 70 CE. The interest in connecting with rabbinic Judaism was also motivated by the realization that those who reject a part of their past impoverish their souls and deny themselves valuable cultural resources.

What began as a reaction to the anti-rabbinic bias of secular Zionism in the 1960s persisted throughout the subsequent decades of the twentieth century and has continued to be a factor in Israeli culture to the present day. The title of this book, *The Charm of Wise Hesitancy*, is taken from a 1999 essay by Ruth Calderon, one of the important leaders of the rediscovery of post-biblical Judaism in Israel in recent decades. In that essay, Calderon wrote that she was motivated to participate in this cultural trend after she came to question the marginalization of the post-biblical textual tradition in her education in secular schools. Her shift, and that of others of her generation, to a more positive attitude toward this tradition was the product of their realization that secular Zionism had unfairly condemned rabbinic Judaism as the source of the very qualities and values of Diaspora Jewish life against which

Zionism had rebelled. "We knew," she wrote in a rather sarcastic tone, "that the Talmud was distanced from us and we were distanced from it so that we would not catch the 'viruses' of the 'non-productive' and 'pale' Diaspora Jews."[1]

Furthermore, she and other members of her generation had difficulty identifying with the heroic Zionist culture that had been presented to them as the antidote to Diaspora life. No longer worried about being pulled into aspects of Diaspora culture and no longer enamored of the alternative Zionist culture in which they were educated, they were open to seeing that which was positive in the rabbinic culture central to the Jewish Diaspora existence that had been so denigrated by their educators: "We met for the first time new kinds of role models: alongside the hero of the Six-Day War who 'did not hesitate for a moment,' alongside heroes of 1948 … and their eternal youth, we met old heroes, sitting on the benches of the study house. Like the grandfathers we never had. By means of them were uncovered the charm of wise hesitancy, of a Diaspora liberated from the bounds of provincialism and religiosity. The virtual reality of the Talmud became for us a ready-made option."[2]

Parallel to the positive reappraisal of rabbinic literature by secular Israelis, some religious Israelis have undertaken a positive reappraisal of legendary texts belonging to the genre of rabbinic literature known as *aggadah*, a genre which had been largely marginalized at the highest level of text study in yeshivot and therefore had been of lower cultural status than legal texts belonging to the genre of rabbinic literature known as *halakhah*. Just as secular Israelis began to realize how much they were missing by not engaging in rabbinic literature in general, these religious Israelis began to realize how much they were missing by not engaging in any serious way with rabbinic legendary texts. In response, they sought to revive the dialogic relationship between *halakhah* and *aggadah* that had come to be abandoned in previous generations. In doing so, they discovered a new way to deepen their understanding of the religious truths embodied in traditional Jewish texts.

The turn of religious Israelis to *aggadah* and the turn of secular Israelis to post-biblical literature, with a focus on *aggadah*, has led to a shared interest in the positive reevaluation of rabbinic legendary texts. A sub-genre of *aggadah* in which both religious and secular Israelis have been engaged is that of what has come to be known as Talmudic stories, which tell of the life and times of the sages who established and developed rabbinic culture in the Land of Israel and Babylonia before, during, and following the period of the destruction of the Second Temple.

The idea to write a book about the resurgence of interest in Talmudic stories began in the bookstores of Jerusalem that I frequent every time I visit Israel. Beginning in the early 2000s, I noticed a number of recently published books that were anthologies of Talmudic stories. My own previous books have been about the relationship of modern Hebrew belles-lettres (primarily Israeli poetry) to the Bible, post-biblical Jewish texts, and traditional Jewish religious experience.[3] It occurred to me that what the authors of these anthologies of Talmudic stories were attempting to do was similar to what the writers I had studied in my previous scholarship had aspired to accomplish. Both sets of writers sought ways to bridge the gap between traditional texts and contemporary consciousness. The writers of fiction and poetry, about whom I had written, did this by turning to the Bible and other traditional Jewish sources with the purpose of creating versions of these texts that reflected contemporary concerns; the authors of the books I was now discovering were collecting and writing interpretations of Talmudic stories that reflected contemporary concerns. The genre was different, but the cultural impulse was the same.

In addition, a central theme of my scholarship has been the breakdown of the barriers between religious and secular culture in Israel in recent decades. I have written on secular Israelis engaging with classical religious texts and exploring the nature of religious experience, and I have written on religious Israelis adopting literary genres developed primarily by secular writers and exploring themes found in secular literature that had once been taboo in religious culture. I was therefore delighted to discover another manifestation of the convergence of the interests of religious and secular Israelis as they came to appreciate the relevance of a genre of rabbinic literature that both, for different reasons, had once ignored.

I have set for myself two primary goals in writing this book. I have sought to convey to readers an understanding of the growing interest among Israelis in the study of Talmudic stories in the latter half of the twentieth century and the beginning of the twenty-first century. I have also aspired to present a wide range of contemporary Israeli interpretations of selected Talmudic stories. To my knowledge, no one has attempted to present such an overall picture of the reinterpretation of Talmudic stories in Israel today. In presenting these interpretations, it is my hope that readers will learn about how these readings have been shaped by contemporary Israeli concerns and also how they themselves might read these stories in light of their own experiences.

In anticipation of questions about terminology that may arise in the minds of readers, I offer two points of clarification. First, I use the term "Talmudic stories" to refer to legends about rabbis of the periods in which the Mishnah and Talmud were developed in the Land of Israel and in Babylonia. This genre is often referred to as *ma'asei ḥakhamim* ("sage legends"). Not all sage legends were published in the Talmud; some appear only in collections of rabbinic Midrash. Nevertheless, since the Talmud is such a vast repository of these stories, they are often referred to as "Talmudic stories," and I have adopted that practice. In fact, almost all of the stories on which I focus in this book are from the Talmud.

Second, any sophisticated analysis of Israeli culture will recognize the inaccuracy of the view held by many Israeli Jews that they can be neatly divided into two categories based on their relationship to the Jewish tradition: *dati* (religious) and *ḥiloni* (secular). There are many so-called *dati* Israelis who participate actively in secular society and culture, and there are many so-called *ḥiloni* Israelis for whom religious faith and at least some traditional ritual practice are central to their lives. In this study, I have made use of these terms when I have sought to distinguish between Israelis who in principle accept the authority of the system of traditional Jewish law (for whom I use the term "religious") and Israelis who do not (for whom I use the term "secular").

I would like to acknowledge the following people who generously agreed to meet with me and provide insights into the resurgence of interest in Talmudic stories in Israel and the larger contexts of the secular return to the study of post-biblical Jewish texts and the religious turn to the study of legendary texts: Ronen Ahituv, Mordechai Bar-Or, Yehuda Brandes, Ruth Calderon, Dov Elbaum, Ari Elon, Shmuel Faust, Shlomo Glicksberg, Micah Goodman, Ido Hevroni, Admiel Kosman, Chani Kroyzer, Binyanim Lau, Yehoshua Levinson, Yehudah Mirsky, Nira Nahliel, Inbar Raveh, Tsafi Sebba-Elran, Naama Shaked, Avigdor Shinan, Amram Tropper, Ruhama Weiss, Oded Yisraeli, Anat Yisraeli-Taran, and Be'eri Zimmerman. In particular, I want to express my gratitude to Tsafi Sebba-Elran, whose comments on the manuscript have been invaluable. I also thank Brown University for a sabbatical in the academic year 2012-2013, during which I was able to make substantial progress in my research and in writing this book. In addition, I am grateful to the Program in Judaic Studies and the Brown University Faculty Travel Fund for financial support that enabled me to undertake research travel to Israel. Finally, I want to express my love for my wife Shelly and my deep gratitude for our steadfast commitment to living as mutually supportive partners in the beautiful life we share.

INTRODUCTION

RECOVERING A REPRESSED PAST

On February 12, 2013, Ruth Calderon was invited to the dais of the Israeli Knesset to deliver her first speech as a newly-elected member of parliament.[1] The speech was unlike any given in the history of deliberations in Israel's legislature in that it consisted primarily of her reading and interpreting a Talmudic story. The Talmudic story that Calderon read before the Knesset, first in the original Aramaic and then in Hebrew translation, was, as is typical of these stories, very brief:

> Rabbi Rahumi studied under Rava in Mehoza. He would regularly come home to his wife on the eve of Yom Kippur. One day [on the eve of Yom Kippur] the topic [he was studying] drew him in. His wife anticipated him, "He is coming. He is coming." He did not come. She began to grieve. She shed a tear from her eye. He was sitting on a roof. The roof collapsed under him, and he died. (B. Ketubot 62b)[2]

The story reflects what appears to have been a common practice among rabbinic scholars in Babylonia: to absent themselves from home for long periods of time to study Torah. The author of the story expresses his disapproval of this custom by portraying empathically the emotional stress experienced by Rabbi Rahumi's wife when he was so engaged in Torah study that he forgot to return home for the sacred holiday. The excitement captured in her cry of anticipation, "He is coming. He is coming," dissipated when she realized he had failed to appear. The tear that she shed in response to her profound disappointment was followed immediately by Rabbi Rahumi's death when the roof on which he was sitting collapsed, thereby suggesting that in the end he received a well-deserved divine punishment for being so immersed in Torah that he abandoned his wife.

Why, one might ask, would a secular Israeli politician devote her first parliamentary speech to reading and interpreting a selection from the Talmud, a compendium of rabbinic teachings that is at the center of religious Jewish study in yeshivot, but largely ignored by secular Israelis? Furthermore, how could a story critical of a husband who has neglected his wife hundreds of years ago possibly be relevant to the political discourse of Israel's parliament?

In her speech, Calderon signaled to her fellow parliamentarians and to Israelis as a whole that the Talmud was no longer just for religious Israelis and that as a secular Israeli, she advocated studying it outside the confines of the yeshiva. She also made clear that she believed that the Talmud was a relevant source to which one could turn to find solutions to the issues faced by contemporary Israelis. In particular, in her speech she declared that this text could serve as the basis for a discussion of one of the burning political issues of the day: whether the military draft exemption of ultra-Orthodox yeshiva students, dating back to the early years of the State of Israel, should be eliminated or at least modified.

The drafting of ultra-Orthodox yeshiva students had been one of the central political issues during and in the immediate aftermath of the recent election, due largely to two factors: (1) Before the election the Israeli Supreme Court had struck down the yeshiva draft exemption law, which meant that the Knesset was obligated to replace it with a law that did not grant such an exemption. (2) For the first time in many years, no ultra-Orthodox party was included in the governing coalition. Therefore, there was a high likelihood that a new law passed by the Knesset would define the obligation of ultra-Orthodox youths to serve their country in a way that would infuriate that segment of society. The dominant ultra-Orthodox leaders were determined to fight to preserve the draft exemption. Their fierce opposition to eliminating the exemption was due largely to the fact that the ultra-Orthodox feared that if their youths were engaged in either military or civilian national service, they would be exposed to a larger cultural world that might alienate them from the ultra-Orthodox way of life in which they were raised.

Calderon had just been elected to parliament as a member of the Yesh Atid (There is a Future) party, headed by Yair Lapid, which had campaigned on a platform opposed to the fact that ultra-Orthodox Israeli men were allowed by law to engage in extended periods of time studying in yeshiva rather than submit to compulsory military service. Israelis of a wide range of political orientations opposed this draft exemption, because it resulted in a high percentage of ultra-Orthodox Israeli men not sharing equally with other Israelis in the responsibility of defending their country. Opponents of the draft exemption also disapproved of the fact that in their full-time yeshiva study, these ultra-Orthodox men did not typically learn skills that would make them employable citizens, causing them and their families to become unnecessarily dependent on government welfare throughout their lives. As Calderon explained in her interpretation of the story, Rabbi Rahumi represents for her the typical ultra-Orthodox Israeli man who, in choosing to devote his entire life to studying Torah, neglects his other human obligations. In the case of Rabbi Rahumi, the neglected party is his wife; in the case of the ultra-Orthodox Israelis, the neglected obligation is military or at least civilian national service and contributing to Israel's economy.

Despite the association she suggested between the story's critique of Rabbi Rahumi and the negative image of the ultra-Orthodox found in Yesh Atid's campaign rhetoric, Calderon was careful not to make use of the story in her speech to excessively fan the flames of political controversy. She magnanimously declared that she learned from the story "that often, in a dispute, both sides are right."[3] In her reading of the story, both secular Israelis, represented by the wife, and ultra-Orthodox Israelis, represented by Rabbi Rahumi, could be seen as justified when they asserted the value of their way of life and criticized the way of life of their political opponents: "Many times we [secularists] feel like the woman, waiting, serving in the army, doing all the work while others [the ultra-Orthodox] sit on the roof and study Torah; sometimes those others [the ultra-Orthodox] feel that they bear the entire weight of tradition, culture, and Torah on their backs while we [secularists] go to the beach and have fun."[4] It is only when she could come to appreciate the point of view of both sides, she declared, that she would be able to contribute to finding a solution to this much debated political issue.

Calderon then went on to advocate an alternative to the existing dichotomy between ultra-Orthodox Israelis spending their time studying Torah and not serving in the army and secular Israelis serving in the army and neglecting the study of Torah. In her ideal world, the ultra-Orthodox would fulfill some form of national service and the secularists would engage in the study of Torah. "I aspire," she announced, "to bring about a situation in which Torah study is the heritage of all of Israel … in which all young citizens of Israel assume the responsibility of both

Torah study and military and civilian national service."[5] In addition to the obvious implication of this statement that she favored a law that would draft ultra-Orthodox young men into the army or some form of civilian national service, she stated explicitly that she would work for financial support from the government for Torah study by secular Israelis equal to that provided to religious Israelis who study in yeshivot.

Calderon's speech evoked a number of strong reactions from Israelis along the political and cultural spectrum. Many responded enthusiastically to this Talmud lesson by a secular Israeli, which publicly broke down the barriers between secularism and religiosity that have dominated Israeli culture for so long. Others, particularly those on the two cultural extremes of ultra-Orthodoxy and secularism, were taken aback by this highly unconventional speech; it confirmed their political anxieties evoked by the establishment of the new government coalition led by Binyamin Netanyahu, of which Yesh Atid became a member in early 2013.

In an article in "Kikar Shabbat," an ultra-Orthodox web site, Yaakov Blau wrote that he believed that Calderon's speech revealed a strong connection between her party's support for proposals to draft ultra-Orthodox men and her encouragement of Torah study from a secular perspective, both of which presented dangers to the future of the ultra-Orthodox way of life.[6] Blau argued that the speech represented a contemporary revival in Israel of the efforts of the modernizing, anti-traditional, late eighteenth and nineteenth-century European Jewish movement known as the Haskalah to destroy traditional Judaism. This new Haskalah, in his opinion, is more dangerous than the original one. It had been clear in its day that the older Haskalah was determined to undermine the authority of the Torah and encourage Jews to assimilate into gentile society, asserted Blau, and so one could understand it as an enemy force to be resisted. While the newer Haskalah is also an enemy of tradition, Blau maintained that it presents itself more ambiguously than the older Haskalah did, and thereby deceives people about its true purpose, causing them to let down their guard. "[It] is not at all like the Jewish Haskalah in Europe," argued Blau, "it understands religious faith and does not reject it out of hand. … [It] does not want to transform us into a nation like all the nations. On the contrary, [it] wants to increase Torah study."[7] From Blau's point of view, however, this newer Haskalah resembles the older Haskalah in one way. Just as the older Haskalah resorted to the deceptive use of rabbinical figures (presumably here Blau includes not only Haskalah-oriented traditional rabbis but also rabbis identified with Reform Judaism) to seduce Jews away from tradition, so the newer Haskalah makes use of the secular Talmud teacher Calderon (whom he mockingly refers to as a "woman rabbi," which she is not) and two other Yesh Atid members of Knesset, the religious Zionist Rabbi Shai Piron and the ultra-Orthodox Rabbi Dov Lipman, as "fig leaves who use our weapons [i.e. sacred rabbinic texts] ... against us."[8]

On the other end of the political spectrum, secular left-wing journalist Uri Misgav felt threatened by Calderon's speech for a different reason.[9] For him, the speech confirmed the dangers inherent in the joint participation in the government coalition by the Yesh Atid party, led by Yair Lapid, and the religious Zionist Habayit Heyehudi (The Jewish Home) party, led by Naftali Bennett. Misgav argued in an opinion column in the daily newspaper *Haaretz* that it is likely, due to this political cooperation between the two parties, that Yair Lapid will sell out the political principles that are so important to his secular supporters. Indeed, he maintained, a significant sign of this selling out can be discerned in Ruth Calderon's speech. The speech, he declared, followed the typical pattern of alliances between the secular and the religious, which he believed always involved the self-denigration of the secular and the compromising of their principles to satisfy the religious. He sarcastically critiqued the "excited song of praise sung with a trembling voice ... [and] the bending of knees" in submission to the values of the religious that he discerned in Calderon's speech.[10]

Misgav then went on to refer to a famous 1952 meeting between a leading ultra-Orthodox rabbi Avraham Yeshayahu Karelitz, known as the Hazon Ish, and then Prime Minister David Ben-Gurion. At this meeting, it was reported, the Hazon Ish had insisted that secular Israelis would have to accommodate the needs of religiously observant Israelis, for just as when a full wagon (which to him represented the religious culture) and an empty wagon (which to him represented the secular culture) meet on the road, the empty wagon should give way to the full wagon. Calderon's speech, in Misgav's opinion, demonstrated the degree to which she agreed with the Hazon Ish's position that secular cultural is "empty," in the sense of worthless, and that religious culture is "full," in the sense of containing much meaning and significance: "Once again the empty wagon accompanied by self-denigration and feelings of inferiority. ... Calderon went up on the stage with a book of the Talmud, devoted her speech to a Talmud lesson, and finished it with a prayer."[11] Even Yair Lapid, the leader of Calderon's party, he noted, indicated his willingness to sell out secularism when he "declared recently that his dream is that every child in Israel would learn a page of Talmud along with mathematics."[12]

When it comes to compromise between the religious and the secular, complained Misgav, "[t]here is not and never is symmetry."[13] All attempts at reconciliation between these two cultural orientations, he declared, inevitably end up with the secularists compromising their values, while the religious refuse to compromise theirs. In this speech, he noted, Ruth Calderon had read a selection from a classic work of traditional Jewish religious literature, but he was certain that no religious member of the Knesset would ever read in public from the writings of secular Israeli authors or quote the fiercely anti-religious politician Shulamit Aloni.

It is not surprising that Calderon's attempt to bring together elements of the two extremes of ultra-Orthodoxy and secularism so enraged members of both camps. Political extremes tend to be more comfortable with well-defined positions that clearly distinguish them from those on the opposite end of the political spectrum. They have a vested interest in asserting the purity of their positions, and they feel threatened by the possibility that elements of the opposite position might contaminate their world. Ultra-Orthodox Israelis see themselves as the keepers of the Talmud, and they feel that only the ultra-Orthodox can be trusted to prevent it from being undermined. Secular Israelis see themselves as the keepers of democracy, and they do not trust anyone who studies Talmud to preserve the integrity of Israel's democratic political system. A person such as Ruth Calderon, who seeks to build bridges between the two camps, blurs important differences between them and, from the perspective of extremists, makes it more possible for the other side to take power. From an ultra-Orthodox perspective her speech could contribute to the pulling of ultra-Orthodox young men away from traditional faith and practice, and from a secular perspective her speech could contribute to Israel becoming a society dominated by traditional Jewish faith rather than by democratic values.

The Return to the Jewish Bookcase

Ruth Calderon's controversial speech was not simply the idiosyncratic expression of an individual out of step with accepted political and cultural categories. She spoke as one of the leaders of a cultural trend that has been developing in Israel over the past five decades. This trend, which has come to be known as "the return to the Jewish bookcase" (*haḥazarah la'aron hasefarim hayehudi*), has consisted of secular Israeli Jews rediscovering the treasures of the post-biblical Jewish textual tradition that had played only a marginal role in the secular Israeli school curriculum as well as in secular Israeli culture as a whole. I describe this tradition as playing a "marginal role" in secular Israeli education and culture due to the fact that the post-biblical Jewish textual tradition was never fully absent from either the secular Israeli school system or the cultural consciousness of Israeli society. Even Prime Minister David Ben-Gurion, a vocal champion of the secular Zionist rejection of post-biblical Judaism and Diaspora Jewish life, came to see that the lack of an awareness of the entire span of Jewish history in secular Israeli youth was problematic. In 1955, he charged Zalman Aran, the Minister of Education, to develop a Jewish consciousness curriculum for the secular school system. Over the years, various attempts were made to increase the teaching of post-biblical Jewish texts in secular schools. Such efforts, however, never succeeded in fully overcoming the marginalization of the post-biblical textual tradition in secular Israeli culture.[14]

The return to the Jewish bookcase as a significant cultural phenomenon can be said to have begun in the early 1960s, led by a group of secular Israeli kibbutz intellectuals constituting themselves as "Ḥug Shedemot." The name of the group signified their association with the journal *Shedemot* (originally *Shedemot lamadrikh*), which was established at that time. Among the most notable early members were Avraham (Patchi) Shapira, founding editor of *Shedemot*, Muki Tsur, and Yariv Ben-Aharon.[15] Members of this group, who belonged to the second generation of kibbutz members, along with others of their contemporaries, experienced a discomfort with the kibbutz ideology of the generation that had founded the kibbutz movement. Gad Ofaz makes the point that this younger generation's challenge to established kibbutz ideology took place in the context of a perceived decline in the viability of the kibbutz ideology at the time that this second generation was emerging into adulthood: "Many of the beliefs that motivated and sustained the generation of the pioneers collapsed, along with [ideological] struggles and splits. Youths of the second generation felt more and more that a different spiritual basis was needed" to maintain the viability of the kibbutz movement.[16]

At the same time, to the extent that the first generation had been able to maintain the influence of kibbutz ideology, the members of the second generation resisted its imposition on their lives. As Alon Gan observes, their resistance followed a pattern that is often repeated in the relationship between revolutionaries and their offspring. "The generation of the parents," writes Gan, "lived the transition from the dream (the utopian vision) to the reality [of the kibbutz] and sought to preserve it by means of ideology. Individuals in the next generation sought to conduct a reverse process from that of their parents: the parents turned utopia into ideology [and] their children sought to break open the lock that preserved the ideology and to form for themselves dreams (utopian visions) of their own.... they began a journey in search of new dreams."[17]

As Gad Ofaz observes, one of the central elements of kibbutz ideology challenged by members of the second generation was the rejection of the Diaspora Jewish religious culture and the determination to replace it with a culture in which the main role model was that of a "new Jew, muscle-bound working his land and defending it."[18] Ofaz explains that the younger generation came to question the anxiety that their parents had felt, which drove them to an extreme hostility toward Diaspora culture: "[The older generation] had a feeling that the Disapora and its religious culture was lurking, as it were, in the corner like a trap for the weak, the less determined, and the overly sensitive."[19] This rejection of Diaspora religious Jewish culture, writes Ofaz, had a significant effect on the curriculum of secular kibbutz schools. While the Bible, with which they felt an affinity, was taught, "[t]he teaching of Jewish history was cut off at the Bar Kokhba rebellion [in 132-135 CE], and then picked up anew with the emergence of the early Zionists. Thus, the oral Torah [of rabbinic Judaism] was omitted from the curriculum."[20]

Some members of the second generation of kibbutzniks, argues Ofaz, came to believe that this selective, Bible-centered approach to the Jewish cultural heritage left them without the kinds of resources they needed to help them meet the ongoing existential challenges of the immediate pre-State period and of the early years of the State. "The years in which the native-born sons [of the second generation] grew up did not spare them trying moments," writes Ofaz.[21] "From the time that the first sons born in the kibbutzim grew up, until today, Israel has never experienced calm or peace. Its sons have found themselves in the constant tension of struggling for their very existence."[22] A culture that limited itself to the Bible as its main source did not, Ofaz argues, provide them with the resources to face these existential challenges: "The giving up of all the cultural assets that were collected during thousands of years of challenges in which the people of Israel persisted meant that [this generation had to] stand and come to terms [with its existence] completely naked [in a spiritual sense]."[23] One of the most important potential roles of the post-biblical tradition for members of this new generation was that it could provide a conceptual framework in which to grant meaning to the self-sacrifice to which they were called in the defense of their country. Members of this younger generation, writes Ofaz, "who were aroused to ask about the meaning of national existence and its value in relationship to the life of the individual, were amazed at the strength of persistence that drove the people of Israel during the generations."[24] Ofaz quotes Eli Alon, a kibbutz poet of that generation: "I feel a great hunger to contemplate the nature of this faith for which Jews were ready to die for the sake of the continuity of generations."[25] This is why, Alon has written, he felt driven to retrieve the wisdom of the Jewish tradition that had been excised from the secular education he and his peers received: "We are cut off from Judaism and from its answers . . . years of education to disparage the Diaspora have succeeded in severing us from it and from its culture in which we might perhaps have found an answer to our existential questions."[26]

In addition, for members of this second generation of kibbutzniks, the study of the entire history of Jewish sources was seen as a necessary process to achieve a much needed Jewish cultural renewal. As Yariv Ben-Aharon puts it, "If you want to be who you are, you want to renew life from within, and you want to reveal the hidden forces of inner renewal . . . you cannot dismiss the heritage of the past. You have to come to terms with it. You have to draw from it. You have to create from within it."[27]

Alon Gan points out that initially, Ḥug Shedemot played a marginal role in kibbutz society, advocating rebellious ideas that were subversive of the cultural status quo. "*Shedemot* and the group that solidified around it," observes Gan, "were like secret agents who undermined the behavior code of native-born Israelis, while seeking ways to form a spiritual identity that would be an alternative to that of the generation of the fathers."[28] As Gan sees it, the tense period leading up to the Six-Day War in 1967 and Israel's sweeping victory in that war opened up many more second-generation kibbutzniks to seeking the kinds of alternative cultural paths advocated by Ḥug Shedemot. This became very evident, Gan notes, when members of Ḥug Shedemot engaged in a project to interview young kibbutz members who had fought in the Six-Day War. Transcripts of these interviews were published in a book titled *Siaḥ loḥamim* (*Discourse of the Warriors*), which was widely read at that time.[29] Muki Tsur observes that in the course of conducting these interviews, they discovered "a crisis and a spiritual turning point" in their generation, as demonstrated by the agonized responses to war of the soldiers with whom they met, which stood in stark contrast to the celebratory atmosphere that was dominating Israel at the time.[30] "The newspapers and victory volumes, the ecstatic hikes in the conquered territories, the euphoria that broke out after the deep fears during the period of waiting [before the war] were not compatible with what we revealed," writes Tsur about himself and the others who interviewed these soldiers.[31]

Much inspiration for Ḥug Shedemot's cultural revolution of return to post-biblical Jewish sources came from the writings of the Zionist intellectual leaders and writers of the early twentieth-century wave of immigration to the Land of Israel, known as the Second Aliyah, including Yosef Hayyim Brenner, Aharon David Gordon, and Berl Katznelson. It was the ongoing relationship of these figures to the Jewish tradition that provided a model for members of Ḥug Shedemot of how they could find a path to that cultural heritage. As Gad Ofaz observes, while it is true that these Second Aliyah figures rebelled against the religious Diaspora culture in which they were raised, their relationship to Jewish tradition was more nuanced than that of the generation immediately preceding that of Ḥug Shedemot.[32] When members of Ḥug Shedemot began to explore "the inner life of these [Second Aliyah] pioneers by means of their personal writings—diaries, letters, conversations—[they uncovered] the complexity of a push-pull relationship [with the Jewish tradition], a drive to cut themselves off combined with longings for the Diaspora home and its culture, study, prayer, [and] community relations."[33] Yariv Ben-Aharon recalls that he and his peers were taught only about the rebellion against tradition of these earlier ideological and cultural leaders. However, after he began to explore post-biblical Jewish texts, Ben-Aharon set out to challenge that mistaken notion and to assert that "these leading figures were experts in the language of the sources, made use of it, and depended on it."[34] Indeed, he recalls, he realized later in life that he had never fully understood their writings until he had studied the traditional sources to which they referred.

Muki Tsur has written that a key discovery of members of Ḥug Shedemot in their attempt to reconnect with post-biblical Jewish texts was that throughout Jewish history, each generation has reinterpreted past sources to make them relevant. This process, they came to realize, is central to rabbinic Midrash, but is also present in the "midrashic" way members of the Second Aliyah recast Jewish concepts as applicable to modern Zionism. Tsur declares that just as earlier generations felt they had the "the right to interpret" (*hazekhut lidrosh*), so too did members of his own generation. The declaration of this right, according to Tsur, has made it possible for them to "accept the yoke of the tradition, but we see for ourselves the right and the ability to express our world by means of it; there is in the right to interpret a recognition of the eternity of the Torah and a recognition of the historical contexts of its manifestations .... There is in the right to interpret a recognition of the fact that the dream of one generation depends on the interpretations of another generation."[35]

Berl Katznelson was one of the most outspoken Second Aliyah advocates of the importance of Zionists staying connected with the heritage of rabbinic Judaism. A representative example of his approach to this issue may be found in an essay he published in the Labor Zionist newspaper *Davar* in 1934, "Ḥurban utelishut" ("Destruction and Uprootedness"). In this essay, he wrote that it made him very uncomfortable to learn that a Zionist youth group went off to its summer camp on the night of Tisha B'Av, the fast commemorating the destructions of the First and Second Temples in Jerusalem, "the very night on which the people of Israel laments its destruction, its enslavement, and the bitterness of its exile," as he put it.[36] The youth group's disassociation from this fast day was, for Katznelson, a most unfortunate instance of the tendency of secular Zionists to distance themselves from all that is associated with the vulnerability of Jewish Diaspora existence.

In an article he wrote shortly afterward, "Meqorot lo-akhzav" ("Reliable Sources"), Katznelson made clear why he was so disappointed in what he saw as the youth group's desecration of Tisha B'Av. "A generation that renews and creates," he declared, "*does not* throw on the trash heap the inheritance of past generations."[37] Instead, Katznelson asserted, a truly creative generation "sometimes grabs on to existing tradition and adds to it; sometimes it descends to the junk pile, uncovers that which was forgotten, polishes off its rust, and revises an ancient tradition which has the ability to nourish the soul of the renewing generation."[38] Indeed, he asked rhetorically, "If there is in the life of the people something that is very ancient and very deep, that has the ability to educate people and to strengthen them for the future, would it be appropriate for revolutionaries to reject it?"[39]

Once their curiosity about the post-biblical tradition from which they had been deprived was aroused, the challenge facing the members of Ḥug Shedemot was how to make up for their lack of education in post-biblical Jewish texts and thereby gain access to them. For the most part, they did not seek to be taught these texts by rabbis fully versed in post-biblical Judaism. Instead, members of Ḥug Shedemot turned to academics of European origin at the Hebrew University, including such figures as Shmuel Hugo Bergman, Martin Buber, Nathan Rotenstreich, Gershom Scholem, and Ernst Simon, who could serve as models of how to study traditional Jewish texts from a modern perspective.[40] Gad Ofaz notes that these scholars served well the need of secular kibbutz members to explore post-biblical Jewish sources because, as he puts it, "in their thinking and writings they combined the traditional Jewish sources with modern culture and thought."[41] Muki Tsur writes that the fact that these scholars were conscious of the "spiritual void" of the breakdown of religious faith in the modern period made them more appropriate teachers of Judaism for Ḥug Shedemot than traditional rabbinic scholars unwilling to acknowledge the contemporary spiritual crisis of Judaism.[42] In addition, Avraham Shapira developed a close relationship with the intellectually open faculty of the Jewish Theological Seminary of the Conservative Movement in the U.S, and as a result they served members of Ḥug Shedemot as another source of access to traditional Jewish texts.[43] Eliezer Schweid, a native-born Israeli, the son of parents who arrived in the Land of Israel during the Third Aliyah, had spent a period of time as a young adult as a member of a kibbutz, during which he published articles in the journal *Shedemot.* After completing a doctorate in Jewish studies at the Hebrew University in 1963, he joined the faculty of that university and thereby became an important role model for members of Ḥug Shedemot seeking to engage in the study of Judaism. In 1984, for example, Avraham Shapira received a Ph.D. at Tel Aviv University based on his doctoral thesis on the writings of Martin Buber.

Secular kibbutz members who sought to return to the Jewish bookcase also gained knowledge of the post-biblical Jewish tradition from older kibbutz members who had come as young men to Israel after having studied in yeshiva in Europe. One important example of such a figure was Meir Ayali (1913-2001), who had attended yeshiva and university in Europe before emigrating to the Land of Israel in 1934. Ayali was deeply concerned about the tendency of members of his generation to dismiss the Jewish post-biblical textual tradition, and he devoted himself to increasing knowledge of that tradition among his fellow kibbutzniks. In 1971, he wrote that he feared that one day kibbutz culture would be based only on the Bible, with no reference to rabbinic texts. He dreaded the loss to Israeli Jewish culture if, in his words, "the entire connection to Jewish values will be solely based on the Bible … skipping over all that was created in the intervening periods and ignoring it."[44]

Ayali insisted that "the Bible is not what distinguishes Jewish culture from other cultures and it did not in itself determine the character of Judaism."[45] What became Judaism, he argued, was based on "the interpretation [of the Bible] that the sages of the generations presented, the spiritual and practical meanings that were concluded from them."[46] He believed that it would be culturally disastrous if kibbutzniks did not learn about the ways that rabbinic interpretations of the Bible moved Judaism in a more humanistic direction, adjusting the original biblical meanings to reflect contemporary perspectives and concerns.

In keeping with his conviction of the importance of engaging in the full range of the traditional Jewish heritage, Ayali studied with a number of the leading scholars of Jewish studies at the Hebrew University, and he completed a doctoral dissertation at the Hebrew University under the direction of Ephraim Urbach, titled "The Status of the Hired Worker in the Talmud," in which he combined his socialist commitments with his intense interest in rabbinics.[47] He also published works of scholarship on post-biblical texts, including the Talmud and Responsa literature, and he was the founding editor of a series of books in Jewish studies, Helal Ben-Hayim, issued by the kibbutz-sponsored publishing house Hakibbutz Hameuchad.[48]

As an educator, Ayali encouraged kibbutzniks to study the post-biblical textual tradition. When he was principal of a regional kibbutz high school, for example, he organized a voluntary Talmud study group for students. In 1966, at Kibbutz Yifat, he established what appears to have been the first all-night Shavuot study session (*tiqqun leyl shavu'ot*) for secular Israelis. This tradition continued throughout his life and was eventually widely adopted throughout the country by secular Israelis seeking to participate in the return to the Jewish bookcase.[49]

In establishing the Shavuot study session, Ayali radically challenged the attempt of the secular kibbutz movement to revive the biblical agricultural dimension of the holiday, the bringing of the first fruits, at the expense of the meaning the rabbis had attributed to the holiday as a commemoration of the giving of the Torah at Mount Sinai.

In 1968, Ayali wrote about why he opposed the way that secular kibbutzim observed Shavuot: "Out of an honest and enthusiastic desire to renew the youthful period of the nation, we [kibbutzniks] chose to restore the original agricultural dimension and the return to nature, but out of an exaggerated zealousness 'to return to the sources' we threw out the spiritual dimension that had aroused soulful contemplation and the experience of holiness."[50] In effect, he explained, the secular kibbutzim reversed the process in which the rabbis had moved the holiday away from being "a primitive cultic holiday."[51] He noted that he experienced anxiety every year when he witnessed an older kibbutznik symbolically "sacrificing the first fruits to the Jewish National Fund, following which our beautiful daughters go out in a charming dance of thanksgiving, as if they were priestesses of [the pagan god] Baal . . . ."[52] He simply could not understand why his fellow kibbutzniks were not aware "of the danger that by exaggerating the natural dimension and eliminating the spiritual meaning, we are returning to a primitive paganism, the enemy of culture, even if only in a symbolic manner."[53]

David Zimmerman (1911-1984), a contemporary of Meir Ayali, was a yeshiva-educated European Jew who emigrated to Israel in 1935 and became a member of two secular kibbutzim in the course of his adult life: Na'an and Mishmar Hasharon. David Zimmerman's son Be'eri, a teacher in institutions devoted to the return to the Jewish bookcase, told me in an interview that his father was part of what Be'eri called an "underground" of fellow former yeshiva students living in secular kibbutzim who maintained an active interest in rabbinic literature, quietly defying the dominant anti-rabbinic ethos of secular Zionism. During our interview, Be'eri proudly pointed to the full set of the Babylonian Talmud that he had inherited from his late father and fondly recalled how, as a small child, he had been very impressed by the large volumes of the set placed on the bottom shelf of the bookcase, which were taller than he was. David Zimmerman taught kibbutzniks selections of rabbinic legends, and he began publishing such legends with interpretive comments in the journal *Shedemot.*

Eventually, the appeal of post-biblical Jewish texts spread considerably beyond the secular kibbutzim, and since the late 1980s, study houses devoted to drawing secular Israelis to these texts have been established to provide an institutional framework for satisfying the need of secular

Israelis to discover these repressed elements of their culture. The most influential of such institutions, sometimes referred to as "pluralistic study houses," include two which grew out of earlier programs of Jewish studies initiated by members of Ḥug Shedemot, Hamidrashah Be'Oranim in Kiryat Tivon, and Beit Hamidrash Bina in Ramat Efal. Other important pluralistic study houses are Elul in Jerusalem, Alma in Tel Aviv, Kolot in Jerusalem, Ein Prat—Hamidrashah Be'Alon near Jerusalem, and three secular yeshivot established by Bina, in Tel Aviv, Jerusalem, and Beersheva. Additionally, among the pre-army year programs available to high school graduates, a number are devoted to introducing secular Israelis to the study of traditional Jewish texts. Midreshet, an umbrella organization of pluralistic study houses, has a web site which offers source sheets with discussion questions that can be used by anyone engaged in the study of traditional Jewish texts.[54] Other popular manifestations of the study of traditional Jewish texts are the annual festival of study Lo Bashamayim at Kfar Blum in the summer and the study conference Hakhel in Jerusalem during Sukkot, which is organized by Panim, an umbrella organization for groups devoted to new approaches to Judaism in Israel.[55]

One of the most important developments that facilitated the study of Talmud among secular Israelis was the project undertaken by Adin Steinsaltz from 1965 to 2010 to publish a new edition of the Babylonian Talmud with a vocalized text, all of its Aramaic passages translated into Hebrew, and explanatory notes. This edition, designed to make the Talmud accessible to those without a yeshiva education, is the one generally used for the study of Talmud in the pluralistic study houses and other non-yeshiva settings. Ruth Calderon, who as a secular Israeli studied traditional Jewish texts at Hamidrashah Be'Oranim and at the Hebrew University and eventually was involved in the founding of both Elul (together with Mordechai Bar-Or) and Alma, has testified that, "If the Steinsaltz edition of the Talmud had not been created during the period I was growing up, I would not have been able to study [Talmud] at all. Not only I, but all of the [participants in the pluralistic] study houses have been dependent on it."[56]

Calderon has explained that she began to explore post-biblical Jewish texts because she found that she identified with them more than she did with the Bible itself. She found herself drawn to the radical reinterpretation of the Bible in rabbinic Judaism, in which priests were replaced by sages, location in one territory was replaced by location anywhere, and sacrifices were replaced by prayer and study.[57] The Bible, she argues, served well the focus of Zionism on the assertion of Jewish power and territorial sovereignty in the Land of Israel, but she and others of her generation needed post-biblical Judaism to provide them with the path that they sought to "compassion, humility, [and] delicacy, which did not have a place in [Zionist culture]."[58] This was particularly true, Calderon relates, in the aftermath of both the Six-Day War and the Yom Kippur War. "[Both wars]," she argues, "taught the Israeli public … that [they] did not bear enough memory in order to build an Israeli culture that could come to terms with such challenges as conquering and victory, the crisis of leadership, and the bitterness of war. Hebrew consciousness needed to recognize itself as part of a much longer process. The comfort, the prayer, the long and patient Jewish dream were needed so that the Jewish community in Israel would awake from its pridefulness and its pain, recognize itself anew, and continue to build itself."[59]

Calderon attributes the growing interest in post-biblical Jewish texts among secular Israelis in part to similarities between the historical experiences of the Jews in the rabbinic period and those of contemporary Israeli Jews. Both, she notes, have lived in the aftermath of national tragedy—the destruction of the Second Temple and the Holocaust respectively. The experience of the rabbis, that the Jewish people had been abandoned by God when the Temple was destroyed, led them to think of God's involvement in human existence as much more limited than had been reported in the Bible. Contemporary Israelis who doubt that God plays a role in history and may even doubt His actual existence as a result of the Holocaust, she argues, could therefore identify more with the rabbinic view of a God less involved in the world than with the biblical view of a God who regularly intervenes in human affairs.

Furthermore, Calderon observes, as opposed to the Israelites' experience in the biblical world, in which people received revelations of absolute truths by prophets, the rabbis no longer counted on the possibility of a divine revelation to human beings. Instead, they turned to human deliberation on how to understand sacred texts in order to decide how they should live their lives. Calderon cites the moment in the Talmudic story "The Oven of Akhnai" when Rabbi Yehoshua stands up to God and refuses to make a legal ruling according to a voice from Heaven that supported the position of his opponent Rabbi Eliezer. In this statement, argues Calderon, Rabbi Yehoshua makes clear that "[t]ruth [based on divine revelation] is no longer decisive, and perhaps there is no absolute truth … and in a place of communal learning the process, the discussion, and the vote [provide] the only relevant truth," a notion that resonates with the post-modern skepticism of contemporary Israelis.[60]

Calderon also observes that when, in this story, God is portrayed as smiling in response to Rabbi Yehoshua's challenge to His authority, one finds a rabbinic view of God that differs radically from the view of God found in the Bible, which is potentially attractive to her contemporaries. "It is difficult to imagine the biblical God smiling," she observes, "Smiling is a delicate response and behind it is a complex personality. … The biblical God rarely appears like this. The biblical God is a force of nature. He is the Creator of the world; He intervenes in it at His will with great gestures—the flood, the destruction of Sodom, the splitting of the Sea of Reeds. The smile testifies to a transition from the biblical image of God painted in oil colors … to the Talmudic image of God, drawn in pencil and hints of water color with a delicate line."[61] In addition, she suggests, the God in this rabbinic story is now prepared to turn much of His power over to human beings. "God … is proud of His creatures who stand before him in maturity and not in submission," she observes. "God is impressed and proud of His creatures who create a world in which He does not have the possibility of intervening, like a father who rejoices in his son when he beats him in a game of chess."[62] This, according to Calderon, is an image of divinity that is more appealing to contemporary Israelis with their anthropocentric humanistic worldview than that found in the Bible.

Calderon cites another reason why she and other secular Israelis who returned to the Jewish bookcase considered it to be of central importance to study rabbinic literature, especially the central text of that literature, the Talmud. As long as secular Israelis are ignorant of the Talmud, she argues, they will not have the ability to forge the kind of Jewish culture that best meets their needs and reflects their worldview. In effect, she declares, "the secular and pluralistic study [of Talmud] is a struggle for liberation [from the authority of the religious]," who claim an exclusive prerogative to define what Judaism is, based on their knowledge of the Talmud.[63] It is only by knowing this text on which Jewish culture is based, she maintains, that secularists can "participate at all levels in the formation of our culture … to live [our lives] as [Jews] in an authentic manner: to marry, to celebrate a Bar Mitzvah, to study, to create, and even to bury, God forbid, in an authentic manner" on their own terms.[64]

In the early years of the pluralistic study houses, many secularists resisted the notion that there was value in studying the post-biblical Jewish tradition. Yariv Ben-Aharon reports that when he declared that he wanted to commit himself to teaching traditional Jewish sources, members of his kibbutz "related to me a bit as if I were the village idiot."[65] He goes on to recall that his father, Yitzhak Ben-Aharon, a leader of the kibbutz movement, "was never interested" in his pursuit of Jewish learning and teaching.[66] He surmises that this was because his engagement with the post-biblical Jewish tradition raised in his father's imagination the "images of rabbis and Hasidic rebbes whom he had known in Romania [before immigrating to the Land of Israel], with all of their superstitions."[67]

Muki Tsur recalls that when Avraham Shapira first introduced the study of traditional Jewish texts at the Kibbutz Seminar at Oranim, which eventually led to the creation of Hamidrashah Be'Oranim, the faculty members of the seminar were greatly concerned that "the coming out of the closet of Judaism could perhaps create a new orthodoxy and perhaps even bring about a return to traditional Jewish observance (*ḥazarah beteshuvah*) or insert cracks in the secular orthodoxy and bring harm to liberalism and socialism."[68] Sara Shadmi-Wortman, an early leader of Hamidrashah Be'Oranim, writes of how challenging it was at first to disseminate the study of the Jewish tradition to secular Israelis. The teachers were forced to make efforts "to create a change in consciousness, to break the emotional barriers of the young secularist before his Jewish identity. The assumption was that these barriers are not just a matter of lack of knowledge, but also a deep alienation from the substance [of the identity] and a lack of a feeling of being at home in the Jewish tradition, stemming in part from the suspicion that opening up to it would obligate one to transform one's personality, to change one's way of life, and to become someone else."[69]

Micah Goodman, founder of Ein Prat—Hamidrashah Be'Alon, has stated that he believes that the secular alienation from tradition with which leaders of the pluralistic study houses originally had to deal is less of a factor in today's Israeli youths. "Today," he explains, "there is a new generation [of Israelis] who are secure in their secular identity."[70] Unlike members of previous generations, he claims, "they do not have to base [their secular identity] on a negation of Judaism."[71] He reports that "many young secularists I meet say, 'I am a secularist who is connected to Judaism.'"[72] The current generation of young secularists, he notes, "[t]the descendants of those who rebelled against the tradition, have found that they have nothing against which to rebel. The grandparents and parents of the current generation sought to liberate themselves from the heavy yoke of the Jewish tradition that limited their personal growth, while today, after there is nothing left of this tradition, the current generation is seeking a tradition that will help them to grow in new areas."[73]

At times, the pluralistic study house movement has aspired to overcome the social, cultural, and political barriers between secular and religious Israelis. One of the goals of Elul, when it was first founded by the secular Ruth Calderon and the religious Mordechai Bar-Or, was to attempt to break down those barriers by creating a space in which secular and religious Israelis could study traditional texts together. As Ruth Calderon recalls, their hope was to replace the typical model of religious-secular learning in which the secular Israeli comes to the religious Israeli to learn traditional texts from him. They wanted what Calderon refers to as "an egalitarian learning" in which the secular and religious Israelis would engage together in the study process.[74]

Following the assassination of Prime Minister Yitzhak Rabin in 1995 by a religious Zionist, a political conflict erupted between secular and religious Israelis. Secular Israelis accused religious Israelis and the Jewish texts they studied as being responsible for this national tragedy. Bina was founded shortly after the assassination in part as an attempt to address the emergence of this secular alienation from religious Israelis and from the Jewish tradition, as a result of which, in the words of Bina's founder and director, Eran Baruch, "many Israelis refrained from touching what was perceived as religious or ultra-Orthodox and felt this was not theirs."[75]

Some pluralistic study houses have begun to explore how the study of post-biblical Jewish texts can contribute to efforts to improve Israeli society. At the secular yeshivot founded by Bina, students devote a considerable period of time during the week engaged in helping to improve the lives of residents in the city where their yeshiva is located. This turn to social action has given rise to an effort to complement the original emphasis of the pluralistic study houses on the study of rabbinic legendary texts (*aggadah*) with the study of rabbinic legal texts (*halakhah*). Mordechai Bar-Or, Head of Kolot, has argued that the Jewish tradition can change the way people in Israel conduct their lives for the better, but only if their study of that tradition includes the rabbinic legal texts that speak of what obligates a Jew. In keeping with this approach, the Kolot program Bar-Or designed is made available to professional leaders in such areas as economics, government, and the army who, he hopes, will bring the values reflected in traditional Jewish legal and legendary texts to their work and thereby make positive changes in the way Israeli society functions.[76]

Hamidrashah Be'Oranim has also moved in this direction. In 2013, it published a commentary on a Talmudic discussion of the laws designed to control male sexual desires and to channel them into their proper expression in marriage and related stories embedded in that discussion.[77] This is the product of a group of women in a program called Niggun Nashim, who undertook what they call a feminist reading of this Talmudic discussion and a consideration of its relevance to the demand of some religious Israelis to enforce a greater separation between men and women in the public sphere, which has the effect of marginalizing the role of women in that sphere.[78] The goal of this project was to open up discussion of this issue and arrive at a reasonable public policy that takes into account both the need for standards of sexual morality and the importance of allowing women equal participation in Israeli society.[79]

In the early 2000s, some secular Israelis involved in the return to the Jewish bookcase began to move beyond the mere study of traditional Jewish sources to the establishment of communities of secular Israelis that would, along with the study of traditional Jewish texts, undertake Jewish religious practice, including Sabbath and holiday celebrations, prayer services, life cycle events, and social action. Their practice draws on Jewish traditions and elements of modern Israeli culture and is not necessarily guided by traditional Jewish law. In 2000, Bini Talmi, Shay Zarchi, and Moshe Yitzhaki, instructors at Oranim, established a community named Nigun Halev, which meets in Moshav Nahalal in Emek Yizrael.[80] Similar communities have been established throughout the country.[81] One of the best known of these communities is Beit Tefilah Israeli, founded in Tel Aviv in 2004.[82] That community organizes a Kabbalat Shabbat service by the Mediterranean port of Jaffa on Friday evenings in the summer.[83]

Religious Israelis Rediscover Rabbinic Legends

Religious Israelis had no need to "return to the Jewish bookcase," during the second half of the twentieth century because they had never left it. The post-biblical Jewish textual tradition that had been largely marginalized in secular Israeli culture has played a central role in the culture of religious Israelis, as it did for generations of Jews. Nevertheless, one genre of post-biblical Jewish texts, that of rabbinic legends (*aggadah*), found in the Babylonian Talmud, the Jerusalem Talmud, and midrashic collections, was not always taken seriously in the culture of religious Jews in the Diaspora.

Yair Lorberbaum argues that early rabbinic literature was characterized by an integrated approach to *halakhah* and *aggadah*, with both genres viewed as valuable sources of religious truth. "The Mishnah," he writes, "freely intertwines halakhah and aggadah, drawing no distinction between the two; the same holds true with respect to *midreshei halakhah* and the Tosefta. The Babylonian Talmud abounds with challenges to the *aggadah*, while relying upon it in halakhic matters."[84] It was during the post-Talmudic Geonic period, he observes, that some religious scholars began to make a clear distinction between *halakhah* and *aggadah* and to assert that *aggadah* was not a reliable source of religious knowledge, especially when it came to the all-important challenge of determining Jewish law. Lorberbaum captures this approach in a statement by Rabbi Hai Gaon (939-1038):

> It should be known that the words of aggadah do not have the status of oral tradition, and each person conjectures as he pleases, employing such terms as "perhaps" and "it could be said," so that the issues are not clearly defined. For that reason we cannot rely upon them. … And these *midrashot* are not tradition and not halakhah, but were only stated by way of conjecture (Otsar Hage'onim, Hagigah, Commentaries Section 14a).[85]

As Lorberbaum notes, some rabbinic scholars followed this trend to isolate *aggadah* from *halakhah* and to denigrate its value, while others "adhered to the Talmudic tradition, viewing aggadah as an authoritative source and as a subject for study and extrapolation."[86]

In Eastern Europe, where the majority of religious Zionist immigrants to the Land of Israel were born, rabbinic legends primarily played a role in the more popular religious culture. Less learned Jews found in rabbinic sermons drawing on legends or in the direct study of legendary texts a spiritual sustenance that was not available to them from the legal texts more central to the yeshiva curriculum, which they found difficult to understand. In Eastern European yeshivot, following the approach introduced in the Geonic period, legendary texts (*aggadah*) were viewed as much less significant than legal texts (*halakhah*), and it was typical for those learning in the yeshivot to skip over legendary passages in the Talmud. The late nineteenth and early twentieth-century Hebrew writer Micha Yosef Berdyczewski recalls this disdain for legends in his fellow yeshiva students: "I heard with my own ears from the highest ranked students of the yeshiva, who think that the whole world was created only for them, saying, 'If we printed [the Talmud], we would skip the legends and not print them at all, because of what use are they? Legends were only created for the simple people ... but not for us.'"[87]

Rav Avraham Yitzhak Kook (1865-1935), the spiritual father of religious Zionism, strongly argued that *aggadah* was as religiously significant as *halakhah*. In a diary entry Kook wrote in the early twentieth century, he asserted his belief in the important religious value of legendary texts, and he argued for a method of Talmud study in which both legal and legendary passages would be taken with equal seriousness: "Legal and legendary texts must be unified together. The need to study them together of necessity will also bring about their spiritual unity."[88] In keeping with his general philosophical quest for that which unites opposites (*aḥdut hahafakhim*), Rav Kook argued here that his advocacy of integrating the study of legal texts and the study of legendary texts was not his own invention, that they are actually deeply intertwined. "This joining together," he wrote, "is nothing less than the revelation of the unity hidden within them that has always existed."[89] Rav Kook signaled the importance he saw in legendary texts by writing a partial commentary to *Eyn Ya'akov*, a compilation of legends found in the Babylonian Talmud.[90]

Rav Kook's attempt to raise the status of legendary texts had little impact on those engaged in the highest levels of traditional study in the yeshivot of his day, and the longstanding neglect of *aggadah* has persisted in most Israeli yeshivot until the present. As recently as 2009, Binyamin Kelmanson, Co-Head of Yeshivat Otniel, lamented the fact that even as religious Zionist yeshivot have engaged in revising the curriculum of study to supplement the centrality of the study of the legal passages in the Talmud, "*aggadah* is still neglected."[91] He made this statement in the Introduction to a book based on classes he taught at his yeshiva in which he engaged in a detailed analysis of rabbinic legends about the destruction of the Second Temple in Jerusalem, thereby challenging the trend in yeshivot to refrain from engaging in any serious way with *aggadah*. There are other signs of a trend among religious Israelis to value the study of legendary rabbinic texts. In 2006, Galei Masekhta, a religious study house devoted to *aggadah*, was established in Jerusalem and later became associated with Yeshivat Yafo. Since 2009, Yeshivat Ahavat Yisrael in Netivot, which is committed to the inclusion of *aggadah* in its curriculum, has held an annual day devoted to the study of *aggadah*, and the papers presented at that event are published in a journal titled *Asuppot.* In addition, the religious Zionist Mikhlelet Efrata in Jerusalem has an Aggadah Teaching Center and publishes a journal of studies on rabbinic legends, *Derekh aggadah.*

Contemporary religious Israelis advocating a return to *aggadah* have found inspiration in the insistence of Rav Kook that Jewish study could be complete only if both *halakhah* and *aggadah* were studied in tandem with teach other. They are particularly taken by Rav Kook's notion that the integration of *halakhah* and *aggadah* would be a central characteristic of the way Torah would be studied in the Land of Israel, referred to by many as *torat erets yisra'el*. In its programmatic founding statement, Galei Masekhta states clearly that their approach directly follows Rav Kook's "call for a general renewal of Torah study, at the center of which is the systematic and deep study of *aggadah*, which he considered to be the key to a transition from the Torah of the Diaspora to the Torah of the Land of Israel—a Torah that would be the fountain and heart of the culture of the people of Israel returning to its Land."[92]

Religious Zionist rabbi and Talmudic scholar Yehuda Brandes published a two-volume series, *Aggadah lema'aseh* (2005, 2011), in which, in the spirit of Rav Kook's teachings, he sought to counter the tendency in the yeshiva world to denigrate the value of studying legendary passages in favor of the study of legal passages in the Talmud. In the Introduction to the first volume he challenges the accepted notion that law and legend play two distinct functions. "The separation of *aggadah* from *halakhah*," he writes, "is an impossible task."[93] Instead, he argues, legend plays an indispensable role in the rabbis' legal discussions of how one should act in life. Legal texts, he suggests, cannot adequately teach all that one needs to know to understand how to live. "Legend completes what is missing [in the legal text] with spiritual and ideational contexts and provides people of the law—sages, legal decisors, teachers of law, and also the simple person obeying the law—the overview and the depths of consciousness that will guide their teachings, decisions, and actions in order that they will not miss the correct path of the law and become lost in the thicket of details."[94] Such an understanding of the spirit of the law that legend presents is particularly needed, Brandes observes, "especially in legal topics in which it is necessary to bring to bear human sensitivity beyond the letter of the law."[95] In the two volumes, Brandes analyzes selected Talmudic passages in which law and legend are intertwined and legend serves to deepen one's understanding of the complexities of the law. From time to time, Brandes steps away from his textual analysis to suggest how the Talmudic passages may have something to say about contemporary issues.[96]

Religious Zionist rabbi Binyamin Lau has also made an important contribution to the revival of interest in rabbinic legends among Israelis. During the years 2006-2012, he published a four-volume series, *Ḥakhamim*, in which he drew on Talmudic stories and reported sayings of the ancient rabbis to write a history of how rabbinic Judaism developed. *Ḥakhamim* began in a traditional Jewish context, a series of talks Lau gave in his synagogue about the Talmudic tractate Pirkei Avot, which he delivered beginning in the summer of 2004 in the afternoon of the Sabbath when it is customary to read from that tractate. In subsequent years, he drew increasingly on the whole range of Talmudic stories, and periodically he would transform his talks into the volumes that became part of the series.

Lau writes in the Preface to the first volume that he aspired in the work to synthesize between the traditional yeshiva approach to Jewish texts and that of modern academia, taking into account both the religious teachings of the stories about the sages and the historical contexts in which the sages functioned.[97] Lau sees these stories as dealing with larger religious issues that could be of relevance to contemporary readers. "It is my prayer," he writes, "that the results of this study will draw us nearer to the world of the sages and by understanding their world we will better understand our world and improve it."[98] Indeed, in the earlier volumes of the series, he interrupts the flow of the historical narrative to comment on how one can find contemporary religious lessons in the lives and thought of the rabbis.

Aggadah is the genre of rabbinic literature that has most appealed to secular Israelis returning to the Jewish bookcase, largely due to the fact that the narratives of rabbinic legends are more accessible to them than the more complex and specialized legal discussions of *halakhah*. And so, as religious Israelis have begun to reevaluate the significance of *aggadah*, these two cultural groups' interests have converged. These interests meet in particular in the subgenre of *aggadah*, the Talmudic story, of which the story about Rabbi Rahumi and his wife, cited by Ruth Calderon in her Knesset speech, is a prime example. Indeed, as we follow Israeli interest in Talmudic stories and the interpretations of those stories by contemporary Israeli readers, we will discover a wide range of secular and religious readers engaged in what amounts to the same project: the cultural re-appropriation of a neglected but valuable resource and the attempt to understand that resource in terms of contemporary perspectives and concerns.

CHAPTER 1

THE REDISCOVERY OF TALMUDIC STORIES

Early in the twentieth century, several decades before the emergence of a new interest in Talmudic stories in Israel, the Hebrew poet Hayyim Nahman Bialik (1873-1934) and the writer and editor Yehoshua Hana Ravnitzky (1859-1944) devoted themselves to composing an anthology of rabbinic legends, including Talmudic stories. In this anthology, *Sefer ha'aggadah* (*Book of Legends*), the first edition of which appeared in Europe in 1908-1911, the editors sought to make rabbinic legends accessible to secularized Hebrew readers who had become distant from traditional Jewish learning and from the religious worldview reflected in these legends.

In an essay by Bialik, "Lekhinusah shel ha'aggadah" ("Toward the Ingathering of Legends," 1908), which served as the Introduction to *Sefer ha'aggadah,* he expressed his strong conviction that rabbinic legends were relevant to the concerns of the secularized Jewish Hebrew readers of his day. One of the classic rabbinic statements about the value of rabbinic legends proclaims that they are a source of divine knowledge: "If you wish to know the One who spoke and the world came into being [i.e. God], study legends, for from them you will know the Holy One Blessed be He and cling to His ways" (*retsonkha shetakkir mi she'amar vehayah ha'olam, lemad aggadah, shemitokh kakh attah makkir et haqadosh barukh hu umiddabbeq bederakhav* (Sifre, Ekev 49). Playing on the words of this rabbinic rationale for legends, Bialik wrote: "He who wants ... to know the nation of Israel ... against his will should 'go to the legends'" (*mi sherotseh ... lehakkir et ha'umah hayisre'elit ... al korkho 'yelekh etsel aggadah'*).[1] Bialik's argument drew on the romantic notion that had spread throughout Europe in the nineteenth century, that folklore was an important resource for peoples wishing to form a modern national identity. As far as Bialik was concerned, one could discover a wealth of Jewish folklore in rabbinic legends that would provide those who aspired to develop a modern Jewish identity access to the true spirit of the Jewish people throughout its history.[2] As Tsafi Sebba-Elran observes, this rephrasing of the original rabbinic statement about the value of legends reflected Bialik's determination that it was time to transform Judaism from a culture with religion at its center into "a national humanist culture," replacing "the holy spirit as the highest source and purpose of literature" with "the national spirit."[3] It is significant that Bialik wrote that he who wants to know the spirit of the Jewish people would need to go to rabbinic legends "against his will." With that expression, he acknowledged the alienation of his readers from rabbinic texts, especially those who had studied them in yeshiva and had rejected them along with other aspects of traditional Judaism. Nevertheless, Bialik felt that the task before him was to convince them to take another look at rabbinic legends and appreciate their value.

The Talmudic stories in *Sefer ha'aggadah* that tell of the life and times of the rabbis of the Mishnah and Talmud are collected in a section of the anthology titled "Ma'asei ḥakhamim" ("Sage Tales"). In this and other sections of *Sefer ha'aggadah,* Bialik and Ravnitzky allowed themselves extensive editorial freedom. While they were aware that among secularized male Jews of their generation there were those who had been trained in yeshiva in reading rabbinic legends, they were also conscious of the fact that many men and virtually all women had not received such training, and that the ongoing process of secularization was bringing about a growing decline in traditional Jewish learning that made rabbinic legends less accessible to many members of the Hebrew reading public, and presumably would continue to do so in future generations. A substantial number of these legends were written originally in Aramaic, with which the non-yeshiva-trained reader was not familiar, and so Bialik and Ravnitzky translated all of these stories into Hebrew. Rabbinic legends are located throughout the Babylonian Talmud and the Jerusalem Talmud, interspersed with discussions of Jewish law, and many legends appear in midrashic works and traditional anthologies of legends. These sources presented a seemingly impenetrable barrier to modern Jews not familiar with them and ill-equipped to read them in any meaningful way. Therefore, the editors of *Sefer ha'aggadah* set out to extract rabbinic legends from the texts in which they were embedded and thereby make them more available to the general Hebrew reading public.

Another issue addressed by the editors was their sense that not all of the legends found in traditional texts would appeal to contemporary readers. "In our day," Bialik wrote, "not everyone is familiar with ancient books, and not everyone can or wants to pick through the piles of material that grew to be mountains during several generations in order to find pearls beneath them. And even more so, not everyone can bring together scraps and patches to create a full garment and scattered pieces of rock to create a building."[4] The readers of his day, Bialik argued, needed editors who could find the best of the stories and present them in a form that would meet contemporary readers' literary expectations. In collecting stories about a particular rabbi, for example, Bialik and Ravnitzky gathered legends spread throughout rabbinic literature and constructed as best as they could a biography of that rabbi with events presented in chronological order, conforming with contemporary approaches to retelling the story of an important figure.

Bialik and Ravnitzky's *Sefer ha'aggadah* was enthusiastically received by the Hebrew reading public in Europe and in the Land of Israel. The editors proudly proclaimed in the Introduction to the 1929 revised edition of the work, "*Sefer ha'aggadah* has become a popular book (*sefer am*) in the fullest meaning of the term. We would be amazed if there was one educated Hebrew [reading] household among the Jewish people that has not embraced *Sefer ha'aggadah.*"[5] This assessment is confirmed by Israeli scholar Yonah Fraenkel, who wrote several decades later, "There was not one educated Hebrew [reading] household and not one Zionist school class between the two world wars in the Land of Israel and in the Diaspora in which *Sefer ha'aggadah* did not have an impact. Bialik made it possible for legends to be a national treasure of the people of Israel, as it was building its renewed national independence."[6]

Sefer ha'aggadah had a more significant impact on secular Hebrew readers than on religious Hebrew readers, because the former were not as familiar with rabbinic legends as were the latter. As secular kibbutz educator and scholar Meir Ayali has observed, "Who knows what would have been the fate of rabbinic legends if [secular readers] had had to labor to search for them in the mines of the Talmud, to sift through them, and to purify them of the dross of legal discussions and the complexities of the arguments, and if they had not been presented to us in [Hebrew] translation, formulated and ordered by Bialik and Ravnitzky [in *Sefer ha'aggadah*], so that we could read them without great effort?"[7]

The secular Israeli writer Yoram Kaniuk (1930-2013), a first generation native-born Israeli who grew up in the later years of the British Mandate before the establishment of the State of Israel, testified to the role that *Sefer ha'aggadah* had in the secular education of his generation when he wrote, "We were sons of the Bible, but also sons of *Sefer ha'aggadah* by Bialik and Ravnitzky."[8] His contemporary, secular kibbutz-born poet and lyricist Yoram Taharlev (b. 1938), has declared that when he was growing up, "almost every secular home had three obligatory books: the Bible, *Sefer ha'aggadah*, and [the moralistic Talmudic tractate] Pirkei Avot."[9]

Although it succeeded in increasing the awareness of rabbinic legends among secular Hebrew readers, in the end *Sefer ha'aggadah* was not able to establish a central role for these legends among secular Zionists, due to the inherent contradiction between the ethos of rabbinic legends and that of secular Zionism. Legends about the life and times of the rabbis take place mainly during the Roman occupation of the Land of Israel, including the late Second Temple period, the period of the destruction of the Temple in 70 CE, and the aftermath of that destruction and that of the unsuccessful Bar Kokhba revolt. During these periods, Jews had relatively little political power and were subject to religious persecution. The other major locale of rabbinic legends is the Diaspora Jewish community of Babylonia. Furthermore, the leading characters in rabbinic legends are cerebral figures primarily preoccupied with the study of Torah. Stories about this vulnerable, intellectually-oriented, spiritualized existence which persisted in the time of the rabbis, not only in the Diaspora but also in the Land of Israel, did not provide Zionists with heroic models from the past that could inspire the nationalist ethos of the Zionist aspiration for sovereignty in the Land of Israel and later the struggle to maintain Jewish independence in the newly established State of Israel. Thus, even though *Sefer ha'aggadah* was an important part of Yoram Kaniuk's education, it is also clear from what he writes of the period of his youth that much of the politically moderate ethos reflected in rabbinic legends was at odds with how he and his fellow first-generation of native born Israelis were being educated: "Our teachers thought that we would revive our ancient land, our national home, and we would avenge the history of the Jewish people, avenge the pogroms. They wanted us to undertake a giant retaliatory raid against Jewish history. ... They wanted us to begin to create a new masculine Jewish history of our own so that we would no longer live at the mercy of the history of someone else."[10]

As Tsafi Sebba-Elran has observed, certain editorial changes introduced by Bialik and Ravnitzky in *Sefer ha'aggadah* emphasized politically moderate, even pacifist trends in rabbinic legends, thereby portraying this part of the Jewish heritage as significantly incompatible with the more militant Zionist ethos on which Kaniuk and his contemporaries, members of the first generation born in the Land of Israel, were raised. A prime example of this characterization of rabbinic culture in *Sefer ha'aggadah* is the selection of legends about the destruction of the Second Temple in the anthology that portray the departure of Rabban Yohanan ben Zakkai from Jerusalem during the Roman siege as a political approach preferable to that of the Jews who insisted on remaining in Jerusalem and continuing to resist the Romans, the figures of history with whom Kaniuk's generation would much more readily identify.[11]

Sefer ha'aggadah has never fully lost its iconic status as a classic of Hebrew literature. Avigdor Shinan, editor of a recently published new edition of the book, has estimated that about two thousand copies of the book are sold each year in Israel, but these are, as he puts it, primarily for Bar Mitzvah presents and school libraries.[12] Over time, the influence of *Sefer ha'aggadah* on Israeli culture has waned significantly. Observing the status of that work toward the end of the twentieth century, Yonah Fraenkel lamented the fact that, in contrast to the situation earlier in the century, one could no longer say "that in every educated Hebrew [reading] household in our time *Sefer ha'aggadah* is found, and also the number of children in Hebrew schools who encounter *Sefer ha'aggadah* as living learning material certainly is not large today."[13]

The Contribution of Academic Studies to the Positive Reevaluation of Talmudic Stories in Contemporary Israel

Yonah Fraenkel's comments on the decline of the impact of *Sefer ha'aggadah* on contemporary Israeli culture are significant, because he played such a central role in reversing that trend and restoring the cultural status of one subgenre of rabbinic legends, the Talmudic story, toward the end of the twentieth century. Fraenkel (1928-2012), a religiously observant Jew, emigrated to the Land of Israel with his family in 1937, received a yeshiva education, and completed a doctorate at the Hebrew University, where he eventually was appointed to a faculty position in the Department of Hebrew Literature.[14] Beginning in the

1970s, Fraenkel challenged the assumption of scholars of rabbinics in the nineteenth and much of the twentieth century that Talmudic stories were of interest primarily as sources for the writing of the history of the rabbis in the Land of Israel and in Babylonia. The historical approach that Fraenkel questioned, explains Amram Tropper, was based on the belief of scholars that "the creators of the stories sought to describe events that they saw with their own eyes or reliable traditions that they heard from others and therefore the foundation of the story reflected an event that took place in reality and had a grain of historical truth."[15] These creators, scholars believed, "were also blessed with artistic skills that led them to enhance their works with legendary and literary embellishments," which, it was thought, could be set aside to arrive at "the pure historical kernel" at the heart of each story.[16]

In opposition to this approach, Fraenkel insisted that Talmudic stories were not reliable historical sources. He questioned the historical accuracy of Talmudic stories for a number of reasons: (1) The accomplished artistry of the storytelling is such an integral part of each of these texts that it is impossible to set it aside and arrive at a kernel of historical truth. (2) There are often too many contradictory stories about the same event or historical figure to allow one to determine which version was the more historically accurate. (3) Many stories were composed generations after the events which they purported to relate. In effect, argued Fraenkel, Talmudic stories were works of fiction that should be submitted to close readings and analyzed as self-contained, well-crafted aesthetic creations with the methods of the New Criticism that had been popular in literary studies in the middle of the twentieth century.[17] Even as he lamented the failure of *Sefer ha'aggadah* to maintain its influence in Israeli culture, Fraenkel was proud of the way that his new literary approach to Talmudic stories and other rabbinic legends became increasingly popular in institutions of higher learning in Israel. "Every year," he declared, "large numbers of men and women, young and less young, religious and secular, native born and non-native born Israelis, city dwellers and settlement dwellers alike, sit pouring over legendary texts and attempting to decipher their hidden meanings."[18]

In subsequent decades, there has been an explosion of Israeli scholarship on Talmudic stories, including a significant number of works continuing the literary approach of Fraenkel, other works of a more historical nature that largely take into account Fraenkel's skepticism of the factual accuracy of these stories, and works applying the methodology of folklore studies to this genre. Among the most significant works of such scholarship are books by Azaria Beitner, Nurit Beeri, Galit Hasan-Rokem, Admiel Kosman, Ofra Meir, Aharon Oppenheimer, Inbar Raveh, Amram Tropper, Shulamit Valler (and one she co-authored with Shalom Razabi), Ruhama Weiss, Eli Yassif, Anat Yisraeli-Taran, and Yaffa Zilkha. In addition, some books by Israeli scholars have been published in English, including those by Alon Goshen-Gottstein, co-authors Tova Hartman and Charlie Buckholtz, Galit Hasan-Rokem, and Dalia Hoshen.[19]

Making Talmudic Stories Accessible to the General Public

Even as new approaches to Talmudic stories developed in the world of Israeli scholarship, a significant number of books designed to make Talmudic stories more accessible to the general reading public were published. Like *Sefer ha'aggadah* in the early twentieth century, these books, composed by academic scholars and other learned writers, presented selected Talmudic stories that the authors deemed to be of potential relevance to contemporary Israelis, repackaged them in formats easily read by contemporaries seeking to connect with this genre, and interpreted them with the goal of suggesting that one can find in them insights about human existence to which readers could relate. With the publication of this genre of books, secular Israelis no longer had to view these stories as embodying an arcane rabbinic Judaism that was at best irrelevant and at worst decadent, while religious Israelis were offered a fresh new approach to a genre that was not taken seriously in their culture.

As a result of the efforts of the writers of these books on Talmudic stories, Israelis could begin to appreciate Talmudic stories as good works of fiction that were enjoyable to read and significant resources on which to draw to enrich their lives. They came to appreciate these stories for a number of reasons: (1) They are short, well-crafted narratives that draw in readers the way that any good story will. (2) They are written in a minimalistic style that focuses mainly on dialogue and actions; the narrator rarely reveals what is going on in the inner life of the characters, and so these stories tend to leave considerable room for imaginative attempts by the reader to decide why characters do what they do. (3) They are about universal human situations with which all readers can identify, such as marriages, relationships between parents and children, power struggles between people, and the successes and failures of those who try to live good lives. (4) They raise central moral questions about how people should relate to each other in society and in intimate relations. (5) The stories are often highly critical of the rabbinic protagonists portrayed in them, a characteristic which is both surprising and attractive to contemporary Israeli readers who tend to assume that the Talmud would tell only stories that hold up rabbis as examples of goodness and purity. (6) As Yehoshua Levinson, a student of Yonah Fraenkel, observes, there is something about the typical plot of a Talmudic story in which an individual struggles with a personal issue that appealed to Israelis toward the end of the twentieth century when Israeli culture was turning away from collectivism and focusing more on the interests and needs of the individual, a trend also reflected in the Hebrew literature of that period.[20]

The first two significant books that sought to introduce the general Israeli reading public to Talmudic stories were both published in 1981: *Iyyunim be'olamo haruḥani shel sippur ha'aggadah* (*Studies in the Spiritual World of the Legendary Story*), by Yonah Fraenkel, and *Shemonah sippurei ahavah min hatalmud vehamidrash* (*Eight Love Stories from Talmud and Midrash*), by David Zimmerman (1911-1984), the kibbutz educator mentioned in my Introduction.[21] In the Introductions to their books, both writers state that Talmudic stories are of significant value to contemporary Israelis because they portray concrete situations in which characters seek to come to terms with the most challenging experiences of human existence. "There is hardly a moral, theological, or historical-national question," argues Fraenkel, "that does not appear in the [Talmudic] story."[22] Zimmerman writes that many Talmudic stories carry a significant message. "The narrator presents to us an event," he writes, "and he sets it up—sometimes explicitly and sometimes implicitly—as an example for the listening or reading audience."[23] Zimmerman emphasizes that in the stories he selected to present in his book, "the message is always *moral*, growing out of an existence that is saturated with humane values."[24]

The attempts by Fraenkel and Zimmerman to draw Israelis to a greater appreciation of Talmudic stories had nowhere near the influence on Israeli culture that *Alma di*, by Ari Elon (b. 1950), had when it was published as an issue of the kibbutz journal *Shedemot* in 1990.[25] Elon was born in Jerusalem to a prominent religious Zionist family. As a young man, he ceased observing religious rituals, but he continued to be very attached to the study of traditional Jewish texts. He completed an M.A. thesis on Talmudic stories under the supervision of Yonah Fraenkel, and he currently teaches at pluralistic study houses.[26] In *Alma di,* playing on the similarity between the Hebrew term for "rabbinic," *rabbani,* and the Hebrew term for "autonomous," *ribboni,* Elon makes much of the distinction between those whom he calls *rabbani* Jews, religious Jews who accept the divine authority of Jewish law, and those whom he calls *ribboni* Jews, secular Jews who do not accept that authority and assert their autonomous right to choose their own path in life. The approach of the *ribboni* Jews that he undertakes in his readings of Talmudic stories involves what he refers to as "transforming the Torah of Israel from a source of authority to a source of inspiration."[27] Elon writes that he is troubled by the fact that those who have identified with the secular Zionist transformation of Jewish identity, the *ribboni* Jews, have given up any claim to the sources of the post-biblical Jewish tradition and have allowed the *rabbani* Jews to maintain a monopoly over them, rather than "fighting for their right and obligation to liberate the Torah of Israel from the embrace of the rabbis."[28] Elon argues that traditional Jewish sources can be of great value to the secular Jew: "He can learn a lot from them about himself, his people, his collective memories, his desires, his repressions."[29]

Dov Elbaum, the editor of a new edition of *Alma di,* published for the first time as a book in 2011, who himself has been active in furthering the aims of the return to the Jewish bookcase, writes that "[t]he reactions to the appearance of *Alma di* [in 1990] were extensive and strong; conferences, study sessions, and many pages of thought and reflection were written in reaction to the surprising and exciting words of *Alma di.*"[30] It had an important impact, explains Elbaum, by "pointing to the refreshing challenge that [traditional Jewish sources could present to] Zionism and to Israeli society and culture."[31] It was, declares Elbaum, "one of the first and most important formulations of the secular Jewish renaissance in Israel."[32]

One of the most enthusiastic readers of *Alma di* when it first appeared was secular kibbutznik Yariv Ben-Aharon (1934-2016), mentioned in my Introduction as a key figure in the establishment of the second-generation kibbutz movement known as Ḥug Shedemot. Ben-Aharon was born in the secular kibbutz Givat Hayim, and his father, Yitzhak Ben-Aharon (1906-2006), was an important kibbutz leader belonging to the generation against which Yariv Ben-Aharon and others rebelled as part of Ḥug

Shedemot. In an article Yariv Ben-Aharon published in an issue of *Shedemot* after the publication of *Alma di*, titled "Higanukh pumbedita" ("We Have Arrived at You Pumbedita"), he marvels at how Elon succeeded in the section on rabbinic legends in *Alma di* in restoring the connection of contemporary Israeli Jews to the largely repressed rabbinic culture of the Diaspora. Ben-Aharon suggests in his article that Elon's reclamation of rabbinic legends was able to have an impact on secular Israelis precisely because the most recent generations had engaged in a "rebellion against rabbinic authority and the ideal of the sage," clearing the way for a new view of the value of rabbinic legends, and thereby figuratively allowing Israelis to return to the Torah of the Exile as taught in the Babylonian center of Torah study in Pumpedita.[33] Ben-Aharon observes that Elon discovered an "alternative spirituality" in rabbinic Diaspora culture, which allowed the rabbis to transcend history—a welcome change from all that Israelis have had to endure as a result of the Zionist return to history. Now, he declares, they could "return to encompass some talmudic discussion or legend, to absorb and drink in the full extent of the spiritual satisfactions within this richness."[34]

Ben-Aharon made his own contribution to a greater appreciation of Talmudic stories in his work, *Aggadat pumbedita*, which was published in 2000.[35] As a secular kibbutznik, Ben-Aharon had had no previous training in the study of rabbinic texts. After taking a leave from his kibbutz to study traditional Jewish sources in Jerusalem, he returned to his kibbutz with the conviction that the post-biblical Jewish heritage offered contemporary Israelis much that was relevant to their lives. In 1975, following his period of study in Jerusalem, he wrote, "I plan to encourage large numbers of people to read our ancient and marvelous literature, to imbibe and be revivified by it. There is no greater literature."[36] In an attempt to fulfill that mission he designed *Aggadat pumbedita* as a contemporary commentary on a Talmudic chapter, known as "Hasokher et hapo'alim" (B. Bava Metzia 83a-87a), which is replete with stories. Ben-Aharon writes in his Introduction that his work is presented "to those who seek their personal path in the world of the spirit, to wanderers and tortured souls, as well as to lovers of *midreshei aggadah* and Talmud, who see in these sources part of their language, their literature, their cultural identity, and even their faith; to those whose eyes are open who know that under the wings of Talmudic legends take place bitter struggles about direction and meaning in the lives of human beings of flesh and blood."[37]

In the early decades of the 2000s, several books in which selected Talmudic stories were presented and interpreted appeared in Israel. In each of these books, the writers sought to introduce readers to the genre of the Talmudic story as well as demonstrate the relevance of Talmudic stories to contemporary concerns. Published by leading Israeli publishers, these books made a significant contribution to the revival of interest in this genre among secular and religious Israelis. As we consider each of these books and relevant background information about the writers who selected and interpreted the Talmudic stories, we will gain a greater understanding of the variety of approaches the writers took, thereby creating a richly diverse discourse on how to read Talmudic stories in our day.

Hashuq. habayit. halev: aggadot talmudiyyot (*The Market. The Home. The Heart: Talmudic Legends*) was published in 2001 by Ruth Calderon (b. 1961), whose Knesset speech in which she taught a Talmudic story I discussed in my Introduction.[38] Calderon was born in Tel Aviv to a Sephardic father from Bulgaria and an Ashkenazic mother from Germany. She has described her home as having been "a very Jewish, very Zionist, secular, traditional, religious home that combined Ashkenaz and Sepharad, [Revisionist] Betar and [Socialist] Hashomer Hatzair ... in the [Israeli] mainstream of the 60s and 70s."[39] She received a secular education through high school, but subsequently began to pursue the study of traditional Jewish texts at Hamidrashah Be'Oranim, the Shalom Hartman Institute, and the Hebrew University, from which she received a doctorate in Talmud in 2007. She was involved in the founding of two of the most prominent of the Israeli pluralistic study houses, Elul in Jerusalem (together with Mordechai Bar-Or) in 1989 and Alma in Tel Aviv in 1995.

Massekhet gevarim: Rav vehaqatsav ve'od sippurim al gavriyyut, ahavah, otentinyyut besippur ha'aggadah uvasippur haḥasidi (*Men's Tractate: Rav and the Butcher and Other Stories: On Manhood, Love, and Authentic Life in Aggadic and Hasidic Stories*) and *Massekhet nashim: ḥokhmah, ahavah, ne'emanut, teshuqah, yofi, min, qedushah: qeri'ah besippurim talmudiyym verabbaniyym ushenei midreshei shir* (*Women's Tractate: Wisdom, Love, Faithfulness, Passion, Beauty, Sex, Holiness: A Reading of Talmudic and Rabbinic Stories and Two Midrashic Poems*), were published in 2002 and 2007 respectively by Admiel Kosman (b.1957), who was born in Haifa and raised in a religious Zionist home.[40] Kosman's father is a European-born textile worker who fled the Nazis during World War II before immigrating to Israel, and his mother is a Mizrahi Jew. After a period of yeshiva study, Kosman pursued the academic study of Talmud at the undergraduate and graduate levels at the religious Zionist Bar Ilan University, receiving a Ph.D. in 1993 and continuing there as a faculty member in its Department of Talmud. In 2003, he left Bar Ilan University to accept appointments in Potsdam, Germany as a faculty member in the School of Jewish Studies at the University of Potsdam and as Academic Director at the Reform rabbinical seminary Abraham Geiger College. In addition to his academic career, Kosman is also a poet. During the late 1990s and early 2000s, Kosman wrote a column in the daily *Haaretz,* known as "Otsar qatan" ("A Small Treasure"). In this column he presented traditional Jewish narratives, including Talmudic stories, Hasidic tales, and stories drawn from works of rabbinic responsa, and his interpretations of their relevance to contemporary readers, which became the basis for his books *Massekhet gevarim* and *Massekhet nashim.*

Mitḥayyevet benafshi: qeri'ot meḥuyyavot batalmud (*Committing My Soul: Committed Readings in the Talmud*) was published by Ruhama Weiss (b.1966) in 2006, and in 2012 she published together with psychologist Avner HaCohen *Immahot betippul: massa psikhologi-sifruti im gibborot hatalmud* (*Mothers in Therapy: A Psychological Look at Four Talmudic Women*).[41] Weiss was born to a religious Zionist family in Jerusalem, but eventually she ceased identifying with the way of life in which she was raised. Having not been allowed to study Talmud as a girl, she eventually received a doctorate in rabbinics at the Hebrew University. She teaches rabbinics at Hebrew Union College in Jerusalem and at the Secular Yeshiva in Jerusalem. At Hebrew Union College, she is also the director of The Life Texts-Talmudic Bibliotherapy Program and she teaches in the Blaustein Center for Pastoral Counseling. In addition, she has published a number of books of poetry.

Aggadeta: sippur haderamah hatalmudit (*Legends: Stories of Talmudic Drama*) was published in 2011 by Shmuel Faust (b. 1968).[42] Faust was born to a religious Zionist family in Jerusalem. He holds a doctorate in rabbinics from Bar Ilan University and is the literary editor of the Musaf Shabbat of *Makor rishon* and Head of the Graduate Studies Program and Director of the Aggadah Teaching Center at Efrata College of Education. During the years 2005-2008, he had a column in *Makor rishon*, "Aggadeta," in which he introduced readers to Talmudic stories. Articles from his column became the basis for his book.

Ḥalom shel bein hashemashot: iyyun uderishah besippurim talmudiyyim (*A Dream at Twilight: A Study and Inquiry in Talmudic Stories*) was published in 2013 by Yaara Inbar (b. 1996).[43] Inbar was born and continues to live in Jerusalem. She studied Talmudic, kabbalistic, and Hasidic texts at the Hebrew University. Before she completed her doctoral dissertation in the Department of Jewish Thought at the Hebrew University, she decided to leave the world of formal academic scholarship and pursue her writing and teaching in informal settings so that she could explore the more personal connections readers of traditional Jewish texts may have with these sources.[44] *Ḥayyot haqodesh: yetsurei hapere beveit midrasham shel ḥazal* (*Holy Beings: Wild Creatures in the Rabbinic Academy*) was published in 2016 by Ido Hevroni. Hevroni holds a doctorate in rabbinics from Bar Ilan University and is the Educational Director at Shalem College in Jerusalem.[45]

In their reflections on the writing of each of their books, these writers make clear what they see as the nature and purpose of their contemporary selection and interpretation of Talmudic stories. Ruth Calderon writes that she composed her book in order "to tell stories close to my heart from Talmud and Midrash, out of a desire and need to bring them together with members of the secular Israeli community to which I belong."[46] She declares to her readers that her book is not to be seen as having an educational, religious, or scholarly purpose, but rather as one that seeks "to present [these stories] as moving texts that can motivate people, as literature."[47] She finds "in these legends an intuitive, emotional, and artistic formation of those great questions with which culture deals."[48] She sees particular value in seeking to understand these stories because, as she puts it, "entering the world of the Jewish imagination allows one to touch the underlying foundation of this culture, and at the same time something personal and internal."[49]

Inspired by twentieth-century Jewish thinker Martin Buber, the underlying message of Admiel Kosman's story selection and commentary is that the stories he presents provide powerful examples of the human need for dialogue with the other, in which one may discover God.[50] Kosman believes that the stories he has collected also provide important observations about gender relations: "The Jewish demand for dialogue [expressed in these stories]," he argues, "allows no place for the development of solely masculine or solely feminine qualities. Both [genders] are called upon to fulfill their independent identities … by turning their face to the other gender in order to melt to the extent possible into one unity."[51]

Writing as a secularist who left the religious Zionist culture of her youth, Ruhama Weiss distinguishes her approach to the Talmud from that of religious Jews. "The committed learning I am suggesting in this book," she explains, "does not involve a return to traditional learning ... because one can never return and I am not sure I want to do so."[52] Secularists, she explains, feel as if they have a freedom of choice that affects the nature of their learning. "For the person who does not see himself obligated to observe the Torah and the commandments going to the study house is no longer a naïve going; it is a going that recognizes the possibility of not going."[53]

In her book, *Mitḥayyevet benafshi*, Weiss presents legal and legendary selections from the Talmud, including Talmudic stories, and interacts with them in a process to which she refers as "a mutual influence of the Torah text and the learner."[54] She makes clear that she does not worry that by allowing herself to interpret traditional texts in a freely imaginative way, she will negate the significance of those texts. She considers herself free "to dare to suggest independent interpretations, so personal that at first glance they appear to be excessively beyond the meaning of the text, because one may assume that the Torah will know what to do with the interpretations I suggest and so it will know how to set boundaries; it will take care of itself."[55] In keeping with her notion of a mutual interaction between learner and text, she declares that "alongside [her] expansion of interpretive freedom ... [she must] develop [her] ability to listen [to what the Torah is saying]."[56] Weiss makes the point that those who are engaged in the study of Torah texts have the opportunity "to bring their hurts to it... [and] to gather together the hurts of generations... to learn from them, to add those hurts to their own hurts and to give birth with them and from them to [an expression achieving] rare literary heights."[57] This approach is particularly evident in her book *Immahot betippul*, in which she draws on the professional knowledge of psychologist Avner HaCohen to discover psychological insights from an analysis of the inner lives of four women characters who are portrayed in Talmudic stories as engaged in difficult challenges of life with which Weiss can readily identify.

One of the important points Shmuel Faust seeks to make in his book draws on his doctoral dissertation, in which he convincingly challenged the accepted wisdom that Talmudic stories are solely for the purpose of presenting the sages in a positive light, and he demonstrated the dominance of negative criticism of the sages in these stories.

This criticism, he believes, is an important component in what makes Talmudic stories so valuable: "[the] instruction filled with wisdom [that they offer] about how to do deeds that are correct, righteous, and good in the eyes of God and humanity."[58] Yaara Inbar also writes of the relevance these stories have for contemporary concerns. She observes that in the lives of the rabbis "there is no cutting of corners, there are no evasions or self-justifications. They look straight [at life] and force us to look straight at them, and thereby also at our own lives."[59] She goes on to write that "The Talmud touches the most intimate unadorned points of each and everyone one of us, and if we only open ourselves up before it we will face ourselves as we have never done previously."[60]

In the Introduction to his book, Ido Hevroni writes of the value he sees in turning to the reading of Talmudic stories and other classical writings: "The person who desires to expand the borders of his world seeks an answer to his questions by means of a dialogue with the great texts of tradition. The questions that the creators of ancient texts asked still trouble us; the answers they have offered allow us to break through the circle of answers available in the context of the time and place in which we live .... [Ancient stories] open before a person new horizons, teach him about alternative existential possibilities, and grant him a tool for self reflection."[61] The official English translation of the Hebrew title of the book, *Ḥayyot haqodesh*, is *Holy Beings*, but it would be more accurate to translate it as *Holy Beasts*. The title, explains Hervoni, reflects his choice to include in the book Talmudic stories that "portray varied encounters between rabbis and 'others,' through whom the [rabbinic] heroes become acquainted with existential possibilities with which they were not aware until then .... The 'other,' who suggests an alternative existence, appears to them at first like 'a beast,' like a strangeness that threatens the organized world of the hero. The process that the heroes experience in the stories will uncover before them 'the holy' in the beast, the opportunity to expand consciousness."[62]

In addition to the books on Talmudic stories we have explored, I would cite two more books published by smaller publishing houses, each of which focuses on a specific theme in Talmudic stories. One book is *Be'avotot hashekhol: iyyunim be'asarah sippurei aggadah al hashekhol be'olamam shel ḥakhamim* (*In the Grip of Bereavement: An Analysis of Ten Aggadic Legends on Bereavement in the World of the Sages*), published by Chaim Licht in 2007.[63] Chaim Licht is Professor Emeritus in the Department of Jewish Thought at the University of Haifa, and he teaches courses in Jewish studies in kibbutz settings. In his book, he presents a study of Talmudic stories about rabbis whose children died, in which he engaged during the year of mourning following the death of his own daughter, shortly before she turned thirty. Having found much value in this study, Licht decided to share his learning with the general public in this book, so that "they would become familiar with the richness of points of view of [the rabbis] about the death of children in the lifetime of their parents."[64]

The second book is *Al mah avdah ha'arets: iyyunim be'aggadot haḥurban* (*Why Was the Land Lost? Studies in the Legends of the Destruction*), published by Binyamin Kelmanson (b. 1957) in 2009.[65] Kelmanson grew up in a religious Zionist family in Haifa. After receiving rabbinical ordination, he eventually became the Co-Head of the religious Zionist Yeshivat Otniel in Otniel. His book is based on a series of classes at his yeshiva in which he taught Talmudic stories of the destruction of the Second Temple in Jerusalem. He writes in the Introduction to the book that although some would assume that legends about the destruction of the Temple would have little or no relevance to Jews living in the State of Israel, which embodies the return to political sovereignty for the Jews, this set of stories is actually of great relevance to contemporary Israel. Kelmanson writes of his personal identification with these Talmudic narratives of catastrophe. His father was a Holocaust survivor who lost his entire family in World War II. In his own lifetime, Kelmanson underwent the traumatic experiences of what was feared to be the impending destruction of the State of Israel in the period leading up to the Six-Day War in 1967 and in the period of the Yom Kippur War in 1973. He was also deeply affected by the deaths of his own contemporaries and his students in the course of the Arab-Israeli conflict. All of these experiences have made him highly sensitive to the possibility that Israel could experience a tragedy as serious as the destruction of the Second Temple, and he therefore is determined to learn from Talmudic stories about that destruction how to avoid a recurrence of catastrophe.

In addition to the books written in an academic context and those written for the general reading public I have already cited, several works by Israeli writers in a wide range of fields have explored the meaning and significance of Talmudic stories. Like the books on this topic, these works are in some cases written for a scholarly readership and in other cases written for the general reading public.

The fields in which these writers work include the academic study of rabbinics and other areas of Jewish studies, psychology, education, film, fiction writing, journalism, cultural development, and yeshiva and communal rabbinic leadership. Authors in these fields include, in alphabetical order: Rachel Ararat, a retired high school teacher of literature, history, and drama who has been a faculty member at Shaanan College; David Asulin, Co-Head of Yeshivat Ahavat Yisrael in Netivot; Brenda Bacon, faculty member at the Schechter Institute of Jewish Studies in Jerusalem; Yehudit Bar-Yesha Gershovitz, faculty member at the Yaacov Herzog Center; Modi Brodetzky, a therapist specializing in children with learning difficulties; Yair Caspi, a psychologist who is the Founder and Director of the Center for Jewish Psychology in Tel Aviv; Yair Dreyfus, a religious Zionist rabbi who is the Head of Yeshivat Siach Yitzchak in Efrat; Shimshon Ettinger, a professor at Bar Ilan University; Shamma Friedman, a professor at the Schechter Institute of Jewish Studies in Jerusalem; Yehoshua Grinberg, a religious Zionist novelist; Ariel Hirschfeld, a professor at the Hebrew University in Jerusalem; Elie Holzer, a professor at Bar Ilan University; Eitam Henkin, a religious Zionist rabbi; Moshe Lavee, a lecturer at the University of Haifa; Udi Leon, a filmmaker; Yael Levine Katz, who holds a doctorate in Talmud from Bar Ilan University; Yehuda Liebes, a professor at the Hebrew University; Hananel Mack, a professor at Bar Ilan University; Pinchas Mandel, a faculty member at the Schechter Institute of Jewish Studies in Jerusalem; Rachel Marani, founder of the Israel Cultural Excellence Foundation; Yifat Monnickendam, who holds a doctorate in Talmud from Bar Ilan University; Gil Nativ, who has served as a rabbi in the Reform and Conservative movements in Israel; Ishay Rosen-Zvi, an associate professor at Tel Aviv University; Aliza Shenhar, a professor at the University of Haifa; Avigdor Shinan, a professor at the Hebrew University in Jerusalem; Yair Schlein, a faculty member at the Open University; Daniel Statman, a professor at the University of Haifa; Oded Yisraeli, a senior lecturer at Ben-Gurion University; and Aryeh Yoeli, editor of the religious Zionist Internet news site Serugim. In addition to works by all of these writers, academic studies by faculty members in American universities, Daniel Boyarin, a professor at University of California at Berkeley, and Jeffrey Rubenstein, a professor at New York University, that have appeared in Hebrew have contributed to the Israeli discourse on Talmudic stories.

As readers consider the contemporary Israeli readings of the Talmudic stories I will present in the upcoming chapters, they may be surprised at my decision to include both academic works and works composed for the general reading public. The purposes of those who write for scholars and those who write for the general public are to a large extent very different. Academics are primarily interested in reconstructing the meaning of a Talmudic story in the historical context in which it was composed, to the extent that that context can be determined. Those who write for the general public often have another purpose in mind, namely to draw on a Talmudic story for insights relevant to contemporary social, political, and cultural issues. Furthermore, the rules of the game that each category of author observes are significantly different. "Ideally," Tsafi Sebba-Elran has observed, "the scholar aspires to be free from any ideological agenda, while [the writer who seeks contemporary insights] proudly declares his ideological affinities. The former is more concerned with historical truth, while the latter is more concerned with a 'usable' truth."[66]

As will be clear from reading the upcoming chapters, I am primarily interested in the way that contemporary interpretations of Talmudic stories contribute to cultural discourse in Israel, an effect closer to what Sebba-Elran characterizes as the search for a usable truth. It turns out, however, that interpretations of Talmudic stories in much of the scholarship on this genre serve not only the academic search for the accurate reconstruction of cultural dimensions of the historical past, but also often suggest the relevance of Talmudic stories to the contemporary reader. Of course, the popularly oriented writing may sometimes take more liberties in creatively re-imagining the meaning of Talmudic stories than the academic studies. Nevertheless, I see the range from the more "straight" readings in the academic writings to the more "creative" readings in the popularized writings as part of a grand conversation transcending the distinctions between the academic and popular discourses. In fact, some works by those with academic training in Talmudic stories, including Ruth Calderon, Shmuel Faust, Yonah Fraenkel, Ido Hevroni, Admiel Kosman, and Ruhama Weiss, are written in a more popular style. Other works by academically trained scholars may be less popular in style, but they too contribute to an understanding of how Talmudic stories can be relevant to Israelis today.[67]

Each of the following chapters focuses on how a wide range of Israeli writers interpret one Talmudic story (or in the case of Chapter

Four, a series of stories about one figure). I chose the stories because they are among those that have been of the greatest interest to people engaged in the study of this genre in Israel today and because I have found myself personally attracted to them. Chapter Two presents a story in which a dispute among rabbis over how to make a ritual ruling raises important questions about the nature of authority and how people treat each other. Chapter Three deals with the story of a relationship that develops between the rabbinic sage Rabbi Yohanan and a robber named Resh Lakish; in this story the latter repents of his ways and becomes Rabbi Yohanan's study partner, but eventually this relationship based on the attraction of opposites breaks down, causing both members of the relationship to die. Chapter Four explores stories about Beruria, the only woman to appear in the Talmud as a learned sage; these stories have much to say about the nature of gender relations in those days as well as our own. Chapter Five presents the story of Rabbi Hiya bar Ashi's struggle to live a life of sexual abstinence until his wife succeeds in tricking him into having sexual relations with her. Chapter Six explores the moving story of the marriage of Akiva, one of the leading rabbis of his time, and his wife and their mutual devotion during the many years in which he is separated from her while studying Torah. Chapter Seven is about the story in which an invitation to a rich man's feast is mistakenly delivered to his enemy Bar Kamtza, rather than to his friend Kamtza; this error leads to Bar Kamtza's public humiliation and to events initiated by him that culminate in the destruction of the Second Temple in Jerusalem.

CHAPTER 2

AUTHORITY, AUTONOMY, AND INTERPERSONAL RELATIONS: THE OVEN OF AKHNAI

The general consensus among the rabbis of the late Second Temple period and the decades following the destruction of the Temple in 70 C.E. was that the age of biblical prophecy had ended and therefore the primary way to know God's will was to engage in an intensive study of His revealed word in the Bible. Many Talmudic stories illustrate the difficulties that can emerge when a group of rabbis seek to determine Jewish law by studying Scripture. In these stories, as well as in discussions of Jewish law in the Talmud, it becomes clear that this process of arriving at divine truth can be problematic due to three factors in particular: (1) the difficulty faced by the rabbis, who are not privy to divine communication, to know for sure that they can determine God's will, which leads to much disagreement about what the law should be; (2) the tension between previous determinations of the law and the need to adjust legal norms to deal with contemporary issues; and (3) the inevitable human conflicts that arise in any group trying to make decisions, in which egotistical self-assertion, competition, and acts of humiliation can all play roles.

Contemporary Israelis can readily identify with these issues. Influenced by trends in modern and post-modern thought, they too are unsure of what is true (and some, unlike the rabbis, are unsure whether truth even exists). They contend on a regular basis with the question of how to adapt established values to contemporary realities. They are also very familiar with what can go wrong in interpersonal relationships as a result of problematic group dynamics. A Talmudic story, known as "The Oven of Akhnai," presents these issues arising at an important juncture in rabbinic history in an effective manner that has captivated many Israelis seeking to come to terms with similar issues in their contemporary context.

"The Oven of Akhnai" takes place in the aftermath of the destruction of the Second Temple in 70 C.E., a time of national upheaval during which the rabbis of the emerging spiritual center in Yavneh were struggling with the question of who has the authority to determine Jewish law and how that law would be applied to the radically changed circumstances in which Jews in the Land of Israel lived. "Very little is known about the way that discussions were conducted and the manner of making decisions in Yavneh," Oded Yisraeli has observed, "but even the little that is before us provides us with enough to understand how problematic the very existence of the process was."[1] This was a time, explains Yisraeli, when "[q]uestions of authority, acceptance of rule, responsibility, and the freedom to teach came to the surface," and clearly these questions were not easily resolved.[2]

The Oven of Akhnai

It was taught there: They cut up sections and put sand between each section. Rabbi Eliezer declared it ritually pure [i.e. not susceptible to becoming ritually impure], and the sages [declared it] ritually impure [i.e. susceptible to becoming ritually impure]. And this is the oven of akhnai. Why [is it called] akhnai? Rabbi Yehudah said in the name of Shmuel: Words surrounded it like an akhna [=snake] and made it ritually impure. It was taught: On that day Rabbi Eliezer brought every argument in the world and they were not found to be acceptable [by the other sages]. He said to them, "If the law is according to my opinion, let this carob tree prove it." The carob tree was uprooted from its place one hundred cubits, and some say four hundred cubits. They said to him, "One may not bring proof from a carob tree." He again said, "If the law is according to my opinion let this channel of water prove it." The water in the channel flowed backward. They said to him, "One may not bring proof from a channel of water." He again said to them, "If the law is according to my opinion, let the walls of the study house prove it." The walls of the study house began to fall. Rabbi Yehoshua rebuked them, saying, "If sages are arguing the law with each other, who are you [to interfere]?" [The walls] did not fall out of respect for Rabbi Yehoshua, and they did not straighten out of respect for Rabbi Eliezer, and they still lean. He said to them again, "If the law is according to my opinion, let Heaven prove it. A heavenly voice said, "Why are you disagreeing with Rabbi Eliezer, for the law is always according to his opinion?" Rabbi Yehoshua stood on his feet and said, "It is not in Heaven [Deuteronomy 30:12]." What did he mean when he said "It is not in Heaven?" Rabbi Yirmiyah said, "That since the Torah was already given at Mount Sinai we do not pay attention to heavenly voices, for at Mount Sinai You already wrote in the Torah, "You shall decide according to the majority [Exodus 23:2]." Rabbi Natan came across Elijah.

He said to him, "What did the Holy One Blessed be He do at that time?" He said to him, "He smiled and said, 'My sons have defeated Me, My sons have defeated Me.'" They say: On that day they brought all [the ovens] that Rabbi Eliezer had declared to be ritually pure and burned them, and they voted to ban him. And they said, "Who will inform him?" Rabbi Akiva said," I will go, lest someone not appropriate will inform him and thereby the whole world will be destroyed." What did Rabbi Akiva do? He dressed in black and wrapped himself in black and sat before him at a distance of four cubits. Rabbi Eliezer said to him, "What is special about this day?" He said to him, "Rabbi, it appears to me that your colleagues have separated themselves from you." He [Rabbi Eliezer] tore his clothing and removed his shoes and went down to sit on the ground. His eyes shed tears, and the world was stricken: one third of the olives, one third of the wheat, and one third of the barley [were ruined]. And there are those who say even the dough in the hands of women was spoiled. It was taught: Destruction happened on that day, for every place to which Rabbi Eliezer turned his eyes was burned. Rabban Gamliel was traveling on a ship, and a wave came up to drown him. He said, "It appears to me that this must be because of Rabbi Eliezer ben Hyrcanus." He stood up on his feet and said, "Master of the Universe, it is revealed and known to You that I did this not for my honor and not for the honor of my father's house, but for Your honor, so that there would not be too many disagreements in Israel." The sea rested from its anger. Imma Shalom was the wife of Rabbi Eliezer and the sister of Rabban Gamliel. From that event onward she did not allow Rabbi Eliezer to prostrate himself [in prayer]. One day it was the new moon, but she was mistaken about whether it was a full or deficient month. Some say a poor man came and stood at the door and she gave him some bread. She came upon him [Rabbi Eliezer] while he was prostrated and said to him, "Get up. You have killed my brother." The sound of a shofar went out to announce to the public from the house of Rabban Gamliel that he had died. He [Rabbi Eliezer] said to her, "How did you know [he died]?" She said to him, "I have a tradition from the house of my father's father that the gates [of Heaven] are locked except for the gates [through which can pass the prayer of one] who is wronged." (B. Bava Metzia 59a-59b)[3]

Authoritative Knowledge vs. Majority Rule

There is a principle in rabbinic law that vessels which are whole and complete are susceptible to ritual purity, and vessels which are not whole and complete are not susceptible to ritual purity. At the beginning of the story, a question arose in the deliberations of the rabbis in Yavneh regarding the status of a particular kind of oven, one consisting of sections with sand inserted to hold them together. Rabbi Eliezer did not consider such an oven to be whole and complete and therefore concluded that it was not susceptible to ritual impurity, while the sages did consider such an oven to be whole and complete and therefore concluded that it was susceptible to becoming ritually impure.

Contemporary Israeli readers of this story have been fascinated by the drama of the intense conflict that arose between Rabbi Eliezer and the sages led by Rabbi Yehoshua and, later in the story, between Rabbi Eliezer and the most authoritative rabbi of the time, Rabban Gamliel, as a result of their differences of opinion. Of particular interest to readers has been the fact that it is not clear why either party took the position it did. They have sought to understand why Rabbi Eliezer was unwilling to bow to the majority opinion and at the same time why Rabbi Yehoshua defied the heavenly voice that supported Rabbi Eliezer, insisting instead that the law be determined by a majority decision of the rabbis. It would appear that Rabbi Eliezer's unwillingness to give his assent to the opinion of the majority was based on his conviction that his legal ruling was the only valid one, and as Yair Schlein observes, he believed that the authority of the law can legitimately stem from "a figure of senior status and the deep inner conviction of this figure" even if he is a minority of one.[4] The statement that Rabbi Eliezer "brought every argument in the world" indicates to Chaim Licht that the story is saying that, in effect, Rabbi Eliezer "possess[ed] all possible wisdom in the world [and] from this the obvious conclusion would be that his words would be accepted and the law would be according to his opinion."[5]

The knowledge that supported Rabbi Eliezer's position came from past teachings that he was sure he had understood and that he believed had to be maintained. As Oded Yisraeli observes, Rabbi Eliezer operated on the assumption that he possessed an "ability and a skill to preserve an early legal tradition in all of its complexities and implications and to pass it on in an authentic and accurate manner to the members of the next generation of teachers of Torah."[6] His teacher, Rabban Yohanan ben Zakkai, extolled Rabbi Eliezer's ability to absorb and retain the teachings he had studied, comparing his mind to "a sealed cistern that does not lose a drop" (Mishnah Avot 2:8).

The division between Rabbi Eliezer on the one hand and Rabbi Yehoshua and Rabban Gamliel on the other hand was not only due to one side asserting the prerogative of a remembered tradition and the other side insisting on the authority of majority rule. The two sides also differed over the extent to which God should have a role in the legal decision-making process. Rabbi Eliezer saw God as playing a central role in that process, while Rabbi Yehoshua and Rabban Gamliel did not see God as playing any role in the process. Rabbi Eliezer, suggests Oded Yisraeli, believed it was important to preserve the tradition handed down from the past, because in that tradition one can find the divine presence. Rabbi Eliezer was apparently convinced, explains Yisraeli, that "he who destroys the purity of the concept of the oral Torah transmitted from generation to generation and mixes into it foreign elements [such as the opinions of contemporary rabbis] ... is actually harming the existential and historical connection to the revelation at Mount Sinai and thereby removes the presence of God from Israel."[7] In contrast, Rabban Gamliel did not see God as central to discussions of the law. "Rabban Gamliel ...," suggests Yair Schlein, "emphasize[d] the distance and separateness of God: [he believed that] from the time that the Torah was given the personal tie between God and his faithful was broken and so one must decide according to the majority" and not look to God as a source of authority.[8]

Autonomy vs. Authority

Daniel Statman notes that many in Israel are attracted to this story because it appears to endorse the legitimacy of human autonomy in making decisions about how to observe Jewish law. "The main and startling expression of autonomy," he writes, "is found [in the story] in the lack of submission of the sages to the word of God and in the determination that the Torah is 'not in Heaven,' and therefore one does not listen to divine messages when it comes to arriving at the appropriate interpretation."[9] This would seem to support the legitimacy of each generation arriving at a new consensus about the law that is in keeping with contemporary values, even if it contradicts previous generations' understanding of the law. "'The Oven of Akhnai,'" writes Statman, "has an almost subversive message. ... The Torah is not in Heaven, and does not even lie in the hands of the one who on the basis of charisma or genius can claim a special relationship with Heaven; the Torah is placed in the hands of sages in every generation, and they have the authority to interpret it according to their understanding ... under changed circumstances."[10] In keeping with this line of interpretation, Shimshon Ettinger suggests that "the dispute between Rabbi Eliezer and the sages was not about the question of the truth of the tradition he possessed, for surely the sages did not disagree with him."[11] Their difference with Rabbi Eliezer was based on the fact that "they wanted to invent another legal ruling in accordance with their opinion," and so all of Rabbi Eliezer's proofs in support of tradition were completely irrelevant to them. [12]

Daniel Statman cautions that the story does not present an unequivocal endorsement of autonomy in the process of rabbinic legal decision making. It is true, he concedes, that if one focuses on the first part of the story, up to the point that it is reported that God "smiled and said, 'My sons have defeated Me, My sons have defeated Me,'" as many contemporary Israeli readers do, one can see the story as strongly endorsing the autonomous right of human beings to decide how to live their lives. However, as the story progresses, it portrays a rabbinic culture that is based on a system that cannot tolerate dissent and is compelled to deny autonomy to those who disagree with the authority of the rabbis in power. "The expectation of [Rabbi Eliezer]," writes Statman, "[was] that he [would] give up his position and bow his head in respect for the authority of the sages. The obvious conclusion is that a sage is permitted to try to persuade his colleagues of . . . his position. If he fails, however, he must submit to their authority, and he is not permitted to undermine them or to go on his own [autonomous] path."[13]

Rabbi Eliezer's Miracles

Contemporary interpreters of the story have not understood the miracles that Rabbi Eliezer brought forth to support his position as actual occurrences, as one would expect in this age of science, but rather as symbols that contribute to the meaning of the story. Oded Yisraeli sees the three miracles as expressing Rabbi Eliezer's strong opposition to the other sages, who he thought were not ruling in an appropriate manner. The uprooting of the carob tree and the reversal of the flow of the water channel refer to what were deemed in rabbinic times to be two of the most basic sources of human physical sustenance, as they are in the legend about Rabbi Shimon bar Yochai and his son Elazar hiding in a cave, living on carobs and water (B. Shabbat 33b). Thus, when Rabbi Eliezer called on Heaven to disrupt their availability it was, Yisraeli asserts, "as if he were cursing the sages [that they will not have their basic physical needs filled]," and when he called on Heaven to bring down the walls of the study house, it was as if he were calling on the walls of the study house to "threaten to bury those who sit in it."[14] Chaim Licht observes that Rabbi Eliezer's call for the walls of the study house to fall down is a declaration that a world "[that is no longer committed to] pure truth has no possibility of existence" and therefore will suffer destruction.[15] In other words, a study house not based on the divine will cannot possibly continue to function as the place for legal decision making. David Asulin sees the water channel as a symbolic representation of how Rabbi Eliezer viewed Torah: "The water channel is built at an incline that conducts water from the source to great distances. It all depends on the strength of the source, of the spring. There is no water source on the way that can renew itself; all of the water comes only from the source. [By analogy, Rabbi Eliezer is saying,] the Torah comes from its source at the revelation at Mount Sinai, from teacher to students in one flow, and no person has permission to invent matters on the way."[16]

Rabbi Eliezer failed to persuade the other sages of his position by arguments based on tradition, by means of miracles, or even by receiving the support of a heavenly voice, yet he still refused to concede defeat. As Aliza Shenhar observes, Rabbi Eliezer's inability to compromise was ultimately intolerable to Rabban Gamliel and the other sages.[17] Rabban Gamliel believed, notes Yair Schlein, that it is "the community . . . which constitutes in effect the only framework that gives legitimization to the individual and his worldview," and therefore he who removes himself from the community cannot be recognized as having a valid opinion.[18]

The sages undertook the extreme actions of burning all the ovens that Rabbi Eliezer had declared to be ritually pure and banning him from future legal deliberations. They apparently could think of no other way to send an unequivocal message that it was imperative that everyone accept the authority of the law as determined by rabbinic consensus. "Their purpose was to make clear to Rabbi Eliezer, and no less importantly to the community of sages in general," observes Daniel Statman, "that the Torah goes out to Israel from the court in Yavneh, in accordance with the majority decision of the legal experts, and no one is authorized to reject it on the basis of private traditions, personal positions, or what he considers to be divine revelation."[19]

Is the Story on the Side of Rabbi Yehoshua and Rabban Gamliel or on the Side of Rabbi Eliezer?

Although in the first part of the story it is Rabbi Yehoshua who spoke in the name of the other sages, it was Rabban Gamliel, the leading sage of his day, who bore the ultimate responsibility for how the sages handled the dissent of Rabbi Eliezer. Indeed, as the story progresses, the original dispute between Rabbi Eliezer and Rabbi Yehoshua is portrayed as an ongoing tension between the authority asserted by Rabban Gamliel and the aggrieved feelings of Rabbi Eliezer, who had been banned from rabbinic decision making.

Contemporary Israeli readings of the story do not present an unequivocal determination of which side of the dispute is favored by the author of the story. Yair Schlein argues that the story embodies a tragic conflict between the points of view of Rabbi Eliezer and Rabban Gamliel, neither of which is fully endorsed.[20] Schlein's interpretation is validated by noting the pattern of God's shifting loyalties to the two points of view during the story, which would seem to suggest the ambivalent attitude of the author toward their conflicting positions. Initially, the supernatural events and the heavenly voice provided strong support for Rabbi Eliezer's position. Then, God seemed to withdraw his support for Rabbi Eliezer by taking delight in the defeat of his argument and by not intervening when the sages banned him. Following this, we see possible evidence of God's support for the banned Rabbi Eliezer when olives, wheat, and dough were ruined as a result of his anguish, and especially when the wave rose up to threaten Rabban Gamliel's life. However, when Rabban Gamliel declared to God that he banned Eliezer not for selfish reasons but in order to prevent controversy among Jews, he succeeded in convincing God to withdraw the wave and allow him to live.

Later, however, in response to Rabbi Eliezer's prayer, God turned against Rabban Gamliel and put him to death. The fact that, at the end of the story, both figures were defeated—Rabbi Eliezer remained banned from the study house and Rabban Gamliel died—suggests to Schlein that the story never makes a definitive statement supporting "one position or the other."[21] The author's inability to reconcile the differences between the two approaches to legal decision making is, argues Schlein, represented as well in the situation of Imma Shalom, caught between her loyalty to her husband Eliezer and her loyalty to her brother Gamliel, and incapable of resolving the conflict between them.[22]

Two religious Zionist rabbis, Binyamin Kelmanson and Yair Dreyfus, both heads of yeshivot, offer different readings of the implications of the story for Israeli Jews committed to the observance of traditional Jewish law. Each reads in it a critique of an aspect of contemporary religiosity which disturbs him, and each calls for change that would improve the quality of religious Jewish life in Israel. In their readings of the legal dispute in the study house, one leans toward the position of Rabbi Yehoshua as the model of religious change he advocates, while the other leans toward the position of Rabbi Eliezer. Kelmanson, who sides with Rabbi Yehoshua, argues that this story may be read as a challenge to the extreme legal conservatism of ultra-Orthodox Jews, which he considers to be a perversion of the true path of Judaism. In response to the undermining of tradition by modern advocates of change, including Reform Judaism, he maintains, ultra-Orthodoxy has insisted that the content of Torah is transmitted in exactly the same form throughout the generations, that "in the final analysis we only summarize, transmit, and recycle the given knowledge," but never allow Jewish law to develop in a new direction.[23] According to Kelmanson's reading, Rabbi Eliezer represents the ultra-Orthodox position that resists change, while Rabbi Yehoshua represents the realization of Jews committed to Jewish law that the sages must adapt the Torah in keeping with contemporary realities. It is the more flexible position of Rabbi Yehoshua that Kelmanson considers to be valid, for he believes that Jewish law is supposed to be open to adjusting itself to the lives of Jews in each generation.

Dreyfus, who sides more with Rabbi Eliezer, focuses his attention on the traumatic break at the time of the establishment of Yavneh in the history of Torah transmission, which is central to understanding the story. This was a time, argues Dreyfus, when the previous concept of "Torah based on prophecy, on spirituality, on imagination and intuition, on a strong push into the realms of the spirit" was replaced with a concept of Torah "that was based on [human] wisdom.[24] In effect, he observes, "'The Oven of Akhnai' is the story of the disappearance of God, the creation of the empty space in which the world exists. The hearing of voices is replaced by the strengthening of humanity; this is the world of a rationalistic humanity that Rabbi Yehoshua represents."[25] In contrast, Rabbi Eliezer cannot make his peace with this godless approach to legal decision making, and so he heroically insists that an ongoing connection with God be maintained in the study house, and the wild disruptions of nature appear to support him.

The ban of Rabbi Eliezer in the story is, Dreyfus argues, analogous to the attempts of the rabbinic establishment of today to stifle the outpouring of religious passion that is challenging its excessive conservatism. In our time, Dreyfus declares, we have the possibility of reversing the exclusion of God from Torah study during rabbinic times and reasserting the experience of the divine presence into religious life. He writes that on the one hand, he finds himself in sympathy with Rabbi Yehoshua, "who signifies in my eyes the stable world, the world of people [committed] to Jewish law."[26] "On the other hand," he writes, "Rabbi Eliezer signifies in my eyes ... the feeling that everyone feels in his bones, the inner burning that demands not to imprison limitless spirit and freedom" and thereby to reconnect with the Divine.[27]

Like Dreyfus, Yair Caspi, a non-observant spiritually-oriented clinical psychologist, views Rabbi Eliezer's position more favorably than that of Rabbi Yehoshua. Caspi, the author of two books advocating the relevance of Jewish religious categories to psychology, *Lidrosh Elohim* (*To Inquire of God*) and *Nissayon: psikhologyah veyahadut: massa tiqqun* (*Challenged: Psychology and Judaism: A Restorative Journey*), is highly critical of Rabbi Yehoshua's declaration that the Torah is no longer in Heaven. He notes that in quoting the biblical expression "it is not in Heaven" (*lo bashamayim hi*), Rabbi Yehoshua distorts the original meaning of the passage in which it appeared: "For this commandment which I command you today is not too wondrous for you and not distant. It is not in Heaven that one would say who will go up to Heaven and take it for us and cause us to hear it and we will do it. And it is not across the sea that one would say who will cross over the sea for us and take it for us and cause us to hear it and we will do it. For the word is very near to you in your mouth and in your heart that you may do it" (Deuteronomy 30:11-14). In effect, Caspi argues, "the verse ... invites everyone, even those who cannot ascend to Heaven or go over the seas, to inquire of God (*lidrosh Elohim*, the name of Caspi's first book) and to hear truth in his heart."[28] However, in Rabbi Yehoshua's use of the term "it is not in Heaven," he "has turned the verse upside down and locked before you the gate of ascent. From now on it is forbidden to inquire of God," and Caspi is very troubled by the barrier to God that Rabbi Yehoshua has erected.[29]

Hurtful Words

The story of "The Oven of Akhnai" is embedded in a Talmudic discussion of the prohibition against engaging in *ona'at devarim*, defined by Yehuda Brandes as "an expression, generally verbal, which hurts another person."[30] According to Brandes, a Talmudic story that is associated with a discussion of a point of law often functions as an illustration of how a law relates to a real life situation. In this case, it appears that the treatment meted out to Rabbi Eliezer by the other rabbis was a vivid example of the commission of this verbal sin of hurtful words coupled with hurtful actions. Indeed, the snake imagery suggested by the term *akhnai* may be, as Jeffrey Rubenstein suggests, a symbolic representation of how the rabbis treated Rabbi Eliezer. "The snake surrounds its prey, crushes and strangles it to death," writes Rubenstein, "so the image alludes to the crude and cruel treatment of Rabbi Eliezer."[31] After all, notes Rubenstein, the way the sages handled the aftermath of the legal disputation was unnecessarily extreme. It does not appear to have been common practice to ban a person who held a minority opinion in a legal discussion, and furthermore it was not necessary for the sages to destroy the ovens they considered to be unclean. They could have just declared them to be forbidden to use.[32]

One may seek to distinguish between the way Rabbi Yehoshua and the other sages conducted their deliberations on Jewish law and the way that they treated Rabbi Eliezer and view their approach to the law favorably while still criticizing them for humiliating Rabbi Eliezer. Tova Hartman and Charlie Buckholtz challenge this idea, asserting that the sages' legal decision-making process and their humiliation of Rabbi Eliezer were more interconnected than might appear on the surface. In fact, they suggest, there may have been a connection between Rabbi Yehoshua's insistence on leaving God out of their deliberations and his moral failing and that of the other sages in the way they treated Rabbi Eliezer. "In a post-destruction world," they write, "there may well exist a compelling need to take greater responsibility for, and marshal greater authority over, the development of Jewish legal tradition."[33] However, in disconnecting from God, one runs the risk of losing touch with the divine imperative to treat other people in a sensitive manner. Hartman and Buckholtz note that there is much emphasis in the discussion of *ona'at devarim* that precedes the story on the particular attention God pays to punishing those who engage in this sin, and this aspect of the preceding discussion, they argue, "seems intent on driving home the message that even though after the destruction God may seem far away, He is never as far away as we think, in particular with respect to our relationships with each other."[34] In the end, they argue, the story can be read as "a cautionary tale about some of the moral and spiritual dangers that can accompany a shift toward a more autonomous self-regard."[35]

Jeffrey Rubenstein observes that the story critiques not only the specific way that the sages treated Rabbi Eliezer, but also the ungodly quality of their legal discussions. When, during the argument between Rabbi Eliezer and the sages, the walls of the study house began to fall, Rabbi Yehoshua called out to them "If sages are arguing the law with each other—what are you doing?" The original Hebrew here for "arguing" is *menatsḥim* (literally: defeating), which suggests that the way the sages treated each other resembled a military battle: in every discussion there was a victor and a loser, and presumably the loser could feel humiliated in his defeat. The walls of the study house, observes Rubenstein, displayed a very different model of relationship than was practiced by the rabbis in their intellectual warfare in their determination to defeat the enemy. When Rabbi Eliezer called for the walls of the study house to fall down and Rabbi Yehoshua called for them to stay upright, the walls refused to take sides in this battle of legal discussion: "[The walls] did not fall out of respect for Rabbi Yehoshua, and they did not straighten out of respect for Rabbi Eliezer, and they still lean." The walls' even-handed respect for both disputants contrasted sharply with the way the disputants treated each other. Furthermore, notes Rubenstein, the story presents God as the ultimate model of how to transcend the war-like character of rabbinic arguments. When He was defeated by Rabbi Yehoshua and the other sages, God did not get angry and did not fight back. He merely smiled and said, "My sons have defeated Me" (*nitsḥuni banay*)—using the same verb as Rabbi Yehoshua when he referred to the disputations in the study house.[36]

Rabbi Akiva and Imma Shalom

Both Rabbi Akiva and Imma Shalom play important roles in drawing the reader's attention to what was so problematic about the sages' treatment of Rabbi Eliezer. Rabbi Akiva, note Tova Hartman and Charlie Buckholtz, appears to be the only one who understood that the sages had related to Rabbi Eliezer in an excessively cruel manner. When he said to his colleagues, "I will go, lest someone not appropriate will go and inform him and thereby the whole world will be destroyed," he "lace[d] his offer to inform Eliezer of the ban with a stinging critique of the entire rabbinic establishment. He [went] because he [was] aware of the violence done to Rabbi Eliezer and the divine consequences this violence [had] the potential to trigger. Given that it was his colleagues who committed this violence in the first place, he [was] dubious that any of them [would] have the wherewithal to extend the type of sensitivity that this moment require[d]."[37]

Yehuda Brandes attributes to Rabbi Akiva a sensitivity to avoid as much as possible the sin of *ona'at devarim* when he went to tell the news to Rabbi Eliezer: "Rabbi Akiva, the great student of Rabbi Eliezer, did not dissent from the need to ban his teacher. The question that stood before him was how he could [inform him] in the most delicate way, so that Rabbi Eliezer would be hurt in the least way possible."[38] Furthermore, he observes, "the sign of mourning—[Akiva's] wrapping himself in black clothing—express[ed] the identification of Rabbi Akiva with the sorrow of his teacher."[39]

Later in the story, we are told of Imma Shalom's desperate attempts to keep Rabbi Eliezer from praying to God to punish her brother Rabban Gamliel for treating him so harshly. In explaining why she was so adamant that her husband not share his pain with God, she declared, "I have a tradition from the house of my father's father that the gates [of heaven] are locked except for the gates [through which can pass the prayer of one] who is wronged." On the basis of this tradition, she was saying, she believed that it was highly likely that if her husband's prayer about his humiliation at the hands of her brother reached God, her brother would receive a divine punishment. Oded Yisraeli calls attention to the irony in the fact that if Imma Shalom received this teaching from her family, presumably her brother Rabban Gamliel did as well and would have been expected to act in accordance with the sensitivity that it advocates.[40] As Tova Hartman and Charlie Buckholtz observe, Imma Shalom comes across as a moral foil to Rabbi Yehoshua and Rabban Gamliel. "If … we understand the … story as emphasizing a critique of the abuses and tragedies that can result from holding autonomous reason aloof from accountability to other values," they write, "then Imma Shalom's reiteration of that tradition [became] … the story's … climax: a stinging rebuke against rabbinic loss of perspective and abuse of power."[41]

Ari Elon goes so far as to suggest that in the story, Imma Shalom presents nothing less than a challenge to the standard approach to Jewish law of the rabbis in the Talmud. He posits the existence of an alternative text, which he calls "Imma Shalom's Talmud." Elon declares that this Talmud, reflecting a feminine perspective, "was written by hidden men who were conscious of the pain in the prominent and clever violence that constitutes an integral part of their Torah wars and is brought to expression in the appearance of explosions of rage, gossip, the enjoyment of the downfall of others, *ona'at devarim*, and humiliation."[42] In a similar vein, Jeffrey Rubenstein writes that the message of the story is that "abstract principles often distract attention from the individual and his situation and belittle the importance of personal human suffering. This danger is even greater when the many—certain in themselves because of their power and correct in their eyes because they are the majority—exercise their control over the individual. The story warns against neglecting the human side: feelings of suffering and shame are important, and one should not ignore them while pursuing legal decision making."[43]

The Contemporary Significance of the Story

The issues in this story of how to know the truth, how to determine communal norms, and how people should relate to each other are of great interest to Israeli readers. Much of the appeal of this story is based on the fact that it explores the complexities of these issues in ways that stimulate considerable thought. It is significant that there is no consensus among readers as to the identity of the real hero of the story. Rabbi Yehoshua and Rabban Gamliel on the one hand and Rabbi Eliezer on the other hand reflect positions that various contemporary readers support. Rabbi Yehoshua and Rabban Gamliel are seen by some to represent the value and perhaps necessity of human autonomy in a time when God's direct presence in the world is not felt. They also represent the desirability of feeling free to innovate in response to changing times. At the same time, they can be seen as affirming the need for the stability of norms established democratically by communal consensus to combat the dangers of the anarchical challenge of a disaffected minority.

Rabbi Eliezer can be appreciated for his reliance on the wisdom of tradition, from which presumably one can learn much that is of value. He may even be considered to be heroic in that he maintains his integrity by insisting on the truth as he sees it. He can also be seen as a person open to the world of the spirit, to an experience of God which challenges the set ways of established institutions. For many, Rabbi Eliezer's main significance in the story is that he is the victim of an inexcusable abuse of power, an experience with which all readers can have much empathy. Of particular interest to readers are the two moral heroes of the story: Rabbi Akiva and Imma Shalom, one of the few women named in the Talmud. Rabbi Akiva is the only one of his contemporaries who truly appreciates the suffering of Rabbi Eliezer. Imma Shalom, caught between loyalty to her brother Rabban Gamliel and her husband Rabbi Eliezer, is impressive in her insistence that God cares deeply that human beings treat each other with utmost sensitivity.

CHAPTER 3

WHEN OPPOSITES ATTRACT: RABBI YOHANAN AND RESH LAKISH

Developing a close relationship with another person is one of the most challenging aspects of human existence. If two people can figure out how to live together, how to work together, and how to play together, it is to the emotional advantage of both. However, even if an initial mutual attraction draws two people together, each person brings to that relationship a distinct background, a set of values, a worldview, and an orientation to life, and their differences will always carry the potential of driving a wedge between them. A Talmudic story about the meeting and coming together of two opposite social types, the Torah scholar Rabbi Yohanan and the robber Resh Lakish, has drawn the attention of many contemporary Israelis who see much in this challenging relationship and its ultimate failure that resonates with their own experience.

Rabbi Yohanan and Resh Lakish

One day, [Rabbi Yohanan] was bathing in the Jordan River. Resh Lakish saw him and jumped into the Jordan after him. He [Rabbi Yohanan] said to him [Resh Lakish], "Your power [should be] for Torah." He [Resh Lakish] said to him [Rabbi Yohanan], "Your beauty [should be] for women." He [Rabbi Yohanan] said to him [Resh Lakish], "If you return [from your evil ways], I will give you my sister, who is more beautiful than I am." He [Resh Lakish] agreed. He wanted to return to get his clothing, but he could not. He [Rabbi Yohanan] taught him [Resh Lakish] Bible and Mishnah and made him a great man. One day there was a dispute in the study house: "A sword and a knife and a dagger and a spear, and a hand sickle and a harvest sickle, at what point are they susceptible to becoming ritually unclean?" [They concluded:] "From the time that they are completely made." "And at what point are they completely made?" Rabbi Yohanan said, "From the time they are forged in the oven." Resh Lakish said, "From the time they are polished in water." He [Rabbi Yohanan] said to him [Resh Lakish]: "A robber would know about his [profession of] robbery." He [Resh

Lakish] said to him [Rabbi Yohanan], "What good did you do me? There [when I was a robber] they called me Master and here they call me Master." He [Rabbi Yohanan] said to him [Resh Lakish], "I did you good by bringing you under the wings of the Shekhinah." Rabbi Yohanan's mind was weakened [i.e. he became depressed]. Resh Lakish was weakened [i.e. he became sick]. His [Rabbi Yohanan's] sister came and wept before him: "Do something for the sake of my children." He [Rabbi Yohanan] said, "Turn your orphans over to me; I will bring them up [Jeremiah 49:11]." [Rabbi Yohanan's sister then said,] "Do something for the sake of my widowhood." He [Rabbi Yohanan] said to her, "Your widows can depend on me [Jeremiah 49:11]." Resh Lakish passed away. Rabbi Yohanan was very saddened about him. The rabbis said, "What shall we do to restore his mind? Let Rabbi Elazar ben Pedat, who has a sharp knowledge of traditions, go." He [Rabbi Elazar] went and sat in front of him [Rabbi Yohanan]. After everything that he [Rabbi Yohanan] said, he [Rabbi Elazar] would say, "There is a teaching that supports you." He [Rabbi Yohanan] said, "Are you like the son of Lakish? Everything I said the son of Lakish would question with twenty-four difficulties, and I would resolve the difficulties twenty-four times until the tradition was expanded, and you say there is a teaching that supports me. Don't I know that what I said is proper?" He [Rabbi Yohanan] would go around tearing his clothes and crying, "Son of Lakish where are you? Son of Lakish where are you?" And he cried out this way until he went out of his mind. The sages sought mercy for him and he passed away. (B. Bava Metzia 84a)

The Meeting of Rabbi Yohanan and Resh Lakish

As Ruth Calderon and Admiel Kosman point out, in a manuscript of the Talmud known as the Hamburg Talmud, it is written that when Resh Lakish saw Rabbi Yohanan, before jumping into the Jordan, Resh Lakish thought that Rabbi Yohanan was a woman. This addition provides a motivation for Resh Lakish's actions, namely, that he was physically attracted to this figure who appeared to be a woman and wanted to engage in sexual relations with her. In B. Bava Metzia 84a, shortly before the appearance of the story of Rabbi Yohanan and Resh Lakish, there are a series of statements that help to explain why Resh Lakish may have thought that Rabbi Yohanan was a woman and why the robber may have been so sexually aroused that he was driven to jump into the water to get closer to him. According to these statements, Rabbi Yohanan was a very handsome man. Rabbi Yohanan identified himself as "one of the beautiful ones from Jerusalem [who have remained after its destruction]." He considered himself to be so handsome that he would sit outside the local ritual bath in the belief that Jewish women, having purified themselves before having sexual relations with their husbands, would see him and as a result they would conceive babies who were as beautiful and learned in Torah as he was. One person declared that Rabbi Yohanan's beauty was so great that it could only be approximated by the aesthetically pleasing image created if one brought a newly forged "silver cup and fill[ed] it with red pomegranate seeds and adorn[ed] it with a crown of red roses and put it between the sun and the shade." In one way, however, Rabbi Yohanan's beauty was said to be marred: he lacked *hadrat panim,* which the medieval commentator Rashi interprets as meaning that Rabbi Yohanan could not grow a beard like other men. If this interpretation of *hadrat panim* is accurate, it would help to explain the gender confusion experienced by Resh Lakish in the version of the story in the Hamburg manuscript when he thought he had come across a beautiful naked woman.[1]

A Surprising Connection

As soon as Resh Lakish entered the water, Rabbi Yohanan called out to him, "Your power [should be] for Torah," to which Resh Lakish replied, "Your beauty [should be] for women."[2] Rachel Marani sees in this brief verbal exchange between Rabbi Yohanan and Resh Lakish (consisting of only four words in the original Aramaic—*ḥelakh le'orayta* and *shufrakh lenashei*) the basis for the mutual attraction that eventually drew them together: each one was in touch with a dimension of human experience which was lacking in the other. When Rabbi Yohanan said, "Your power [should be] for Torah," he was offering Resh Lakish an opportunity to learn about the spiritual dimension missing in his life, and when Resh Lakish said, "Your beauty [should be] for women," he was offering Rabbi Yohanan an opportunity to learn about the physical dimension missing in his life. Another way of seeing the basis for this attraction, Marani suggests, is that the religious figure Rabbi Yohanan offered to teach the criminal figure Resh Lakish the ability to discipline himself within certain boundaries, which he was lacking, while the criminal figure Resh Lakish offered to teach the religious figure Rabbi Yohanan the ability to break through boundaries, which he was lacking. In either case, she writes, each one was saying to the other, "I see the real you [i.e. who you are and what you are missing], beyond your social status, beyond the clothing that identifies your role in life."[3] In other words, their naked encounter signified an ability to discern in each other a potential inner dimension beyond the limited image with which each presented himself to the world.

Another way of reading this brief verbal encounter is to see in it the expression of an insight that each of these men had that the other man had a quality that he could use to succeed in the lifestyle that was the opposite of his. Rabbi Yohanan discerned that Resh Lakish's physical power would enable him to excel as a Torah scholar, and Resh Lakish discerned that Rabbi Yohanan's beauty would enable him to live a life of sexual licentiousness with women.[4] On the face of it, these were inappropriate insights, because the study of Torah could not have been further from Resh Lakish's interests, and the ability to seduce women with his beauty would have been considered sinful by Rabbi Yohanan. It therefore seems highly unlikely that either would be capable of convincing the other to take advantage of the identified quality and cross over to the other side of the cultural divide. Nevertheless, Rabbi Yohanan did succeed in pulling Resh Lakish into his world, and the latter became a great scholar and the designated study partner of Rabbi Yohanan.

Contemporary Israeli readers have wondered how Rabbi Yohanan could possibly see any qualities in the sinful, ignorant Resh Lakish that would make him a good candidate to become a Torah scholar, and for that matter what relevance the physical prowess of Resh Lakish would have for a life in the rabbinic study house. One answer offered is that Rabbi Yohanan's attraction to Resh Lakish was based on an understanding that physical strength can be a factor in the emergence of intellectual and spiritual strengths that would be of great value in the study house. "[Rabbi Yohanan] already saw in his imagination," suggests Ari Elon, "how the presence of Resh Lakish would grant a new power to the Torah being studied."[5] In support of his position, Elon cites a Talmudic saying that uses physical imagery to describe the great intellectual feats of Resh Lakish in the study house: "He who sees Resh Lakish in the study house, it appears to him as if he is uprooting mountains and grinding them together (B. Sanhedrin 24a)."[6] In a similar vein, Ariel Hirshfeld writes, "Rabbi Yohanan [understood] immediately that this [was] a person with a large drive, who [was] able to break through any barrier in his way."[7] According to Hirshfeld, Rabbi Yohanan was aware that all greatness, including that of Torah scholars, is the product of such a drive, and so Resh Lakish's physical strength could be transformed into a spiritual and intellectual forcefulness.

Even if one comes to appreciate why Rabbi Yohanan saw in Resh Lakish the potential of becoming a Torah scholar, it is not clear why Resh

Lakish would repent of his ways and begin to study Torah. It has been suggested that the robber intuited that some quality of Rabbi Yohanan and of his life as a Torah scholar would provide him with fulfillment that he could not attain in his current life. Modi Brodetsky surmises that Resh Lakish realized that Rabbi Yohanan combined both the physical beauty that Resh Lakish celebrated and a spiritual beauty that had not been accessible to him. "When he [saw] the glowing beauty of Rabbi Yohanan," explains Brodetsky, "[Resh Lakish understood] immediately that the beauty and wholeness to which he so aspired [were] not found in the world [of the robbers] in which he had invested most of his efforts until now."[8] In fact, according to Brodetsky's reading, the reason Resh Lakish jumped into the Jordan was that he was driven to seek an understanding of how the person he saw "could realize in his body and soul the ideal of beauty that he so admired."[9]

Admiel Kosman suggests that Rabbi Yohanan presented to Resh Lakish an attractive, alternative, androgynous masculinity infused with qualities associated with femininity that he now realized he had missed in his life as a robber. He saw in Rabbi Yohanan and in the study house, Kosman explains, "a feminine side, soft and inclusive, motherly, forgiving and compassionate, that does not engage all the time—as in his 'masculine' life [as a robber]—in wars with a [phallic] 'spear,'" such as the one he put into the river to catapult himself toward Rabbi Yohanan, according to the version in the Hamburg Talmud manuscript.[10]

Rabbi Yohanan, argues Ari Elon, offered the Torah as a spiritual experience suffused with a sublimated eroticism that would surpass the quality of any sexual relations he had ever experienced with a woman. The notion of Torah study as sublimated eroticism, explains Elon, is suggested by rabbinic texts that portray the relationship between a man and the Torah as analogous to sexual relations between a man and a woman. In the following Talmudic discussion of the meaning of the verse "A love doe, a gracious mountain goat; may her breasts always satisfy you, may you always be impassioned in your love for her" (Proverbs 5:19), it is stated that the experience of Torah study provides a spiritual experience that is always as satisfying as it was the first time one engaged in it:

> Why is an analogy drawn between the Torah and a love doe [*ayelet ahavim,* which can be understood as "a beloved woman"]?

> To teach you that just as the womb of a doe is narrow and the delight of a male who has intercourse with her, for whom each time is like the first time, so the words of Torah are the delight of those who study them, for whom each time is like the first time. (B. Eruvin 54b)[11]

Elon cites other Talmudic passages that compare Resh Lakish's subsequent devotion to Torah study with relations between men and women. He notes that the same verse in Proverbs that was interpreted as comparing Torah study with sexual intercourse is interpreted in a different Talmudic passage (J. Berakhot, Chapter 5), as comparing Resh Lakish's intense loyalty to Torah study with the preoccupation of a man with his lover: "Resh Lakish was so engaged in his study of Torah that he would unknowingly walk beyond the distance from town permitted on the Sabbath."[12] Elon also cites another Talmudic passage (B. Sanhedrin 99b) in which Resh Lakish interprets the biblical verse "He who commits adultery lacks heart" (Proverbs 6:32) as referring to a person who does not study Torah regularly. "Resh Lakish," writes Elon, "was so jealous of his beloved Torah that he defined as a heartless adulterer the one who only sets aside occasional time to it and does not devote his entire self to it."[13] As Elon sees it, when Rabbi Yohanan offered his sister (who he claimed was even more beautiful than he was) to Resh Lakish in marriage, Rabbi Yohanan seduced Resh Lakish into a sexual relationship that would help to pull him into the sublimated erotic relationship that sages have with the Torah.[14] And indeed, writes Elon, in accordance with Rabbi Yohanan's plan, Resh Lakish "found in the Torah what he sought in vain in women. He became one of the great lovers of the Torah of all times."[15]

Some readings discern a homoerotic dimension in the attraction between Rabbi Yohanan and Resh Lakish, which was never expressed in an explicitly sexual relationship but rather was sublimated in the connection between the two when Resh Lakish married Rabbi Yohanan's sister and in their relationship as study partners. While the Hamburg Talmud manuscript adds that before Resh Lakish jumped into the Jordan he "thought that he [Rabbi Yohanan] was a woman," the fact that the classic Vilna edition of the Talmud leaves out those words suggests to Yariv Ben-Aharon that perhaps Resh Lakish knew that the figure in the river was a man, and he was pursuing a homosexual encounter with him.[16] "This is a story," argues

Yehuda Liebes, "about a sexual connection that was changed into the Eros of learners of Torah. It [began] with an attempted rape: Resh Lakish the robber jump[ed] into the Jordan after Rabbi Yohanan, who [was] beautiful but feminine (lacking a beard), and [Resh Lakish] did not relent until Rabbi Yohanan's sister, who [was] more beautiful than [Rabbi Yohanan, was] promised to him. When they [began] to learn Torah together, the sex [was] refined and transformed into a spiritual Eros."[17]

Daniel Boyarin suggests that the sublimated homoerotic relationship that developed between Rabbi Yohanan the teacher and Resh Lakish the student is related to the common pattern of a more explicit homoerotic relationship in the culture of ancient Greece in which "an older man, whose beard marks him as such, takes a youth under his protection, educates him, and prepares him for full participation in the life of the polis, while developing erotic relations between them, [a]t the end of [which] educational process the youth becomes the bearer of the spear [the citizen-soldier known as] the hoplite."[18] In the Talmudic story, Boyarin writes, the pattern is reversed in that "an androgynous man without a beard takes under his protection a powerful man, the carrier of a spear [a detail regarding Resh Lakish present in the Hamburg manuscript], educates him and turns him into 'a great man,' thereby weakening his physical strength and taking the power from his 'spear.'"[19] In order to conform with the traditional Jewish religious prohibition against homosexual relations, observes Boyarin, "it [was] necessary to transfer the homoerotic implications from relations between Resh Lakish and Yohanan to relations between Resh Lakish and the sister of Rabbi Yohanan, and the text accomplish[ed] that transfer in a clear and explicit manner."[20]

The radical transformation of Resh Lakish following his agreement to begin the process of repentance was expressed in a strikingly physical manner. The strong robber who could impressively jump into the Jordan River was now powerless to swim to the shore to retrieve the clothes he had previously removed. Daniel Boyarin and Admiel Kosman both observe that this loss of physical power is in keeping with the rabbinic notion that the study of Torah physically weakens a person (B. Sanhedrin 26b).[21] It is particularly significant that it was his robber clothing that Resh Lakish was unable to recover. "The clothing of a person," notes Modi Brodetsky, "symbolizes his status and social position.

Resh Lakish the penitent [could] no long wear the uniform of the head of a gang. From this moment he [did] not belong to them and they [did] not belong to him—he [had] no psychological ability to continue in the role in which he no longer [believed]."[22] As Elie Holzer puts it, "Symbolically, he [could not] put his clothes back on, because he [did] not want to be (or perhaps he no longer [was]) the same person. The account indicates the deep inner change that Resh Lakish [was] undergoing, disconnecting himself from his social environment and its cultural values, ready to enter a new environment and embrace a very different cultural system, the culture of the [study house]."[23] There is additional significance to the fact that following his decision to repent and study Torah, Resh Lakish emerged from water. This experience can be seen as symbolizing a baby's physical birth from a mother's womb filled with amniotic fluid or a convert's spiritual rebirth following immersion in a ritual bath.[24]

The Break: Mutual Disappointment

One day in the course of a debate on Jewish law in the study house, Rabbi Yohanan insulted Resh Lakish with the words, "A robber would know about his [profession of] robbery." With these words, as Yariv Ben-Aharon notes, Rabbi Yohanan committed three violations of Jewish ethical law mentioned in the Talmud (B. Bava Metzia 58b): hurtful speech (*ona'at devarim*), publicly humiliating another person (*hamalbin penei ḥavero barabbim*), and calling another person by a bad name (*hamekhaneh shem ra leḥavero*).[25] One of the examples of hurtful speech that one should avoid is cited in this Talmudic passage: "If a person is one who has repented, one should not say: 'Remember your past deeds.'" The passage also strongly states that if a person commits the sin of publicly humiliating another person, "it is as if he had shed his blood." Later, the same passage declares that there are three sins that are so unforgiveable that they prevent the soul of a dead person from ever rising out of punishment in Gehenna: "committing adultery with another man's wife, publicly humiliating another person, and calling another person by a bad name." Elie Holzer observes that when Rabbi Yohanan spoke to Resh Lakish as if he were still a robber, his words were "especially insulting because even the readers know that Resh Lakish [had] undergone a profound existential change, symbolized both by his physical weakness and his not being able to retrieve his former clothes [following his decision to follow Rabbi Yohanan to the study house]."[26]

The question of how the relationship suddenly fell apart one day has intrigued many readers of the story, because nothing so far in the story has prepared readers for Rabbi Yohanan's shocking behavior. In fact, up to this point, all they have learned about the development of the relationship between these two characters is contained in a one-sentence summary of events: "He [Rabbi Yohanan] taught him [Resh Lakish] Bible and Mishnah and made him a great man." The only other detail from their life together as study partners is presented later in the story, when Rabbi Yohanan recalled their method of study. The paucity of details from this period of their relationship have provided contemporary interpreters with the opportunity to exercise their imaginations and add details to the story that can be seen as explaining the causes of this tragic break between them.

Some interpreters imagine that as their relationship as study partners developed over time, the expectations Rabbi Yohanan and Resh Lakish had of each other, that their study partnership would be of mutual benefit, became undermined. In Ari Elon's reading, when Rabbi Yohanan introduced Resh Lakish to the sublimated eroticism of Torah study, he envisioned sharing with him the love of Torah, and this he eventually accomplished: "[Resh Lakish] as a sage found in the study of Torah what he did not find as a robber in all the women he conquered. He found it [Torah] good, only good all day long."[27] However, over time, surmises Elon, Resh Lakish's love of Torah completely occupied his consciousness to the degree that "he did not love his children or himself, he did not love his wife, and he did not love Rabbi Yohanan."[28] Elon imagines that Resh Lakish's extreme love of Torah began to agitate Rabbi Yohanan: "Fear mixed with fury began to overtake him," but Resh Lakish was too caught up in his love of Torah to notice the impact he was having on Rabbi Yohanan.[29] While they continued to study Torah together, Elon suggests, they lost the ability to interact as human beings: "They developed between them an intense communication in matters between a person and *his Torah*. Matters between a person and *his friend* they tended to ignore. They did not speak directly about their relationship—about fears, about jealousy, and about mutual desires."[30] Matters came to a head, surmises Elon, when one day there was no way to resolve the differences between them in a dispute about law, and all of Rabbi Yohanan's troubled views of Resh Lakish came out in the insult he hurled at his study partner.[31]

This insult, according to Elon, shattered for Resh Lakish the intense experience of Torah study to which he had completely devoted himself. It revealed to him the true motive of Rabbi Yohanan for bringing him into the study house in the first place, of which not even Rabbi Yohanan was aware. Resh Lakish now understood that the study house was not a place where men engaged in the fully satisfying sublimated eroticism of Torah study, but rather a place where men verbally fought with each other in as aggressive and destructive a manner as men fought physically in the world of the robbers that he had left. It now became clear to Resh Lakish that the reason Rabbi Yohanan had wanted him in the study house was because that institution was violent in nature, and who better to fight the battles of Torah than a strong, aggressive robber?[32]

Admiel Kosman also identifies Resh Lakish's disillusionment with the study house as the source of the break between himself and Rabbi Yohanan. Resh Lakish had thought, surmises Kosman, that "he could substitute the world … of hierarchical struggle who will be more the 'Master,' the great man, than his fellow, with a place in which there is a completely different way of life. He imagined meeting in the study house scholars studying Torah in humility and innocence with no powerful competitive struggles," the world protected by "the wings of the Shekhinah," in the words of Rabbi Yohanan.[33] In such a world, explains Kosman, "no hierarchy would rule, and it would be a place of fellowship and humility, analogous to small chicks gathering under the wings of their mother."[34] Now, with Rabbi Yohanan's insult, Resh Lakish realized that both worlds were dominated by men seeking to control others: "There they called me Master and here they call me Master."[35]

Furthermore, Kosman imagines, this incident in the study house made clear to Resh Lakish for the first time how subordinate he was to the control of Rabbi Yohanan. As evidenced by Rabbi Yohanan's description of their method of study when he mourned Resh Lakish, the latter had always had a secondary role in their study partnership: what he was expected to do was to issue challenges to Rabbi Yohanan's legal arguments in order to increase the understanding of the law as expounded by Rabbi Yohanan, but never to engage in a dispute over legal rulings. Kosman suggests that on that day, in arguing with Rabbi Yohanan over a legal decision, Resh

Lakish was doing something new that seriously threatened the superior status of Rabbi Yohanan. Here, for the first time, Resh Lakish asserted himself as one who had the right to differ with Rabbi Yohanan in such a ruling.[36] "This [presumptuousness] of a student perceived as 'rebelling' against his teacher, the one who 'raised' and developed him with his own hands—and now he [dared] to 'liberate' himself and declare a new way of doing things in the study house—anger[ed] Rabbi Yohanan so much that he [hurled] at him the harsh insult, 'A robber would know about his [profession of] robbery.'"[37]

In the two other verbal conflicts in which Rabbi Yohanan engaged in the story, notes Kosman, he always had to have the last word, signifying the power he had over others and his unwillingness to respond appropriately and listen to the other. He ended the initial discussion with Resh Lakish in the Jordan with the offer of his sister in marriage, and he answered his sister's entreaties to save Resh Lakish with an assertion that he will take care of her and her children. Here, it appears that Rabbi Yohanan had lost his ability to win an argument, and so he resorted to merely putting down the other person.[38] Kosman observes that one can understand, from the extreme reaction of Resh Lakish culminating in his death, that his disillusionment with the study house had been building up over time and that the climactic event of the story constituted the conclusive evidence reinforcing his disillusionment that drove him to his death.[39]

Elie Holzer offers additional support for the imaginative direction suggested by Kosman. He characterizes the subordinate role of Resh Lakish in his Torah study with Rabbi Yohanan as playing the role of a "sparring partner," who will never directly disagree with him, but rather will raise objections to the position taken by Rabbi Yohanan that will lead Rabbi Yohanan to sharpen his arguments in favor of his position. "R. Yochanan," explains Holzer, "[had] no doubt that what he [said] '*[was] correct*' [as he said when he objected to the learning style of Rabbi Elazar ben Pedat], so that there [was] no point for the [study] partner to introduce an alternative view based on personal knowledge."[40] The break between them, argues Holzer, occurred when for "the first time ... Resh Lakish explicitly express[ed] his own personal view, which [was] contrary to R. Yochanan's legal statement."[41] Holzer suggests that "R. Yochanan's response—an ad hominem attack—implie[d] that instead of taking advantage of [the] opportunity for a dialogue on the matter at hand [during which Resh Lakish might make a positive contribution to the study of Torah], R. Yochanan attempt[ed] to extinguish all alternative and relevant voices, by reducing Resh Lakish to his former self, a robber."[42] The break between Rabbi Yohanan and Resh Lakish was, according to Holzer, fundamentally about how they viewed the nature of being study partners and what method of study is most conducive to evoking the presence of God. Holzer points out that a passage elsewhere in the Talmud quotes Resh Lakish as asserting that the presence of God can be discerned between study partners only if they are engaged in an exchange of opinions based on mutual respect:

> Rabbi Abba said in the name of Rabbi Shimon ben Lakish [Resh Lakish]: "When two scholars pay heed to each other in law, the Holy One, blessed be He, listens to their voice, as it is said: 'You who dwell in the gardens, the companions hearken to your voice, cause me to hear it [Song of Songs 8:13].' But if they do not do thus, they cause the divine presence to depart from Israel, as it is said: 'Flee my beloved, and be you like a gazelle like a young deer on hills of spices [Song of Songs 8:14].'" (B. Shabbat 63a)

"Here," Holzer writes, "Resh Lakish stresses the *dialogic* nature of the [study partner] relationship, which is characterized by an exchange of ideas between individuals who share a common purpose of learning from and through each other. This interaction is conducted with forbearance and willingness to learn from one another."[43] As a result of Rabbi Yohanan's attack on him, Holzer explains, Resh Lakish came to realize that Rabbi Yohanan was too self-centered and preoccupied with his own perspective to open up to the perspective of Resh Lakish, and thus the two partners could never experience the divine presence that emerges from a mutual, dialogic method of study.

The Break: Rivalry

A second imaginative direction that has been offered to explain the break between these two characters is to surmise that over time Rabbi Yohanan came to see Resh Lakish as a rival for his position in the study house. Both Rachel Ararat and Ari Elon suggest that Rabbi Yohanan was threatened by the fact that he saw his disciple surpassing him in the ability to study Torah.[44] In effect, Rabbi Yohanan had created a monster who could overtake him in the waters of Torah study even as he had not been able to overtake him in their initial confrontation in the Jordan.[45]

Ruth Calderon imagines that at a certain point Rabbi Yohanan began to perceive that the students were paying more attention to the former robber than to himself, the foremost scholar in the study house: "'Resh Lakish is a friendly person,' he thought, 'no one sits around with me like that.'"[46] When Rabbi Yohanan came upon Resh Lakish learning with the others, no one even noticed him nor did they accord him the proper respect by standing, and as a result Rabbi Yohanan's "jealousy kindled like fire."[47] As Calderon surmises, it was while being in this foul mood that the tension building up in Rabbi Yohanan came to a head, and he turned the legal discussion about the ritual purity of metal utensils into a battle that differed significantly from the way they normally learned together: "Rabbi Yohanan [built] the argument and [did] not look directly at Resh Lakish. He [disagreed] in a professional manner, coldly. Resh Lakish [looked] at him surprised. That which was built hundreds of times with the pleasure of creativity [had] today fiercely become a declaration of war."[48] Resh Lakish then fought back: "certain of his position, he [developed] a winning strategy. … He link[ed] together verses like a magician, like a virtuoso actor."[49] Then, for a moment Resh Lakish pulled back from the battle: "He [saw] the anger of his teacher and for a moment he [was] ready to retreat, as he did many times in his [teacher's] honor."[50] However, Resh Lakish soon recalled that having been transformed from a robber into a sage he had become the equal of his teacher and [did] not have to retreat: "But afterward he [remembered] the 'water' in the Jordan. 'I entered as one kind of person and I came out as another kind of person. Doesn't Yohanan hear? Doesn't he remember?'"[51]

The Break: The Impossibility of a Complete Transformation

A third imaginative direction has been to posit that the assumption that both characters held, that Resh Lakish could fully transform himself from a robber into a sage, was psychologically unrealistic. Ruth Calderon surmises that it was a mistake for both Rabbi Yohanan and Resh Lakish to assume that the latter should give up all aspects of his previous "sinful" life. Due to this flawed basis for their relationship, Calderon suggests, Resh Lakish's disillusionment with the study house had built up over time: "Possibly Resh Lakish [felt] deceived, trapped; after a while he [rebelled] against the attempt to 'domesticate' him and to take his freedom from him. … The promise of a 'rebirth' in the Jordan

[had] crumbled in the routine of the study house, where, as in the robber gang, there [were] power conflicts, doubts, and even evil. He [tortured] himself about whether he lost himself, Resh Lakish, whether his clinging to Rabbi Yohanan was an abandonment of himself."[52]

Calderon also observes that not only did Resh Lakish lose something by trying to repress his past as a robber, but so did Rabbi Yohanan by refusing to allow at least some elements of Resh Lakish's previous life into the study house. "If Resh Lakish had been wise enough to go back and take his belongings [including his] knife, and go into his new life armed with his values and not torn from his past," she writes, "the encounter would have yielded a different essence. The wandering robber would have settled and gained a home, and the learned one would have come in contact with [the] reality [outside of the world of the study house]. [Instead] the two cultures strengthened one element [Torah study] until it conquered everything. The other side [the physicality and freedom of the life of the robber] was forgotten. There was no balance. The people of the book became talking heads, without a body."[53]

Rachel Marani suggests the possibility that Rabbi Yohanan actually believed it was important for Resh Lakish to stay in touch with elements of his previous life as a robber. Rabbi Yohanan's declaration, "A robber would know about his [profession of] robbery," she proposes, was actually not meant as an insult, but rather "almost as [an expression of] joy that Resh Lakish still remember[ed] something of his past, even an attempt, perhaps somewhat awkward, to encourage him not to forget . . . not to lose, after so many years of learning, what always distinguished him from the others: the natural, wild inclinations, 'the qualities of being a robber' in the positive sense, that same quality that enchanted Yohanan [when they first met] in the Jordan, and by virtue of which, at various levels of consciousness, the connection between them [continued to] flourish."[54] Even if her supposition that Rabbi Yohanan's comment was meant to be supportive is an accurate interpretation, Marani admits that it is clear from Resh Lakish's reaction that he took it as an insult.[55]

Daniel Boyarin understands that the break that occurred between Rabbi Yohanan and Resh Lakish raises important questions about whether a teacher can really succeed as a mentor seeking to change the life of his disciple. He notes that this turn of events "forces us to wonder whether one can educate a person or improve human nature."[56] Rabbi Yohanan's insult that Resh Lakish was still in essence a robber and Resh Lakish's declaration that in the study house he saw himself as a Master in exactly the same way he had seen himself when he headed a gang of robbers, Boyarin observes, "express, it would seem, real dissent from the possibility that anything [in the process of transforming Resh Lakish] changed at all."[57]

The Significance of the Topic of the Legal Dispute

The debate about the ritual status of metal utensils, including weapons, provided Rabbi Yohanan with the opening to remind Resh Lakish of his past by sarcastically attributing Resh Lakish's opinion to his having once been a violent robber. From the perspectives of Ido Hevroni, Yehudit Bar-Yesha Gershovitz, and Rachel Marani, the question of whether a metal utensil is considered finished once it has been forged in fire (Rabbi Yohanan's position) or only after it has been placed in water (Resh Lakish's position) can be seen as a metaphorical representation of what so seriously divided the two study partners.

According to Hevroni's reading, the immersion of the utensil in water at the final stage of its being made, a necessary stage in the completion of its creation according to Resh Lakish, adds nothing to its utility; the main purpose of this act is to polish the utensil, thereby improving its external appearance. "In the eyes of Rabbi Yohanan [who did not consider the immersion of the utensil in water to be essential]," Hevroni writes, "the difference between a shiny blade and dull metal [was] rather negligible; in both cases the object [would] maintain its potential as a utensil capable of killing. The thinking of Resh Lakish, in contrast, [fit] the point of view of the robber, for whom external appearance would be important."[58] This seemed to Rabbi Yohanan as a reversion to their original meeting, when Resh Lakish was attracted to him only because of his external beauty. Hevroni suggests that Rabbi Yohanan had hoped that Resh Lakish would develop an appreciation for the internal essence of things, and in this legal argument he saw that Resh Lakish was still thinking more in terms of superficial appearances.[59]

This debate raised the possibility that since Resh Lakish still placed so much importance on external appearances, he had fallen short of a full repentance. Furthermore, argues Hevroni, the dispute reflected a fundamental difference between the study partners about the nature of repentance. Rabbi Yohanan saw it as a process of purification, a rebirth in which the negative elements of the past life were left behind. In contrast, Resh Lakish did not believe he had to reject the life of his past, but rather that it was legitimate for him to use his knowledge of weapons from his evil life as a robber for a good purpose in his new life.[60]

Hevroni notes that a dispute between Rabbi Yohanan and Resh Lakish in another Talmudic passage can be seen as reflecting their different attitudes toward the role of aspects of one's previous life after one has repented:

> Rabbi Yohanan said, "Great is repentance which pushes aside the negative commandments of the Torah." ... Resh Lakish said, "Great is repentance as a result of which transgressions become merits." (B. Yoma 86b)[61]

After Resh Lakish died, suggests Hevroni, it may have become clear to Rabbi Yohanan that he was wrong in his teaching that a penitent needed to "push aside" his sinful actions. It was Resh Lakish, Rabbi Yohanan may have realized, who taught a greater truth, that a penitent can actually make good use of elements from his sinful past after he repented and thereby his "transgressions" can be transformed into "merits." "As a robber," explains Hevroni, "Resh Lakish became accustomed to a life of opposition. A robber is one who is located outside of society and challenges it. In opposition to this external threat, society must defend itself, fortify itself, strengthen itself and in the end if it is sufficiently strong, it develops."[62] By analogy, Rabbi Yohanan came to understand that "when the former robber [Resh Lakish] entered the study house, it is true that he was forced to abandon his weapons, but he did not forsake his survival tactics. Every legal decision by his rabbi [Rabbi Yohanan] called forth within him [Resh Lakish] a devastating attack. His need to defend his opinion forced Rabbi Yohanan to think in a more precise and deep manner, and so the opposition [from Resh Lakish] became a source of growth and development."[63]

Yehudit Bar-Yesha Gershovitz sees the dispute between the two study partners about when a metal utensil is finished as a metaphor for their different understandings of the nature of the relationship between a teacher and his disciple. "According to the educational conception of Rabbi Yohanan," she writes, "the training of a disciple is complete when the disciple is entered into the oven of the Talmud, that is into a formation that the artisan, representing here the teacher, will provide for him.[64] From that moment, the disciple is made proper for his purposes. As Rachel Ararat puts it, Rabbi Yohanan took the approach that one often finds in educational settings in which "the soul of the student [is seen to be] like clay that is formed in the hands of the educator acting as a potter."[65] From the point of view of Resh Lakish, writes Gershovitz, the student must eventually move beyond his role of being formed and achieve an independent existence. The utensil, Resh Lakish was declaring, is ready for use only when it is immersed in water. The role of the water is to cool the utensil from its burning in the fire of the teacher's instruction and thereby to allow it to stand on its own. From that moment on the utensil, i.e. the disciple, no longer needs the power and heat of the fire, i.e. the teacher's instruction, in order to preserve its form, its essence. The utensil is now what it is, and it is made for its purpose. Gershovitz argues that from the point of view of his formation as an outstanding disciple of Rabbi Yohanan, Resh Lakish believed he would be able "to be himself, not dependent on his teacher, [only] when he was liberated from the fire that formed him as a disciple."[66] She goes on to write that when Resh Lakish heard the paternalistic, presumptuous response of Rabbi Yohanan that he brought him under the wings of the Shekhinah, he realized that Rabbi Yohanan wanted to see him as the former Resh Lakish still needing to be educated rather than be willing to let Resh Lakish go as an independent person.

Rachel Marani sees Rabbi Yohanan's ruling that utensils are completed when they are forged in fire and Resh Lakish's ruling that utensils are completed when they are immersed in water as an association that the former has with the qualities associated with the god Apollo—order and reason—and the latter has with the qualities associated with the god Dionysus—chaos and wildness: "Yohanan need[ed] the [Dionysian] fire of Resh Lakish in order to learn Torah, but no less so as a drive that [brought] his soul to life, while Resh Lakish want[ed] Yohanan to play an opposite role, [that of] calming water, water that [would] cool off his stormy soul, that [would] preserve him in the borders that [were] too easily broken."[67] The problem in their relationship, Marani argues, was that if one of them moved too far to the quality of the other, neither would be able to provide the necessary balance to the other. An overly excited Dionysian Yohanan would not be able to provide the restraint that Resh Lakish needed, and an overly restrained Apollonian Resh Lakish would not be able to provide the excitement that Rabbi Yohanan needed.[68]

Rabbi Yohanan's Persistent Insensitivity

As difficult as it is to read of Rabbi Yohanan's violation of Jewish ethical standards when he hurled the insult at Resh Lakish, his insensitive response to his sister's desperate call for him to help save the life of her husband Resh Lakish is infuriating. "The reader cannot help but be stunned by the cruelty and lack of empathy" in Rabbi Yohanan's reaction to his sister's plea, writes Elie Holzer.[69] Indeed, this insensitivity to his sister's feelings can be traced back to the way that Rabbi Yohanan arranged the marriage between her and Resh Lakish without consulting her. As Yariv Ben-Aharon writes, Rabbi Yohanan offered his sister in marriage to Resh Lakish "without asking her permission, as one gives an object."[70] Admiel Kosman goes so far as to compare Resh Lakish's aggressive advance on Rabbi Yohanan in the Jordan with Rabbi Yohanan's violation of his sister's autonomy by offering her to Resh Lakish without her permission.[71] As Daniel Boyarin points out, this arrangement of a marriage without the bride's consent [was] counter to normative rabbinic law.[72]

The words that Rabbi Yohanan used in refusing to fulfill his sister's request are from a biblical verse that convey the words of God (Jeremiah 49:11), thereby displaying Rabbi Yohanan's arrogant assumption that he can play the role of an almighty divinity in her life.[73] Here, observes Elie Holzer, Rabbi Yohanan came across as "a person of self-perceived omnipotence, one who believe[d] himself capable of providing for the needs of all. Like God, he [had] no limitations."[74] The pleading feminine voice of his sister, Admiel Kosman notes, contrasts sharply with the aggressive male voices of Torah discourse in the study house. This Torah discourse turned out to be filled with a power hungry drive that was not at all concerned with the feelings of others and led in its most extreme form to Rabbi Yohanan's insulting words. The sister, in contrast, was asking Rabbi Yohanan to see beyond the self-interested power struggles that characterized his life in the study house and offer aid to those who were vulnerable—she and her children who would become a widow and orphans respectively if Resh Lakish died.[75]

The Inability to Find an Appropriate New Study Partner for Rabbi Yohanan

What is the significance of the failed attempt of the other sages to find for Rabbi Yohanan a suitable study partner to take the place of Resh Lakish? Furthermore, why would they think that the solution to Rabbi Yohanan's need for a study partner was to choose for that purpose Rabbi Elazar ben Pedat, whose approach to the study of Torah was the exact opposite of that of Resh Lakish in that, rather than challenge Rabbi

Yohanan's arguments, he found support for them in the tradition? Yehudit Bar-Yesha Gershovitz suggests that the error of the sages was that they thought that the break between Rabbi Yohanan and Resh Lakish indicated that it would be intolerable to Rabbi Yohanan to have a new study partner who would challenge him the way Resh Lakish had.[76] Admiel Kosman posits that the other sages mistakenly thought that the conflict between Rabbi Yohanan and Resh Lakish indicated that Rabbi Yohanan wanted to conduct the discussions of the study house in an autocratic manner in which no dissent would be allowed. Thus, they chose the "yes-man," Rabbi Elazar.[77] Shmuel Faust surmises that the other sages may have inaccurately concluded that having seen the tragic results of the intellectual sparring in which he engaged with Resh Lakish, it would be best for Rabbi Yohanan to have a partner whose style of study was more affirmative in nature.[78] In fact, writes Gershovitz, Rabbi Elazar ben Pedat was a poor substitute for Resh Lakish: "He was not a person who aroused thinking . . . .He did not have in him the sharp stimulus of thought that Resh Lakish could succeed in raising. . . . .Not only could he not calm the mind of Rabbi Yohanan, but he aroused in him more and more the strong consciousness of the great void that was created with the absence of Resh Lakish from the study house."[79] Gershovitz understands that in the end, Rabbi Yohanan could never recover from the fact that he knew that he had caused the death of his beloved study partner, that "his short sightedness and his inability to rise above his pettiness [were] what caused the death of a person who so influenced the reason for his own existence."[80] With the realization that Rabbi Yohanan's pain was too great to bear, the other sages prayed that death would put him out of his misery.

The Contemporary Significance of the Story

After following the readings by contemporary Israelis seeking to make sense of this story, we can discern the ways that the story in which the relationship between Rabbi Yohanan and Resh Lakish developed and then broke down provides a narrative framework within which to explore contemporary concerns. The openness of each of these opposite social types, the sage and the robber, to elements associated with the other provides a positive vision of the liberating possibility of transcending the differences between what appear to be opposing qualities and values. Resh Lakish is a figure who is completely comfortable with his body, has admirable physical strength, and relates to his sexuality in an uninhibited manner, and yet he feels drawn to the religious world of Rabbi Yohanan. Rabbi Yohanan is far from the stereotypical rabbinical figure of contemporary Israeli culture: he enjoys his sensual bathing in the Jordan; he is proud of his physical beauty, and he is open to welcoming the nonreligious Jew into his community, even such an extreme sinner as Resh Lakish. Furthermore, the religiosity that Rabbi Yohanan offers Resh Lakish is a potentially refreshing synthesis between the physical and the spiritual and the erotic and the intellectual, and Resh Lakish's willingness to incorporate this religiosity into his life is one with which contemporary Israelis can identify in their hunger for a contact with the spirit that does not repress the needs of the body.

For some readers, Rabbi Yohanan represents the ideal of androgyny that challenges rigidly defined gender roles in ways that resonate with contemporary culture. He is a man who could be mistaken for a woman, a man who ostensibly does not play stereotypically masculine power games, but relates to the world in a manner which is more associated with stereotypically feminine qualities. Resh Lakish may have followed him to the study house because he hungered for this breakdown of gender dichotomies as many contemporaries are said to do. It is also possible to see the story as exploring the unconscious homoerotic dimension of relations between men that is often denied and repressed.

Even as the relationship between Rabbi Yohanan and Resh Lakish provides a model of contemporary liberation from cultural, social, and gender dichotomies, other readings call attention to the ways that the failure of their relationship reflects what can often be very wrong in contemporary society. There is a tendency to idealize those who engage in spiritual and intellectual pursuits, as if they have reached the highest level of humanity possible. In reality, according to these readings, that idealization could not be further from the truth. The study house of Rabbi Yohanan displays all of the worst qualities that so often prevail in academia and in the world of the yeshiva: a preoccupation with study to the exclusion of human relations; a hierarchical structure that values people more for their status than for what they might contribute to the enterprise; and the search for truth compromised by power struggles. In these readings, Rabbi Yohanan turns out to be not the ideal synthesizer of the physical and the spiritual, but rather a power hungry, tyrannical bully, who is so lacking in humility that he is unable to reconcile himself with Resh Lakish and relates to his sister as if he were God.

Some interpreters make use of the story to raises serious questions about the problematic nature of human change in the realms of education and of human self-transformation. The story can be seen as providing an example of how teachers and students are not always able to make the transition from their original relationship to one in which teachers let go of the power they have over students and allow students to be free to go out into the world and pursue their own path. Furthermore, as much as some interpreters are initially fascinated by the acceptance of the radically irreligious outsider Resh Lakish in the world of the religious insider Rabbi Yohanan, the story can also be read as evidence for how difficult it can be for both outsiders and insiders to fully trust and accept each other.

CHAPTER 4

WOMEN AND TORAH STUDY: BERURIA

As the only woman who is portrayed in Talmudic stories as engaging in Torah study on the same level as male sages, Beruria has fascinated Israeli readers. Beruria has been of particular interest to those contemporary religious Israelis who advocate women's access to the study of Talmud, from which they had traditionally been excluded.[1] In addition, the significance of the figure of Beruria for many Israelis is that they see in her a powerful proto-feminist pioneer who, by engaging in Torah study, effectively challenged male cultural hegemony in her day.

Due to her iconic status and the fact that she played such an unusual role as a scholarly woman in some Talmudic stories, there has been much discussion about whether Beruria really existed as an historical figure. Contemporary scholars tend to be skeptical of the notion that all of the stories attributed to Beruria are about the same person and therefore the historicity of any stories about her must be called into question.[2] Many who look to Beruria as a heroine relevant to contemporary concerns, however, have not been terribly bothered by the need to find irrefutable proof of her historical existence. Instead, they have related to the stories that feature a character who can be taken to be Beruria as contributing to the portrait of a unified literary figure. There are Talmudic traditions stating that Beruria was the daughter of Rabbi Hanina ben Tradyon and the wife of Rabbi Meir (B. Berakhot 10a; B. Pesahim 62b; B. Avodah Zarah 18a).[3] Therefore, readers of Talmudic stories have identified as the same Beruria not only any female character bearing that name, but also any female character who is unnamed but identified as having either of these relationships.

The stories in which Beruria appears, or at least purportedly appears, place her in a number of different kinds of situations. For the purpose of exploring the range of Beruria stories and how contemporary Israeli readers have understood their significance, I have divided them into categories based on the central qualities of Beruria that each presents, referring to each story with a brief title inserted in brackets at the beginning of the text.

In two stories, Beruria offers a legal ruling that is praised by a male sage:

> [Ritual Purity of an Oven:] An oven, when is it susceptible to ritual impurity? When it reaches a high enough temperature to bake sponge cakes in it. And Rabbi Shimon declares it is susceptible to ritual impurity immediately. Rabban Shimon ben Gamliel says in the name of Rabbi Shila, "[If] one plastered it when it was ritually pure and it became ritually impure, when would it become ritually pure?" Rabbi Halafta of Kfar Hananya said, "I asked Shimon ben Hananya, who asked the son of Rabbi Hanina ben Tradyon, and he said, 'When it will be moved from its place.' And his daughter said, 'When it will be taken apart.' And when this was told to Rabbi Yehudah ben Baba, he said, 'His daughter spoke better than his son.'" (Tosefta Kelim, Bava Kamma 4:17)[4]
>
> [Ritual Purity of a Door Bolt:] A door bolt. Rabbi Tarfon rules that it is ritually impure and the sages rule that it is ritually pure. And Beruria says, "Remove it from one door and hang it on another door." On the Sabbath, when what she said was told to Rabbi Yehudah, he said, "Beruria spoke well." (Tosefta Kelim, Bava Metzia 1:6)[5]

In one story, Beruria is held up to a male sage as an exemplary Torah scholar:

> [Three Hundred Traditions:] Rabbi Simlai came before Rabbi Yohanan and said to him, "Let the master teach me the Book of Genealogies." He said to him, "Where are you from?" He answered, "From Lod." "And where do you reside?" "In Nehardea." He said to him, "One should not conduct a discussion either with Lodites nor with Nehardeans. How much more so with you who are from Lod and who resides in Nehardea." He [Rabbi Simlai] insisted and he [Rabbi Yohanan] agreed. He [Rabbi Simlai] said to him, "Let us learn it in three months." He [Rabbi Yohanan] picked up a clod of earth, threw it at him [Rabbi Simlai], and said to him, "If Beruria, the wife of Rabbi Meir, the daughter of Rabbi Hanina ben Tradyon, learned three hundred traditions in a day from three hundred masters and still did not fulfill her obligation in three years—how can you say [you want to learn it] in three months?" (B. Pesahim 62b).

In two consecutive stories, Beruria rebukes male sages for acting improperly:

> [The Foolish Galilean:] Rabbi Yossi the Galilean was walking on the road and came upon Beruria. He said to her, "Which way should we go to Lod?" She said to him, "You foolish Galilean, did not the sages say, 'Do not speak much with a woman [Mishnah Avot 1:5]?' You should have said, 'Which to Lod?'" (B. Eruvin 53b)
>
> [Kicking a Disciple:] Beruria came upon a disciple reciting his learning in a whisper. She kicked him and said to him, "Is it not written, 'Ordered in all and secured [2 Samuel 23:5]?' If it is ordered by means of your two hundred forty-eight limbs, it will be secured. But if it is not, it will not be secured." (B Eruvin 53b-54a)

In two other consecutive stories, Beruria demonstrates her skill in interpreting biblical verses, once when she teaches her husband how to deal with evil and once when she answers the theological challenges of a heretic:

> [The Hoodlums:] There were hoodlums living near Rabbi Meir and they bothered him a lot. He prayed for mercy for them that they would die. Beruria his wife said to him, "What are you thinking? [Are you acting this way] because it is written, 'May *ḥata'im* [meaning sinners] perish from the earth [Psalms 104:35]?' Is *ḥotim* [meaning sinners] written? [No], *ḥata'im* [which can mean sins] is written. And furthermore, go to the end of the verse, 'and the wicked [*resha'im*] will be no more.' [Is it true that] when sinners will perish the wicked will be no more? So pray for mercy for them that they will repent and the wicked will be no more." He prayed for mercy for them and they repented. (B. Berakhot 10a)
>
> [The Heretic:] A heretic said to Beruria, "It is written, 'Sing out barren woman who has not given birth [Isaiah 54:1].' Because she did not give birth she should sing out?" She said to him, "You fool, go to the end of the verse, which states 'for more are the children of the desolate one than the children of the married woman, says the Lord [Isaiah 54:1].' What is the meaning of 'barren woman who has not given birth?' Sing out community of Israel who is like a barren woman who has not given birth to sons of Gehenna like you." (B. Berakhot 10a)[6]

In one story, Beruria teaches her husband a spiritually elevated way of dealing with grief:

> [The Death of the Sons:] Once when Rabbi Meir was sitting and teaching in the study house on the Sabbath at the time of the afternoon prayer his two sons died. What did their mother do? She placed them both on a bed and covered them with a sheet. When the Sabbath was over, Rabbi Meir came home from the study house and said, "Where are my two sons?" She said, "They went to the study house." He said, "I looked in the study house and did not see them." He was given the cup [of wine] and recited the Havdalah

prayer [concluding the Sabbath]. He said again, "Where are my two sons?" She said. "They went to another place and soon they will come." She brought him food and he ate and said the grace after meals. After he said the grace, she said to him, "Rabbi, I have one question to ask you." He said to her, "Ask your question." She said to him, "Rabbi, in the past a person came and deposited something with me, and now he has come to take it back. Should I return it or not?" He said to her, "My daughter, whoever possesses a deposit must return it to its owner." She said to him, "If it were not for your opinion I would not have given it to him." What did she do? She took him by the hand and brought him up to the room and brought him close to the bed and removed the sheet that was on them, and he saw the two of them lying dead on the bed. He started to cry and say, "My sons, my sons, my teachers, my teachers. My sons in their manner of living and my teachers who would lighten my face with their Torah." At that time she said to Rabbi Meir, "Rabbi, did you not tell me that I am obligated to return the deposit to its owner?" He said, "The Lord gave and the Lord took, may the name of the Lord be blessed forever [Job 1:21]." Rabbi Hanina said, "In this matter he was consoled and returned to his senses, thus it says, 'A woman of valor who can find? [Proverbs 31:10].'" Rabbi Hama bar Hanina said, "Why did the sons of Rabbi Meir have to die at the same time? Because they used to leave the study house and go to eat and drink." (Midrash Mishlei Chapter 31)[7]

In two stories, we learn of the great losses Beruria experienced in her immediate family: the Romans put her parents to death and placed her sister in a house of prostitution, and her brother abandoned the traditional Jewish way of life and was captured and killed by robbers:

[The Parents and the Sister:] [The Romans] brought Rabbi Hanina ben Tradyon to trial, and they said to him, "Why did you teach Torah?" He said them, "As the Lord my God commanded me [Deuteronomy 4:5]." They immediately sentenced him to death by fire, they sentenced his wife to death by the sword, and they sentenced his daughter to go to a house of prostitution. ... [The Romans] found Rabbi Hanina ben Tradyon publicly engaged in teaching Torah with a Torah scroll at his chest. They brought him and wrapped him in the Torah scroll and put around him sticks and lit them with fire and brought wool and dipped it in water and placed it on his heart so that his soul would not leave him quickly. His daughter said to him, "Father, how can I see you like this?" He said to her, "If I were being burned alone it would be difficult for me. Now that I am being burned together with a Torah scroll, He who will avenge the honor of the Torah scroll will avenge my honor." (B. Avodah Zarah 17b-18a)

[The Brother:] Once the son of Rabbi Hanina ben Tradyon followed foreign ways. Robbers captured and killed him. His mangled body was found three days later. He was wrapped and placed on a bier and brought into the city and was praised on account of his father and mother. His father called out the verses: "You roar at your end when your flesh and body are destroyed and you say I despised teachings and refused to hear rebuke and I did not lend my ears to the voice of my teachers or listen to my instructors. Soon I arrived at evil in the community [Proverbs 5:11-14]." He completed the verses and returned to the beginning. His mother called out the verse: "A foolish son angers his father and embitters his mother [Proverbs 17:25]." His sister called out the verse: "Bread from a lie tastes good to a man, but afterwards his mouth will fill with gravel [Proverbs 20:17]." (Massekhet Semahot, Chapter 12)

Beruria the Outsider Who Challenged the Rabbinic Establishment

In some stories, Beruria participated with male rabbis in discussions of Torah, and she surpassed them in knowledge and religious insight. At times, she even had the courage to directly challenge the way they conducted themselves. In two stories, she is portrayed as surpassing her own husband, Rabbi Meir, in her approach to the challenges of life. In "The Hoodlums," Beruria's approach to the hoodlums is portrayed as superior to that of Rabbi Meir. Rabbi Meir, observes Yifat Monnickendam, comes across as rather egocentric, as he prayed for an easy solution to his problem—their death. "His portrayal in the story as seeking mercy," she writes, "evokes immediately the question of mercy for whom? For him or for them? There is in this more than a little irony. In contrast to him, Beruria represents here a wider view that relates to the complexity of the problem. She [did] not ignore the distress of her husband Rabbi Meir, who [was] suffering from the hoodlums, but she present[ed] her appreciation of the ability of the hoodlums to change."[8] Tova Hartman and Charlie Buckholtz note that when Beruria argued that Rabbi Meir should pray against the sins of the hoodlums rather than against them, she called upon him to live up to the highest religious ideals. They understand her argument to be based on two rhetorical questions: "How can people on society's margins be judged for summary execution? How can a spiritual leader use prayer as a weapon of personal vengeance?"[9] It is significant, observe Hartman and Buckholtz, that Beruria's argument was not based on ethical abstractions, but rather on the question of how to interpret a word in a biblical verse. "Clearly motivated by an alternate intuition about human nature and an alternate vision of prayer," they suggest, "Beruriah stage[d] her criticism not as an ethical rebuke but as a hermeneutical conversation. Her bona fides as a Rabbinic authority [were] taken for granted as their conversation [took] on a clear Talmudic cast."[10]

Both Yifat Monnickendam and Shmuel Faust remark on how "The Death of the Sons" reverses stereotypical gender images: the wife's emotionally restrained clear-headed rational functioning is stereotypically associated with men, and the husband's emotional breakdown is stereotypically associated with women.[11] Chaim Licht suggests that initially Bruria's restrained response to the death of her sons might come across to readers as not completely to her credit: "The shocking picture of the mother," he writes, "placing her two dead sons on the bed and spreading a sheet over them arouses mixed feelings: on the one hand wonder and admiration, on the other hand astonishment and dismay. Had she no motherly feelings? Was it possible that she did not shed a tear in private?"[12] Shulamit Valler agrees that initially the reader would question the seemingly cold and calculating response of Beruria to the death of her sons: "How is it possible that she did not call Rabbi Meir back from the study house immediately upon the death of the children, which would be expected in accordance with human nature and also correct according to Jewish law, which states that mourning cancels the obligation to study Torah?"[13] This questioning of her humanity may continue as the reader observes her lying to her husband about the whereabouts of the sons and delaying telling him that they have died.

As the story progresses, Valler argues, what at first raises questions about Beruria's character can be seen as a display of an inner strength necessary to design a scenario that will facilitate Rabbi Meir's emotional coping with the death of the sons. When one reads of the extreme emotional reaction of Rabbi Meir to this tragic event, she observes, "the reader now understands that her familiarity with her husband's weakness is what caused her to delay announcing the tragedy for a period of time, which would give her the opportunity to strengthen him physically by means of food and wine and spiritually by means of providing an ideological framework that would enable him to be comforted," when she made an analogy between the obligation to return a deposit and the imperative to affirm the justice of God taking their sons from them.[14] Her sensitivity to her husband's emotional vulnerability was evident when, as Yifat Monnickendam notes, she took some time to present him with the truth: "She [grabbed] him by the hand, [brought] him up to the room, in the room she [brought] him close to the bed, and only then [did] she allow him to see his two dead sons for himself."[15]

Shmuel Faust and Chaim Licht suggest that Beruria's reaction to Rabbi Meir's ruling that she must return the deposit, "If it were not for your opinion I would not have given it to him," may indicate that she was having more difficulty justifying God's taking of the life of her children than she let on. As Licht puts it, Beruria was saying to Rabbi Meir that "she disagree[d] with [his ruling], but respect[ed] it and will fulfill it to the letter of the law," in other words she knew that the tradition teaches her she should make her peace with this tragedy, but inside she was resisting meeting that expectation.[16]

In two of the stories, observes Yifat Monnickendam, Beruria is far more impressive than male Torah sages in taking on the challenges of religious polemics and of mastering Torah study as a whole. Beruria's success in arguing with the man in "The Heretic" contrasts sharply with Rabbi Meir's failure in arguing with his heretical teacher Elisha ben Abuya (e.g. in B. Hagigah 15a).[17] In "Three Hundred Traditions," when Rabbi Yohanan declared to Rabbi Simlai that he could not expect to master Torah any faster than Beruria, the implication was that she was a most accomplished scholar.[18]

Given the degree to which men have felt threatened in modern times by the growing entrance of women to professions once dominated by men, it is not surprising that Moshe Lavee discerns in his readings of "Ritual Purity of an Oven" and "Ritual Purity of a Door Bolt" evidence of the male rabbis' discomfort when Beruria upended accepted gender roles by engaging with them in Torah discourse.[19] In these stories, Lavee sees "two elements that ... struggle ... in the formation of her image: on the one hand amazement at a woman speaking in a legal discussion and on the other hand a consciousness that this is an exceptional case and an attempt to limit or minimize it."[20] The statement "Beruria spoke well" in "Ritual Purity of a Stove" can be read as praise, but since, as Lavee notes, it is generally not used in response to the stated legal opinion of men, it may be an expression of surprise at the rare occasion of a woman making a plausible legal argument.[21] In "Ritual Purity of a Door Bolt," in which Beruria is said to have presented a more correct ruling than her brother, Lavee discerns a suggestion of how uncomfortable the male rabbinic establishment was with this instance of a woman besting a man in the realm of study which men saw as belonging exclusively to them.[22] Furthermore, observes Lavee, the choice to refer in these stories to legal discussions about household items, with which a woman would be particularly familiar, indicates that whoever composed them may have wanted to make the point that Beruria's opinion stemmed more from her experience doing housework than from her deep knowledge of Jewish law as a whole.[23]

Stories that portray Beruria as aggressively challenging men, in one case even to the extent of physically attacking a male figure, are read as celebrations of her courage and of the effective means she used to make her case. Beruria is seen as masterful in the sarcastic way that she challenged the misogynist attitudes of the rabbinic establishment in "Rabbi Yossi the Galilean," calling Rabbi Yossi to task for not using the absolute minimum number of words to ask her for directions. "In her words filled with irony" observes Yifat Monnickendam, "she express[ed] in fact her opinion about the saying, 'Do not speak much with women,' and suggest[ed] that from her point of view it [was] ridiculous."[24] Furthermore, argues Monnickendam, she undermined the rabbinic establishment by beating them at their own game: "In her words she reveal[ed] that even though she [was] 'only' a woman, she [was] very familiar with the words of the sages, and [knew] how to study them carefully, to quote them, and to make conclusions from them. It emerge[d] from this that there [was] in her words a certain challenge to the established world of the sages who [thought] she [was] light headed and that one should not speak much with her. In order to prove to the establishment its mistake she demonstrate[d] learned abilities."[25] Furthermore, as Tova Hartman and Charlie Buckholtz argue, when Beruria quoted the rabbinic dictum "Do not speak much with a woman," she issued what they call "a stinging indictment of [r]abbinic hypocrisy."[26] In effect, they see her as saying to Rabbi Yossi: When the sages warn against speaking too much to women, they thereby exclude them from engagement in Torah study, and yet you as a sage do not even follow this dictum.

Hartman and Buckholtz suggest that Beruria's strong response to Rabbi Yossi's inquiry about directions can be seen as a biting critique of what may lie behind that request. His use of the word "we," ("Which way should we go to Lod?") may have come across to Beruria as an improper violation of sexual modesty. "Whether she [took] R. Yossi's words as a flirtation or [was] concerned to point out that they *could* be taken as a flirtation, we now understand that her reaction . . . [was] of great consequence, as it [shut] down these immodest possibilities of R. Yossi's question and defuse[d] their potential sexual charge."[27]

In "Kicking the Disciple," Beruria forcefully made use of a biblical verse to instruct a Torah student how to study. Hartman and Buckholtz note that Beruria [felt] fully confident in the role she played in educating a student of Torah. "She [saw] herself," Hartman and Buckholtz argue, "as possessing authority in this setting and she [did] not hesitate to use it. In the world of the Rabbis she too [was] a teacher of students."[28] Hartman and Buckholtz are impressed by her insistence that the student be physically engaged in his study of Torah: "She want[ed] him to learn using his whole voice, his whole body. Her kick [was] intended as a physical disruption of his intellectual reverie, forcing him to remember that there is a body attached to the learning mind which must be felt and engaged, which must be penetrated and animated by what the mind discovers, in order for such discoveries to be translated into normal behavior."[29]

Beruria as a Genuine Torah Scholar

Although she recognizes that Beruria "is the only female scholar who appears in Talmudic literature," Dalia Hoshen dissents from the consensus that Beruria's learnedness was an extreme exception that challenged and perhaps even threatened the male sages presiding over the world of Torah study.[30] Hoshen argues, in fact, that Beruria's identity as a Torah scholar was completely consistent with the normative teachings of her time. It is true, Hoshen concedes, that there was a significant distinction made between men and women in terms of the limited obligation of women to participate in ritual observance. A clear confirmation of this fact, she observes, may be found in the legal discussion of whose life to save first if more than one person is in danger: "Whatsoever is more sanctified than another precedes the other. . . . A man takes precedence over a woman in life saving (Mishnah Horayot 3:6-7)," due to the fact that the woman is not obligated to fulfill most of the positive ritual commandments.

However, asserts Hoshen, in rabbinic times women were not irrevocably limited to an inferior status in the area of Torah study. There is evidence in rabbinic literature, she insists, that in those days Torah scholarship provided an avenue for people to raise their religious status no matter how low it originally was. The law of priorities in saving lives, she notes, goes on to provide a list of priorities in terms of status: "A priest takes precedence over a Levite, a Levite over an Israelite, an Israelite over a *mamzer* [the product of an illicit sexual union]. ... This order of precedence applies only when they are all equal, but if a *mamzer* is a scholar (*talmid ḥakham*) and a High Priest is ignorant (*am ha'arets*) the scholarly *mamzer* takes precedence over the ignorant High Priest" (Mishnah Horayot 3:8). From this, Hoshen concludes that in tanaitic times, "Sociology pale[d] when countered by scholarly achievement. ... When entering the circle of Torah study, there [was] no preconditioned status, rather all [were] (potentially) equal: Priests, Levites, Israelites, *mamzerim*, gentiles, and so on."[31] Although Hoshen cannot cite an explicit statement in rabbinic literature about a woman raising her status by becoming a Torah scholar, she insists on viewing the Beruria stories as based on the notion that if even a *mamzer* could be respected as a Torah scholar, so could and so was the woman Beruria, at least in terms of "the figure emerging from the texts" of the stories about Beruria.[32]

Psychoanalyzing Beruria

Ruhama Weiss makes use of the Beruria stories to reconstruct her biography with an emphasis on her emotional development from childhood until maturity. In her book *Immahot betippul* Weiss, in partnership with psychologist Avner HaCohen, attempts to understand the psychology of four women characters in the Talmud. The format of each section includes an analysis by Weiss of Talmudic stories about each of these women, email correspondence between Weiss and HaCohen, and the content of discussions they had about each figure. The fourth section of the book is devoted to Beruria. While Weiss and HaCohen accept the scholarly consensus that the stories commonly assumed to be associated with Beruria are not likely to be about the same figure, their psychological analysis of Beruria is written as if she were the same person in all the stories, as Weiss puts it, "a literary figure, and more accurately a mythic figure."[33] Most of the interpretations in the book are based on observations by Weiss that she shared with HaCohen or that she made in response to HaCohen's observations, and it is on these observations that we will focus.

Weiss sees evidence in "Ritual Purity of an Oven" and "Ritual Purity of a Door Bolt" that Beruria's study of Torah began in her household when she was a child. Both of these stories "deal with laws of home life, and both of Beruria's legal decisions are accepted and accompanied by a festive praise, a conclusion that also indicates the wonderment of a teacher at a student who was advancing and developing in his studies."[34] The compliment of her making a ruling superior to that of her brother, which appears nowhere else in the Talmud in connection with a woman, argues Weiss, would seem to belong to a scene when she still lived in the same household as him.[35] Citing the statement in "Three Hundred Traditions" that Beruria spent over three years studying three hundred traditions, Weiss concludes that already as a maturing youth, under the guidance of her father, Beruria began to become intensely engaged in Torah study.[36]

In tracing the later psychological development of Beruria, Weiss cites stories that tell of the tragic fates of the members of her family. In "The Parents and the Sister," we learn of the executions of her father and mother and the forced placement of her sister in a house of prostitution, all punishments issued by the Romans in response to her father's insistence on defying the government ban on publicly teaching Torah. On seeing her father being burned alive by the Romans, Beruria cried out, "Father, how can I see you like this?" In response, her father made no reference to the emotional pain she had expressed. He merely stated, "Now that I am being burned together with a Torah scroll, He who will avenge the honor of the Torah scroll will avenge my honor." In responding this way to his daughter, the father expressed no regrets for the pain he was causing his family by violating the Roman ban on teaching Torah. The message which Beruria internalized from his words, surmises Weiss, was that loyalty to religious ideology was more important than emotional ties to the members of one's family.[37]

In response to her sister's forced entrance into a house of prostitution, Weiss notes, there are indications of Beruria having been trained well to repress her emotional responses to the suffering of family members if they violated the accepted religious norms. In seeking to understand why God would allow the Romans to punish the sister, the Talmud tells that she was being punished by God for engaging in flirtatious behavior before the Romans: "Once the daughter [of Rabbi Hanina ben Tradyon] was walking before the important men of Rome. They said, 'How nice are the footsteps of this young lady.' Immediately she paid more attention to her footsteps" (B. Avodah Zarah 18a). Thus, like the brother, the sister had departed from Torah values, albeit in not as extreme a manner as he did. In a story to be discussed later in this chapter, Beruria sent Rabbi Meir to rescue her sister from the house of prostitution. Weiss does not discern in Beruria any empathy for her sister as a victim of Roman persecution. If Beruria lacked empathy for her sister it may be because she thought that her sister brought it on herself by acting licentiously. Beruria appears to be concerned only about the effect of her sister's fate on her own social standing: "The reason for [Beruria's] desire for her [sister's] release [was] tied to the status of Beruria," [as she stated,] 'I am ashamed that my sister sits in a house of prostitution.'"[39] Furthermore, as we will see in our later consideration of this story, Beruria went along with Rabbi Meir's insistence that he would save the sister only if he could determine that she had not yet engaged in forbidden sexual relations, and Weiss sees in Beruria's tacit support for this approach by her husband a reinforcement of the impression that religious loyalty was more important to Beruria than any emotional connection to her family.[40]

Weiss presents Bruria's emotionally restrained response in "The Death of the Sons" as additional evidence for her focus on religious ideology rather than on the feelings she might have for family members. She never cried, and similar to her parents and herself at the time of her brother's death, she led Rabbi Meir to the conclusion that this family tragedy was in keeping with God's just ways. Indeed, notes Weiss, at the end of the story Beruria's conclusion is reinforced by the statement that the sons' deaths came about as a punishment for neglecting their Torah studies.[41]

Understanding the "Beruria Incident" in Rashi's Commentary

Perhaps the most discussed Talmudic story about Beruria in Israel in our time is the one presented in Rashi's commentary to explain a comment at the end of the story about Beruria sending Rabbi Meir to rescue his sister from the house of prostitution:

> Beruria, the wife of Rabbi Meir, was the daughter of Rabbi Hanina ben Tradyon. She said to him [Rabbi Meir], "I am ashamed that my sister sits in a house of prostitution [into which she was forced by the Romans]." He took three kavs of dinar coins and went [to Rome]. He said, "If no forbidden thing has been done to her, a miracle will occur. If she has done what is forbidden, no miracle

> will occur for her." He went and presented himself as a horseman. He said to her, "Submit to me." She said, "I am menstruating." He said to her, "I will wait." She said to him, "There are many women that are more beautiful than I am." He thought, "I can conclude that she has not committed a forbidden act. She must speak this way to every man who comes here." He went to her guard and said, "Release her to me." He [the guard] said, "I fear the government." He [Rabbi Meir] said to him, "Take the three kavs of dinar coins. Use half for bribes and keep the other half." He said, "When the half [for bribing] is gone, what shall I do?" He said to him, "Say, 'God of Meir, answer me,' and you will be saved." He said to him, "How can I know that this will work?" Some attack dogs were there. He [Rabbi Meir] picked up a clod of dirt and threw it at them. They came to bite him, and he said, "God of Meir, answer me," and they left him alone. So he [the guard] gave her to him. Eventually the matter became known to the palace. They brought him [the keeper] and put him up to be hung. He said, "God of Meir, answer me," and they brought him down. They said to him, "How did this happen?" He told them what happened. They carved a picture of Rabbi Meir on the gates of Rome and said that whoever sees this face should bring him [to the authorities]. One day they saw him and ran after him. He ran away from them and went into a house of prostitution. Another version is that he saw gentile food, dipped one finger in it, and licked another. Others say that Elijah appeared looking like a prostitute and embraced him. They said, "Heaven forbid, Rabbi Meir would never have acted this way." He rose and fled to Babylonia. Some say it was because of this matter, while others say it was because of the Beruria incident. (B. Avodah Zarah 18a-b)

In response to the urging of his wife Beruria, Rabbi Meir succeeded in liberating her sister who had been forced into a house of prostitution. When the Roman authorities found out what he did, he escaped arrest by appearing to violate the Torah, perhaps by entering a house of prostitution, perhaps by seeming to embrace a prostitute, or perhaps by seeming to eat non-kosher food, thereby disguising his true identity as a pious rabbi. He then fled to Babylonia. If the text had only read that he fled "because of this matter," it would have appeared that he fled out of fear of being arrested by the Romans for liberating his sister-in-law. However, the text also refers to "the Beruria incident," which may be taken as another possible reason why he fled. Rashi's commentary contains a narrative of "the Beruria incident" which purportedly was an alternative motive for Rabbi Meir's flight:

> Once she [Beruria] made fun of the saying of the sages, "Women are light headed." And he [Rabbi Meir] said to her, "I swear, in the end you will have to admit they are right." And he [Rabbi Meir] ordered one of his students to tempt her to [commit a sexual] sin, and the student kept insisting for many days until she consented. And when it became known to her, she strangled herself, and Rabbi Meir fled in shame. (Rashi in B. Avodah Zarah 18b)

Contemporary Israeli readers have sought to make sense of this "incident," with its salacious details of a rabbi sending his student to tempt his wife to engage in an act of adultery, the wife's eventual succumbing to the sexual advances of a man to whom she was not married, and her subsequent suicide. Yifat Monnickendam claims that the story presents a positive portrait of Beruria and that it is consistent with the trend she discerns in other stories in which Beruria is presented as superior to Rabbi Meir. She cites the similarities between the story of Beruria being tempted by the student and one about Rabbi Meir being tempted by Satan in the guise of a woman.

> Rabbi Meir used to make fun of transgressors. One day, Satan appeared to him in the form of a woman on the opposite bank of the river. There was no ferry, so he [Rabbi Meir] seized a rope and proceeded across. When he had reached half way along the rope, he [Satan] let him go, saying, "Had they not declared in Heaven, 'Take heed of Rabbi Meir and his learning,' I would have valued your life at two small coins." (B. Kiddushin 81a)

"The point of departure of [the story in Kiddushin and the story in Rashi's commentary]," writes Monnickendam, "[was] the same. The heroes [Rabbi Meir and Beruria] dismiss[ed] the possibility that they would succumb to sin. They demonstrate[d] self-confidence, each one in a different way. Rabbi Meir express[ed] it by making fun of sinners, while Beruria express[ed] it by dismissing the words of the sages."[42] Monnickendam makes the point, however, that there is a significant contrast between the way that the husband and wife reacted to an attempted seduction: Rabbi Meir succumbed right away and even went to the trouble of overcoming a barrier to reach the figure with whom he desired to sin. In contrast, it took a while before Beruria succumbed to temptation. Furthermore, the consequences of their actions and the ways they reacted to the sexual trial were different. Rabbi Meir was saved from sin because of his Torah learning and never once expressed any regret or shame, whereas Beruria was appropriately troubled by her sin and even went so far as to punish herself. It would seem, Monnickendam argues, that although he may have been the greater scholar, Rabbi Meir did not internalize the religious lessons of Torah learning, while Beruria did.[43]

Ruhama Weiss responds to the story with much empathy for Beruria's failure to uphold the standards of sexual morality to which she was committed and her response to this moral failure, which was to commit suicide. As we saw in Weiss's psychological analysis of Beruria, the experiences she had with her family of origin reinforced the message that it was of utmost importance to repress her deepest feelings in favor of religious ideology. She was taught by her father that rather than feel anguish over his suffering at the hands of the Romans, she should take comfort in the religious significance of his martyrdom. When her wayward brother was killed, her parents modeled for her a declaration that his death was in accordance with divine justice. As she developed, her internalization of this emotional repression was evident in the detached and apparently judgmental way she related to the persecution of her sister by the Romans and in her unemotional theological justification of her sons' sudden deaths. In that latter story and in "The Hoodlums" one sees that her marriage was based more on Torah discourse than on passion.

At a certain point in her life, suggests Weiss, Breruria felt the need to rebel against her training in emotional repression that had been so effective. This is why, according to Weiss, she began an argument with Rabbi Meir over the expression "women are light headed." "The argument with Rabbi Meir," suggests Weiss, "was actually a call for help. 'My mind is light,' she cried out to him and to herself, 'my mind is broken and has given up on the hardness that it acquired for itself. My mind is finally light, it seeks support, it seeks a *ḥaver* [friend] not a *ḥevruta* [study partner], it seeks a supportive man.'"[44] As Weiss sees it, due to all the losses she suffered in her life with the deaths of her father, mother, brother, and sons, which were explained away by theological justification, and the lack of emotional connection between her husband and herself, she was left with a "terrible loneliness ... that envelope[d] all the years of [her] life."[45]

That is why she succumbed to the seduction of the student, who reconnected her with the passion within her that she needed to express. After she did so, she felt shame before her husband who tested and defeated her, her sister who remained virtuous under much more trying circumstances, the student who would likely brag to his friends about his sexual conquest, the neighbors who would delight that this learned woman had her downfall, and thus, Weiss surmises, she was driven to suicide. By deciding to strangle herself, observes Weiss, she affirmed her sexual misdeed as a violation of God's law: the punishment in Jewish law for adultery is strangling.[46] In the end, however, Weiss is proud of Beruria for succumbing to the seduction of the student, for by doing so she "exploited the opportunity for softness and love," for which she was starved throughout her life.[47]

The Rejection of the Authenticity of the Rashi Story

The story of Beruria's seduction and suicide, which appears in no other known source, is evidently of post-Talmudic composition, perhaps transmitted by Rashi, perhaps added to his commentary after his time. Some argue that the fact that the story does not appear in the text of the Talmud and the fact that the Tosaphists who comment on Rashi seem not to have been aware of it point to a relatively late date of composition. Very likely, it first appeared in a marginal comment in a manuscript of the Talmud that was embedded by a later scribe into the Rashi commentary. Dalia Hoshen posits that it is one of many post-Talmudic tales featuring the sages that are not always consistent with the stories told about them in the Talmud, the authenticity of which can be easily dismissed. However, as she rightly observes, "[t]he reason for the attention given this story is its appearance within Rashi's commentary on a page of Talmud."[48]

Unlike Yifat Monnickendam and Ruhama Weiss, who see Beruria as portrayed in a relatively positive light in this story, a number of readers have raised questions about the authenticity of the story because they do not think that its tale of the seduction of Beruria orchestrated by her husband, her succumbing to the seduction, and her death by suicide can be easily integrated into the overall narrative suggested by the other Beruria stories, nor is it consistent with other stories told about Rabbi Meir. As Daniel Boyarin puts it, this is a "repulsive story that contradicts everything told about Beruria in other sources of the talmudic-midrashic literature."[49] Tova Hartman and Charlie Buckholtz emphasize that the portraits of Beruria and Rabbi Meir in the Rashi story are so at odds with their portraits in the Talmud, that they give "a sense that Rashi is taking some other, unfamiliar characters and dressing them up as the Talmudic Beruriah and Rabbi Meir, putting familiar names on strangers to advance an agenda that seems totally external to the source texts."[50] Eitam Henkin finds it hard to believe this rather extreme story. "Is it plausible," he asks, "that because of a one-time mockery by Beruria of the words of the sages Rabbi Meir would decide to pursue a situation in which she would succumb to betraying him with another man? This is not the behavior of a person of sound mind, and even more so of one of the greatest of the early sages."[51] Henkin goes on to note that the story portrays both of them as violating Jewish law, Rabbi Meir as one who placed a moral stumbling block before a person (*netinat mikhshol*) and deceived a person (*ona'at devarim*) and Beruria as one who committed suicide (*hame'abbed atsmo lada'at*).[52]

Some who reject the authenticity of the Rashi story present explanations for the statement in the Talmud that Rabbi Meir fled to Babylonia because of "the Beruria incident" that differ from that in the Rashi commentary and therefore make the explanation in Rashi unnecessary. Tal Ilan suggests that the reference to "the Beruria incident" may refer to the fact that Hanina ben Tradyon really had only one daughter, Beruria, and that it was Beruria who was the daughter sent to the house of prostitution, an event that drove Rabbi Meir to flee to Babylonia, although it was later covered up by the Talmud stating that it was Beruria's sister who was sent to the house of prostitution.[53] Dalia Hoshen argues that the Talmud presented two possible reasons why Rabbi Meir fled to Babylonia, neither of which involved the story told in Rashi's commentary. "Because of this matter" referred to Rabbi Meir's self-consciousness at having been seen by the Romans as being involved with prostitution and/or eating non-kosher food, and "because of the Beruria incident" referred to the entire story of the rescue of

Beruria's sister, as a result of which Rabbi Meir was wanted for arrest by the Romans.[54]

Contemporary readers have sought to determine what point the author of the story was seeking to make. Daniel Boyarin argues that the story was invented for the purpose of advocating a strong opposition to women learning Torah that emerged in Babylonia, long after the period in which Rabbi Meir and Beruria lived in the Land of Israel. While it may be that the early Beruria legends indicate it was possible, if not usual, for a woman to study Torah in the Land of Israel, this raised an issue in Babylonia, "for there a learned woman was a most rare phenomenon, which threatened the social order and all that pertained to relations between the genders."[55] Boyarin also argues that the story raises a serious question about the advisability of women studying Torah when it is read in comparison with the story about Beruria's sister in the house of prostitution. By drawing a contrast between the two sisters, the story is emphasizing the point that it was the sister, who did not study Torah and in fact acted flirtatiously in front of Roman men, who maintained her sexual purity, even under duress in the house of prostitution, while Beruria, the sister who did study Torah, succumbed to sexual sin.[56]

Although Tova Hartman and Charlie Buckholtz agree that the story in the Rashi commentary may have been composed with the purpose of denigrating Beruria as a religious hero, they speculate that perhaps the purpose of the story was to criticize Rabbi Meir "for his outrageous abuse of power" by using his authority to send his student to commit adultery and by placing his wife in such an uncompromising circumstance.[57] They believe that in the conclusion of the story in Rashi's commentary, one can discern a ratification of Beruria as a moral hero: "In this reading, Rashi assigns Beruriah a martyr's death, killing her in order to revitalize her legacy not only as a formidable, learned social critic but as one willing to stand as an example by taking ultimate responsibility for her own mistakes (in contrast to her disgraced husband, whose response to the incident [was] to run away)."[58]

Avraham Grossman has called attention to a version of the story of Rabbi Meir and Beruria found in an eleventh-century work, *Ḥibbur yafeh min hayeshu'ah*, by the North African rabbinic scholar Rabbi Nissim ben Rabbi Yaakov, who lived approximately two generations before Rashi. This version suggests that there is an alternative tradition that may in fact be more authentic than the controversial version of how Beruria met her end in the Rashi commentary.[59] The version in *Ḥibbur yafeh min hayeshu'ah* makes no reference to Rabbi Meir testing his wife's sexual morality nor to her committing suicide. Instead, it relates that following Rabbi Meir's rescue of Beruria's sister and the consequent dangers he experienced when pursued by the Romans "Rabbi Meir took his wife and all that he owned and moved to Iraq [meaning Babylonia]."[60]

While Yoel Bin-Nun understands the appeal of the notion that the more authentic version of the story of Breruria is the one in *Ḥibbur yafeh min hayeshu'ah,* he suggests that it may be possible to preserve the validity of Rashi's version and avoid the negative view it presents of Rabbi Meir and Beruria. He points out that in the Rashi story in the Parma manuscript of the Talmud, one letter that appears in the classic Vilna edition of the Talmud is missing, thereby potentially changing one's understanding of what happened in the story. In the classic Vilna edition of the Talmud, it is written *vetsivah le'eḥad mitalmidav lenassotah ledevar averah* ("and he [Rabbi Meir] ordered one of his students to tempt her to [commit a sexual] sin"). In the Parma manuscript the letter *lamed* is missing from the second word of the phrase making it read *vetsivah eḥad mitalmidav lenassotah ledevar averah* ("and one of his [Rabbi Meir's] students commanded [someone] to tempt her to [commit a sexual] sin").

Based on the version in the Parma manuscript, Bin-Nun suggests that it was not Rabbi Meir who was behind the attempted seduction of his wife, but rather one of his students who, as a collaborator with the Romans, arranged for a man to try to seduce Beruria. Bin-Nun justifies his notion that a student of Rabbi Meir's could have been a Roman collaborator by noting that apparently it was not uncommon for prominent Jewish religious figures to engage in such collaboration. As proof of this he cites the Talmudic story about Rabbi Elazar, the son of Rabbi Shimon bar Yochai, who became involved in arresting Jews for the Roman authorities (B. Bava Metzia 83b). Furthermore, Bin-Nun observes that in the historical context of Roman persecution in which the story takes place, the rabbinic expression that set off the argument between Rabbi Meir and Beruria at the beginning of the story, "women are light headed" (*nashim da'atan qalot*), meant that women were easily susceptible to pressure by the Roman authorities. In support of this notion he cites the fact that according to a Talmudic story (B. Shabbat 33b), Rabbi Shimon bar Yochai and his son Rabbi Elazar hid from the Romans in a cave without telling Rabbi Shimon's wife where they were because "women are light headed," meaning that Rabbi Shimon feared that if pressured by the Romans his wife would reveal where they were hiding. Bin-Nun imagines that in fact Beruria was subject to Roman pressure when the man the student sent on behalf of the Romans said to Beruria that he would save Rabbi Meir from being put to death if she agreed to have sexual relations with him. Facing the dilemma between committing adultery but saving her husband's life or refusing to commit adultery and causing her husband's death, she chose to submit passively to the sexual assault of the man, which in fact is what Jewish law permits a woman to do rather than be killed or allow someone else to be killed. However, when it became known that she had committed adultery, she knew that according to Jewish law she would be forbidden to remain married to Rabbi Meir, and so she felt she had no choice but to commit suicide, and Rabbi Meir felt that he had no choice but to flee.[61]

The Contemporary Significance of the Beruria Stories

Given the contemporary value put on gender equality, it is clear why the Beruria stories have evoked so much interest among Israelis. Readings of these stories provide ways to think about a number of issues in our time. One is the question of gender difference. Beruria is attractive to many as the figure who challenges any residual thought that there are fundamental differences in ability, especially in the intellectual realm, between men and women. For some, Beruria provides a welcome ancient example that repudiates that assumption.

At the same time, the Beruria stories ring true for contemporary readers in that they reflect the difficulty of men opening the realms which they dominate to women, even as they are sometimes forced to acknowledge that women can be as talented as they are or even more so. Beruria is also celebrated as an effective agent of social criticism who shows up the male sages for their hypocrisy and moral obtuseness.[62] It is likely that the story of Beruria in Rashi was written to undermine the figure of the learned Jewish woman, and this is how some contemporary readers interpret it. Yet, this interpretation can be turned on its head and Beruria can be seen as a moral hero. Most poignantly, one reading views Beruria as a victim who when she embraced the religious ideology of men paid a heavy price in emotional repression which led to her tragic downfall.

CHAPTER 5

EROS REPRESSED AND RESTORED: RABBI HIYA BAR ASHI AND HERUTA

It would seem improbable that contemporary Israeli readers would find interest in any of the Talmudic stories about rabbis struggling to control their sexual desires, referred to in these stories as *yetser hara* (the evil inclination).[1] While Israelis are concerned with psychological, social, and moral issues related to sexual relations, regarding one's sex drive as an enemy with which one does battle would presumably be foreign to most of them. Nevertheless, much interest has been expressed by Israelis in a story in which a rabbinic sage, Rabbi Hiya bar Ashi, is so determined to have the upper hand over his sexual desires that he stops having marital relations with his wife. The attraction of this story to contemporary Israelis is due to their discovery that it can be seen to be less about a rabbi's struggle with his evil inclination and more about issues of gender dynamics in marriage with which readers can identify.

Rabbi Hiya Bar Ashi and Heruta

Every time he prostrated himself it was the custom of Rabbi Hiya bar Ashi to say, "May the Merciful One save us from the evil inclination." One day his wife heard him and said, "Since it is already several years that he has withdrawn from me, why is he saying this?" One day he was learning in his garden. She adorned herself and walked back and forth in front of him. He said to her, "Who are you?" She said, "I am Heruta. I returned today." He urged her to have sexual relations with him. She said to him, "Bring me the pomegranate at the top of the tree." He jumped and brought it to her. When he returned home, his wife was lighting the oven. He went up and sat in it. She said to him, "What are you doing?" He said to her, "This is what happened." She said to him, "It was I." He did not pay attention to what she said until she brought him signs. He said to her, "Nevertheless, I intended to violate a prohibition." (B. Kiddushin 81b)

Rabbi Hiya's Supplication

Rabbi Hiya appears at the beginning of the story as a man who regularly prayed to God to save him from his evil inclination, which here, as in a number of other Talmudic stories, is to be taken as a reference to his sexual impulses. It is significant that he prostrated himself (*nafal la'appei* in the original Aramaic) as he prayed for God's aid. The Hebrew term related to this, *nefilat appayim*, is associated with the text of the confession and request for divine forgiveness, Tahanun, traditionally recited on weekday mornings and afternoons while bowing one's head on one's arm in an approximation of prostration. As Yaara Inbar observes, it would appear that the reference to prostration in this story is not to the bowing of one's head during the mandatory daily Tahanun, but rather to Rabbi Hiya's actual prostration of his entire body in a spontaneous personal prayer, a practice that most likely predated the regular recital of the standardized Tahanun prayer.

A number of writers have commented on the intensity of Rabbi Hiya's supplication. Yaara Inbar notes that "[t]he physical prostration in which the prayer was said permitted a different kind of openness to Heaven, with a feeling of total submission greater than in any other position."[2] "A person who prostrates himself with spread limbs on the ground," writes Ido Hevroni, "expresses thereby the helplessness of the supplicant that justifies [his need of] help from the one before whom he prostrates himself."[3] In a similar vein, Yair Barkai observes, Rabbi Hiya resemble[d] a person who [felt] that his sexual drive [was] about to conquer him, to defeat him, to destroy him, almost like a drowning person who cries out, 'Help.' His turning to the Creator also emphasize[d] his feeling that in himself he [was] too weak to come to terms with the problem, that he need[ed] the help of the Almighty."[4]

This story is preceded in the Talmud by two stories about other rabbis struggling with their sexual impulses (B. Kiddushin 81a). In these stories, Rabbi Meir and Rabbi Akiva, respectively, mocked those who succumb to sin, but their spiritual arrogance was undermined when Satan disguised himself as a woman and they were tempted to have relations with that woman until Satan unmasked himself.[5] Shlomo Naeh points out that there is a significant difference between these two stories and the one about Rabbi Hiya. Rabbi Meir and Rabbi Akiva struggled with the temptation to have forbidden sexual relations with a woman who was not their wife, but Rabbi Hiya took this struggle one step further by refraining from having sexual relations not only with women to whom he was not married, but even with his own wife.[6] As Naeh notes, such an extreme denial of sexuality is not supported by mainstream rabbinical teaching. "We have no other testament," he writes, "of a sage who withdrew from his wife in an explicit ascetic struggle against the [evil] inclination, as is told here about Rabbi Hiya bar Ashi."[7]

The Wife Overhearing Rabbi Hiya

After overhearing her husband's daily prayer, apparently for the first time, Rabbi Hiya's wife began to wonder about the connection between their sexless marriage and her husband's desperate plea to God to help him to conquer his sexual urges.[8] Admiel Kosman speculates that by refraining from having sexual relations with his wife, Rabbi Hiya may have created in her the false impression that he had reached an angel-like spiritual level in which he could transcend sexual desire, and it was under this false impression that she had until now accepted the situation.[9] Ruhama Weiss refers to the suggestions of the commentators Rashi and Maharsha that perhaps she thought that he had separated from her because he had lost his sexual desire due to old age.[10] Weiss expresses her amazement that the wife could be so unaware of the internal struggle her husband had been experiencing for so long: "She [was] certain that the external appearance that he present[ed] to her reflect[ed] his inner world. And I think to myself, how blind we can be in a relationship to the inner world of the other. Why did she choose to believe his pretense?"[11] Kosman surmises that now that she knew that he indeed did have sexual urges that he needed to control, she may have been personally insulted that he did not seek sexual satisfaction by engaging in relations with her.[12] Yair Barkai suggests that perhaps she saw a bright side to her discovery in that it revealed to her that her husband still had an active sex drive, and that therefore there was hope that they could resume their marital intimacy.[13]

The Wife's Seduction of Rabbi Hiya

Contemporary Israeli readers have wondered why the wife did not confront Rabbi Hiya directly with her discovery. Furthermore, they ask, why did she decide to dress up and try to seduce him into sexual relations? Her unwillingness or inability to engage in a conversation with her husband about this issue seems to have continued a pattern of non-communication between them that had persisted for some time. It is apparent, suggests Ari Elon, that without ever explaining his reasoning, "the initiative of [sexual] separation came from Rabbi Hiya. It is most likely that this separation was not favored by his wife. Despite this, she accepted the situation as a necessary given and she did not take the initiative to discuss with Rabbi Hiya the explanation for his separation."[14] "Neither," writes Elon, "had the emotional strength to look straight at the other" and come to terms with the issue.[15] Given their long pattern of non-communication, it is not surprising that the issue never came to a head in a direct conversation. Instead, it took the wife's accidental overhearing of Rabbi Hiya's prayer and her attempt to seduce him with no verbal reference to the reality of their sexless marriage to challenge the status quo.[16]

Yair Barkai and Ruhama Weiss suggest two possible reasons why Rabbi Hiya's wife tried to seduce him. On the one hand, she may have been attempting to determine if in his prayer he was asking God to help him to control the sexual desire he had for other women, on which he may have even acted. On the other hand, perhaps now that she knew how torn her husband was between sexuality and holiness, she wanted to try to help him resolve this issue by restoring their sexual life together.[17] Ido Hevroni agrees with the possibility that she took pity on the inner conflict that he was experiencing and therefore took the initiative to help him reconnect with the sexual drive about which he was so conflicted.[18] Similarly, Yaara Inbar posits that Rabbi Hiya's wife hoped that he would allow himself to succumb to his sexual drive either because he was aroused by the temptation of a woman he did not recognize or because he did recognize her "and would suddenly find in his wife another side with which he was not familiar, that [would] finally arouse in him his repressed sexual urges."[19] Ari Elon agrees that Rabbi Hiya's wife may have been attempting an erotic revival in their marriage, but he offers another possibility, that she was trying to take vengeance on him for withdrawing from her under false pretenses.[20]

Another interpretive direction attributes the seduction attempt to a sexual awakening within Rabbi Hiya's wife. Rabbi Hiya's revelation that he had sexual desires, suggests Ruhama Weiss, may have reconnected his wife with her own sexual desires and aroused her to demonstrate them.[21] Ruth Calderon makes the point that this attempted seduction of her husband allowed the wife to release the sexuality within her that she had controlled out of respect for her husband's spiritual aspirations. "In disguise, under the cover of the form of the new figure, the foreign one," explains Calderon, "Rabbi Hiya's wife liberate[d] herself from all prohibitions and made room for powers that she had repressed in accordance with her husband, in accordance with the values of the community and religious commandments."[22] In a similar vein, Yaara Inbar points out that since the root of the original Aramaic term in the story for "adorned herself," *qashtah,* is the same as the root of the Aramaic term for truth, *qushta,* the wife's self-adornment can be seen as an exploration of who her true self is: "In adorning herself, on the one hand the woman [was] covering one truth, that of the known figure [of the modest, pious rabbi's wife], and on the other hand she reveal[ed] another truth, perhaps even more intimate. The act of self-adornment present[ed] an essence that was all the time hidden within her [i.e. her sexuality.]"[23]

In his commentary to the Talmud, Rashi identifies Heruta as "a known prostitute," and as Ruhama Weiss notes, most commentators until the present have accepted this reading. Weiss wonders, however, whether this decision to identify Heruta as a prostitute may say more about the interpreters than about the story itself. "If the name Heruta [with the same root as the Hebrew word for freedom, *ḥerut*] apparently has the one simple and exciting meaning of 'freedom,'" she writes, "why did the interpreters of the story argue for generations that Heruta chose for herself the identity of a prostitute?!"[24] It must stem, she argues, from the tendency people have of associating the sexual freedom of women with prostitution. Weiss prefers to understand the wife's choice of the name as an expression of her determination to be free of the constraints in her sexless marriage. Weiss characterizes her as "a sad and forlorn woman, married to an obsessive ascetic who took hold of herself at an advanced stage of her life and sought to turn her sexuality (and his sexuality) from sorrow to joy, from mourning to celebration."[25]

From the text alone, it is difficult to know why the wife approached her husband in the garden dressed up in the way she did and how she felt about her husband's response to her presence. Ishay Rosen-Zvi considers the possibility that the wife was not trying to disguise herself, but rather she dressed up in such a way that "a woman is expected to do according to Talmudic instruction in order to indicate to her husband that she desires marital relations."[26] If her purpose was to present herself as herself, observes Yair Barkai, one can "imagine the shock and humiliation of the woman, who wore her best clothing for her husband, and it [became] clear to her [when he asked, 'Who are you?'] that he [was] not capable of recognizing her."[27] Yaara Inbar wonders how the question "Who are you?" affected Rabbi Hiya's wife. "[Was] she happy that she succeeded in deceiving him and putting him to the test, according to her plan? Or perhaps she felt pain in her heart when she understood that her husband [could] really not identify her, that he [was] not capable of imagining that there [was] a [seductive] figure like this inside his wife, that it [was] as if he were lifting his eyes before an apparently foreign woman while he had already stopped looking at her for a long time."[28]

The wife's choice to try to seduce Rabbi Hiya in the garden associates their sexual encounter with the biblical story of the Garden of Eden: just as Adam was seduced by Eve to eat the forbidden fruit, so Rabbi Hiya was seduced by his wife to have sexual relations.[29] Readers have commented on other ways that Rabbi Hiya's wife's decision to attempt her husband's seduction in a garden carries significance. Ruhama Weiss notes that the garden was a liminal place between the two realms of Eros and divinity that were warring within Rabbi Hiya's soul. It was neither Rabbi Hiya's home, where his wife lived, representing sexuality, nor was it the study house, which represented the holiness to which he aspired.[30] A place not fully identified with either conflicting realm of human experience had the greatest potential to be a location in which to challenge that conflict. As Yair Barkai puts it, neither the house in which the husband and wife have lived for so long with the routine of sexual abstinence nor the study house which reinforced Rabbi Hiya's striving for holiness would be a promising place to restore the right balance between Eros and holiness.[31]

What was Rabbi Hiya thinking when he urged this woman whom he did not recognize to have sex with him? Was he simply so sexually frustrated that, having found himself alone with a woman, he was compelled to give in to his desires? Did he think she was a prostitute and therefore took advantage of the opportunity to find sexual release with little or no emotional commitment? The narrator's use of the verb *teva'ah*, translated above as "He urged her to have sexual relations with him," can more literally be translated, "he demanded from her," with the understanding being that he was insisting that she submit to him as if she were an object with no consideration of her feelings and no pretense that there was any emotional connection between them. Yair Barkai and Ruth Calderon contrast the use of the verb *teva'ah* here with the use of the verb *mesapper,* which literally means "to tell a story" but refers to loving, consensual sexual relations in another Talmudic story: "Imma Shalom was asked, 'Why are your children so beautiful?' [and she answered] "Because [my husband] has sexual relations with me (*mesapper immi*) not at the beginning of the night or the end of the night, but at midnight" (B. Nedarim 20a-20b).[32]

Another question that arises in this section is why the wife did not immediately give in to Rabbi Hiya's sexual overture. Why did she insist that before she would have relations with him he had to climb up a tree and get a pomegranate for her? Ruhama Weiss suggests that a pomegranate can be seen as resembling the female sexual organ, and by demanding that Rabbi Hiya bring her the pomegranate she was conveying to him the underlying purpose of her attempt to seduce him: "The pomegranate is a symbol of the female sexuality that Heruta allowed herself to lose in her marriage . . . .[H]ow enchanting and exciting to ask for it back from your husband—to get him to jump up to the head of a tree in order to help you return yourself to yourself."[33]

Others, however, see in her demand a darker motivation. Admiel Kosman interprets it as an attempt to humiliate her husband, to bring him down from the spiritual pedestal to which he was aspiring: "She 'brought him down from the top of the tree' to the ground. She returned him to the world of reality from 'the high tree' of 'religious' illusion up which he had climbed."[34] Hananel Mack agrees that her demand indeed made a fool of him: "The description of the respected man making an effort to bring the woman the pomegranate at the top of the tree [made] him look especially silly and calls to the mind of the reader a young man in love prepared to do foolish romantic acts in order to please his beloved."[35] Yair Barkai sees this as an attempt on her part to exact what he calls "a sweet revenge."[36] As he puts it, "She made him prove that he still has power in his loins. An ascetic scholar who prostrates himself [was forced to] jump up in the garden to merit the favors of a prostitute."[37]

As a number of interpreters have observed, the wife's demand of the pomegranate also alludes to the biblical story of Judah and Tamar (Genesis 38).[38] In both narratives, a woman wanted something from a man that she did not feel she could receive in a direct manner. Tamar wanted to have a child, and Rabbi Hiya's wife wanted to have sexual relations with her husband. Both women's desires were presented in their respective stories as justified. According to ancient Israelite practice, Judah should have allowed his youngest son to marry Tamar and father her children, since her two previous husbands, Judah's older sons, had died childless. Similarly, Rabbi Hiya's wife had, by Jewish law, the right to regular conjugal relations with her husband.

Furthermore, according to one reading of this story, both Tamar and Rabbi Hiya's wife disguised themselves in an attempt to seduce the man. Tamar explicitly masqueraded as a prostitute (*qedesah*) and, although it was not explicitly mentioned in the story, many readers have understood this to be what Rabbi Hiya's wife did. In addition, the wife's insistence that Rabbi Hiya give her the pomegranate may have been for the purpose of proving to him what happened. In fact, the pomegranate may have been one of the signs she used once they were back home to prove to her that she was the woman with whom he had had sexual relations. Likewise, Tamar insisted that Judah leave his staff and seal after they had relations to prove that he was the one who fathered her child, so that she would not later be accused of engaging in illicit sex. Both narratives share the image of a person potentially being put to death by burning. Until Judah realized he was the one who had impregnated Tamar, he insisted that she be punished for her act of fornication by being burned at the stake; Rabbi Hiya went into the oven, possibly intending to burn himself to death. A significant difference between the Talmudic story and the biblical story to which it alludes is that the former ends in the failure of the wife's attempts to reconnect with her husband, while the latter has a happy ending: Judah acknowledged that he was responsible for Tamar's impropriety, having put her in the position of never being able to procreate. He withdew his demand that Tamar be put to death and allowed her to give birth to the twins that he had fathered.[39]

The Aftermath of the Seduction

Although the story never explicitly states that Rabbi Hiya had relations with his wife who had identified herself as Heruta, it is clear from what is related later in the story that in fact the wife had succeeded in engaging him in the first sexual encounter they had had in a long time. Yaara Inbar observes that the story does not tell us how the wife reacted to her successful seduction of her husband: "[Was] it anger that fill[ed] her heart? [Was] she grateful to that woman into which she transform[ed] herself or perhaps she [was] jealous of her? [Was] she disappointed in her husband or perhaps actually feeling a new hope about [her relationship with him]?"[40]

As soon as Rabbi Hiya returned home he threw himself into the oven that his wife had lit. Avigdor Shinan surmises that he did so out of a sense of utter spiritual defeat. Having succumbed to the sexual desire he had been seeking to control, he discovered "that his prayers were not accepted, [and] that his power to live a life of withdrawal from sensuality was weak and shaky and his behavior toward his wife was in essence mistaken."[41] Admiel Kosman imagines Rabbi Hiya as unable "to accept the fact that he [had] inclinations like all human beings. And since in his opinion he [had] failed, he despise[d] himself so much that he assume[d] that the only way left for him [was] to sentence himself to the death penalty."[42] As Ido Hevroni puts it, "The rabbi, who believe[d] that his spirit imprisoned in his body was brought to the ultimate nadir, decide[d] to get rid of his body and liberate his spirit from its chains. … Now when the victory [over him] of [his] body [had] become decisive, there [was] no reason to live."[43] Hananel Mack makes the point that Rabbi Hiya "could not release himself from this punishment which to his mind he deserve[d] by law, because the sin he committed with the 'foreign woman' was indeed a full concretization of his main sin: his [sexual] thoughts. He failed completely in his sin, and also his regular prayers did not support him."[44]

It is significant that even after his wife had reassured him that by having sexual relations with her he did not engage in a forbidden act, Rabbi Hiya was not comforted and insisted that he was still guilty because he had intended to sin. Yair Barkai makes the observation that Rabbi Hiya's statement is understandable in light of rabbinic discussions of the importance of a man to be in the right frame of mind when he has relations with his wife.[45] Nevertheless, there is no rabbinic statement that declares that having improper thoughts during sexual intercourse is a capital crime.

In the classic Vilna edition of the Babylonian Talmud, the story concludes as follows: "The rest of that righteous man's life he would fast until he died a particular death." Since the entire story is in Aramaic and this passage is in Hebrew, it would appear that it was added later, and therefore we will not consider it in our analysis. Without this addendum, the original version of the story is open-ended. We do not know if Rabbi Hiya stayed in the oven and insisted on killing himself or if he reconsidered and left the oven, and if so whether he went back to sexual isolation from his wife, or whether what happened between them in fact reinvigorated their marriage. Admiel Kosman sees some measure of hope for the couple. He notes that until the final scene there were no words exchanged between Rabbi Hiya and his wife: in the first scene she overheard him praying to God, and in the second scene they did not address each other as husband and wife but rather as if they were a man and woman having casual sex. In the final scene, for the first time, they really spoke to each other. He admitted to her that he had sinned, and she reassured him that he had not sinned. It is this reading of the ending that leads Kosman to conclude that the central theme of the story is not sexual dysfunction, but "*dialogue, human communication.*"[46] He writes that there is a religious lesson in the story, "that it is not correct to aspire to 'going on high' to seek God in 'heaven,' outside of our world. The aspiration of humanity should be much more modest: to make space for the 'other' and thereby to make space for the presence of God, which is always revealed to us only *here*, in the material world, in the meeting *between two people*, when the dialogue between two people is conducted with honesty, simplicity, and directness."[47]

Like Kosman, Ruth Calderon sees significance in the fact that, for the first time, they were talking to each other as husband and wife. She does not, however, interpret their dialogue as a sign that they would repair their marriage. When the wife said, "It was I," Calderon understands her to be saying to Rabbi Hiya, "I discovered the power, the desire. ... Will you accept me with my many faces? I do not want, I cannot continue to kill a part of me all the time."[48] And when Rabbi Hiya answered, "Nevertheless, I intended to violate a prohibition," he was saying, "I was attracted to the forbidden woman, I wanted you precisely because I did not know it was you. I cannot accept you with your many faces. When I have desire it is for the forbidden. I cannot combine my legal wife with a foreign wife."[49] In other words, Rabbi Hiya was caught between the age-old dichotomy of the woman as Eve and the woman as Lillith, or as is said in Western culture, the woman as Madonna and the woman as a prostitute. He therefore would not be able to have sexual relations with a wife who combined within her the qualities of pious respectability and the qualities of wanton Eros, and so their sexual life could never be resumed.

Ruhama Weiss also reads the ending pessimistically. She imagines Rabbi Hiya leaving the oven "with his body covered with burns and for many years [going] around burned in the study house and in the community and [laying] burned beside his wife in their double bed."[50] If this turned out to be the ending, Weiss laments, then the wife would have gained nothing from what she did and would have lost so much. She would have spent the rest of her life married to a tortured man with whom she would never be able to renew sexual relations.[51]

Ishay Rosen-Zvi sees in this story a subversive attack on the rabbinic association between sexuality and the evil inclination. "It undermines the metaphysical base on which it is built—sexuality as the evil inclination ... [and] uncovers the essence of the problematic status of sexual desire in rabbinic literature."[52] We see in the story, observes Rosen-Zvi, that asceticism and licentiousness are more connected to each other than is conventionally thought. "Rabbi Hiya in our story," writes Rosen-Zvi, "[tried] to distance himself from the evil inclination as best as he could, but actually he [was] dealing with it all the time. Daily in his prayer he gnaw[ed] at it again and again. The ascetic pious person [was] revealed as one who obsessively dealt with the sexuality that he [was] repressing, and therefore he jump[ed] at the first opportunity [for sexual release] that came before him."[53] Shulamit Valler reads the story as a cautionary tale for anyone thinking that he, even with God's help, could repress his sexuality. "Therefore," she writes, "[the story teaches that] the proper way of life is one that allows for giving into the [evil] inclination in the permitted framework—the framework of the family—and to distance oneself from any other possibility of contact with it."[54]

The Contemporary Significance of the Rabbi Hiya and Heruta Story

Contemporary Israeli readers of this story would tend not to have much sympathy for Rabbi Hiya's pursuit of the ascetic ideal of sexual abstinence. Certainly, there is a considerable amount of evidence in the story and in rabbinic literature in general to suggest that the author of the story was also highly critical of Rabbi Hiya. While for most readers of the story, issues of marriage do not include one member trying to refrain from sex for religious reasons, the story may be connected in their minds to one of the great challenges of all marriages: communication and mutual respect for each other's needs. It would appear that contemporary Israelis can relate to the portrait in the story of a marriage in which the husband and wife have drifted apart and live as if they are experiencing no problems. A marriage such as that of Rabbi Hiya and his wife, in which the separation between the husband and wife is due to one spouse pursuing his or her own personal interests to the detriment of the other spouse, is recognizable to contemporary readers. Readers tend to celebrate the brazen action of the wife in taking an erotic initiative that involved tricking her husband into having sex with her, in defiance of traditional norms. By doing so, she asserted the value of the erotic drives of women, which today as well as in ancient times are often not validated by a culture so fixated on male desire. Unfortunately for her, it is very possible that Rabbi Hiya was unable to appreciate and respond to her, and that she therefore would never be able to find the sexual satisfaction that she rightly deserved.

CHAPTER 6

AN IDEAL MARRIAGE: RABBI AKIVA AND THE DAUGHTER OF BEN CALBA SAVUA

"It seems to me," Avigdor Shinan has declared, "that of the hundreds or perhaps thousands of stories scattered throughout [rabbinic literature] ... few are the stories that have been so extensively dealt with and from so many varied directions as the story of the beginnings of Rabbi Akiva."[1] This story, which tells of the humble origins of one of the leading rabbinic sages of his day, Akiva ben Yosef, and the steadfast support of his wife while he studied Torah, has even found its way into Israeli popular artistic productions. The song "Rabbi Akiva," based on a poem by Dalia Ravikovitch about this story, won second prize at the Israeli Song Festival of 1970 and went on to become a very popular song which is still remembered affectionately by Israelis from that era.[2] Some forty years later, the story was used as the core plot of a best-selling historical novel, *Hapardes shel Akiva* (*Akiva's Orchard*, 2012), by Yochi Brandes.

The potential appeal of this story as a romantic narrative is clear: the daughter of a rich man and a lowly shepherd fall in love, but the woman's father refuses to allow her to marry him because he does not consider the man to be of a high enough social status. When they decide to marry in defiance of the woman's father, he disowns her. Discerning in Akiva the potential of becoming a great scholar, the woman encourages him to go to study Torah. Even though he must separate from her for many years to pursue his studies, the wife's loyalty to him never wavers and eventually they are reunited. When Akiva finally returns home as a great sage, he is now of sufficiently high social status that his father-in-law becomes reconciled with him and his wife and agrees to share his wealth with them. The version of the story on which we will focus our attention in this chapter contains most of the elements of the relationship as told by tradition that have been of interest to contemporary readers.

Rabbi Akiva and the Daughter of Ben Calba Savua

Rabbi Akiva was a shepherd who worked for Ben Calba Savua. His [Ben Calba Savua's] daughter saw that he was humble and with excellent qualities. She said to him, "If I am betrothed to you, will you go to the study house?" He said to her, "Yes." He betrothed her in secret and she sent him off. When her father heard, he expelled her from his house and disinherited her. He [Akiva] went and sat for twelve years in the study house. When he returned, he brought with him twelve thousand students. He overheard an old man say to her, "Until when will you live life as if you were a widow?" She said to him, "If he would obey me, he would sit for twelve additional years in the study house." He [Akiva] said [to himself], "I would be doing it with her permission." He returned and sat for twelve additional years in the study house. When he returned [home], he brought with him twenty-four thousand students. When his wife heard, she went out to greet him. Her neighbors said to her, "Borrow clothes and cover yourself." She said to them, "A righteous man knows the soul of his animal [Proverbs 12:10]." When she came to him, she fell on her face and kissed his feet. His attendants pushed her away. He said to them, "Leave her. What I have and what you have is hers." Her father heard that a great man came to town. He said [to himself], "I will go to him; perhaps he will cancel my vow." He came to him. He [Akiva] said to him [Ben Calba Savua], "Did you vow with the understanding that he [your prospective son-in-law] was a great man?" He [Ben Calba Savua] said to him [Akiva], "Even [if he knew] one chapter or even one law." He [Akiva] said to him [Ben Calba Savua], "I am he." He [Ben Calba Savua] fell on his face and kissed his [Akiva's] feet and gave him half of his wealth. (B. Ketubot 62b-63a)

The Betrothal of Akiva and the Daughter of Ben Calba Savua

Contemporary Israeli readers have marveled at the role that the daughter of Ben Calba Savua played in motivating Akiva, a simple, uneducated shepherd, to seek to become a Torah scholar.[3] She saw in him a potential for greatness that he himself did not see. Udi Leon suggests that her powers of discernment may be compared to those of God in the Bible, who saw the qualities of great leadership in such humble shepherds as Moses and David.[4] Oded Yisraeli observes that it is important to note that Ben Calba Savua's daughter's focus on Akiva's inner quality of humility reflected her awareness of how important this quality was for a rabbinic sage, in contrast to the social consensus that the only important quality of a sage is his expertise in Torah study.[5]

Udi Leon notes that if we read the daughter's betrothal proposal as conditional—if you want to become betrothed to me you must go study Torah—it suggests that Akiva really needed this push to begin to train to be a scholar: "The shepherd [did] not learn because he [did] not see the treasure hidden within learning with the same strength and clarity that the woman [saw] it."[6]

The daughter of Ben Calba Savua impresses contemporary Israeli readers because of her willingness to challenge social convention in ways that have been cited by Udi Leon. In defying her father's wishes and proposing marriage to Akiva, she flew in the face of the accepted practice at the time.[7] Also, her openness to crossing the social and economic divide between Akiva and herself, the daughter of his wealthy employer, is very striking.[8] We see how transgressive her insistence on marrying Akiva was in her father's extreme reaction of disinheriting her for this act, which he may have done in an attempt to pressure her not to marry Akiva or perhaps as a test of Akiva to see if he would still be willing to marry her if she were poor.[9] Moshe Lavee observes that the revelation at the end of the story, that Rabbi Akiva had become the great Torah scholar that the daughter of Ben Calba Savua had envisioned, confirmed that her instinct to challenge social conventions was more in line with the truth than her father's insistence on following convention and refusing to grant her permission to marry Akiva.[10]

Akiva's Absence From Home

What do readers make of the self-imposed twenty-four year separation between Akiva and the daughter of Ben Calba Savua? When the old man asked her, "Until when will you live life as if you were a widow?" he was strongly criticizing her for being willing to stay connected to a man who, it would seem, had abandoned her. One might assume that, at least initially, many contemporary readers would agree with the old man. By reading the story in the context of its location in the Talmud, however, some readers have come to appreciate that the old man's negative assessment of their arrangement was distorted and that in fact their decision to consider Akiva's Torah study a higher priority than their living together was a sign that they had a very strong, mutually supportive bond.

The story of Akiva and the daughter of Ben Calba Savua is one of several stories embedded in the Talmud in a legal discussion of how long men of various professions were permitted to be away from home without the permission of their wives.[11] One of the participants in the discussion, Rabbi Eliezer, sets the norm that a Torah scholar should not leave his wife without her consent for more than thirty days at a time. The other stories that appear with the story of Akiva and the daughter of Ben Calba Savua support Rabbi Eliezer's limit on the absence of Torah scholars from home by presenting situations in which the lengthy separation between a Torah scholar and his wife, without taking into consideration the wife's feelings, had disastrous consequences for the couple and/or their family.[12] In contrast to these other stories, although the story of Akiva and the daughter of Ben Calba Savua told of an extremely long absence of a Torah scholar from home—twenty-four years—it had a happy ending in which the man and woman were reunited in a loving manner and were reconciled with her father who had originally opposed their marriage. As Shulamith Valler observes, it would appear that this story ended on such a positive note because not only did the daughter of Ben Calba Savua give permission to Akiva to leave her and engage in Torah study, but she actually urged him to do so.[13]

Despite the long periods of Akiva's absences, during which he and the daughter of Ben Calba Savua were deprived of physical proximity and the ability to express their love directly to each other, the two of them felt powerfully connected. When Akiva returned home after the first twelve-year absence, Yonah Fraenkel points out, they did not even need a direct conversation to realize that they were in full accord that it was acceptable to both of them to be separated for another twelve years so that Akiva could continue to study Torah. All it took was for Akiva to overhear her telling the critical old man, "If he would obey me, he would sit for twelve additional years in the study house," and from that he was able to conclude confidently that his return to study Torah "would be … with her permission."[14]

Akiva's Final Homecoming

One of the most puzzling aspects of the story for contemporary Israeli readers is the portrayal of the reunion between Akiva and the daughter of Ben Calba Savua when he returned home after the second and final twelve-year period of separation between them. Readers have wondered why she refused to heed her neighbors' advice to borrow nice clothes to appear attractive to her husband, and they are not sure how to interpret her response to them: "A righteous man knows the soul of his animal." Why would she refer to Akiva as a righteous man but to herself as an animal? This statement would seem to suggest that she felt inferior to him, an interpretation strengthened when she greeted him by falling on her face and kissing his feet, actions that could be seen as expressions of self-abasement. Akiva's rebuke to his attendants who try to push her away, "Leave her. What I have and what you have is hers," is also puzzling.

Yonah Fraenkel does not interpret the words or actions of the daughter of Ben Calba Savua as indications that she felt inferior to Rabbi Akiva. Fraenkel reads her statement to her neighbors as an assertion that her separation from him did not undermine the bond that had been forged between them at the beginning of the story. "She convey[ed] the contrast between her and him with the help of the expressions 'righteous man' (*tsaddiq*) and 'his animal' (*behemto*), but she [knew] that despite the great external difference [between them—she as a poor under-dressed woman and he as a respected scholar], he [knew her soul]."[15] In addition, Fraenkel suggests that when Rabbi Akiva admonished his disciples, "What I have and what you have is hers," he expressed "the spiritual partnership, or better the spiritual unity between him and her," he who had achieved the status of sage and she who had launched him on this path and unselfishly provided him with moral support for so long.[16]

Admiel Kosman reads the woman's declaration to her neighbors as her confirmation that such a righteous man as Akiva "possess[ed] the ability to see within, penetrating the external appearance and looking into [a person's] soul. Just as [when he was a shepherd] he [could] see what [was] troubling an animal and what its needs [were], even though it [was] unable to express them in words, so he could recognize her relationship with him even without her beautifying herself for him with pretty clothing."[17] In effect, she was saying to them, "Akiva will know my value and the honor I feel for him, even if I appear before him in rags, just as I recognized his qualities when he was a simple shepherd."[18] In a similar vein, Kosman understands Akiva's rebuke of the attendants as a declaration that "behind the screen of the ceremonial, the formality, the hierarchy of the study house stand higher and truer spiritual criteria that you, the students, cannot 'see.' Pure intention and religious devotion are not measured by the outward appearance of a person, and not even by the degree of his learnedness."[19] The truth about the poorly dressed woman who kissed his feet was, he was saying, that she was his worthy partner who deserved as much credit for the Torah study in which he and his students engaged as they did themselves.

Udi Leon, however, interprets the daughter's reference to Akiva as a righteous man and herself as an animal as reflecting some doubt in her mind as to how Akiva will relate to her now that he has returned for good. In pointing out the power discrepancy between them—he as a righteous man and she as an animal—she may have been declaring her desire to test him. Indeed, her refusal to borrow nice clothes and her decision to throw herself at his feet like any common person may suggest that she really wanted to know if he could see into her inner soul despite her external appearance, just as she had seen into his at the beginning of the story.[20]

As Admiel Kosman observes, we can see from Ben Calba Savua's reaction to the news that his son-in-law is the great Rabbi Akiva that he has remained capable of only appreciating that which bears the outer trappings valued by society. Unlike his daughter, who could see the inner potential of Akiva to become a great sage even when he was a humble shepherd, the father could bring himself to honor Akiva by bowing down and kissing his feet only when Akiva could be clearly identified as a sage surrounded by his disciples. Furthermore, there was a great contrast between the ability of the father's daughter and son-in-law to find a spiritual connection even in poverty and the materialistic manner in which the father related to them when he signaled his reconnection with the couple by granting them half of his wealth.[21]

The Married Life of Akiva and the Daughter of Ben Calba Savua

In reading the version of the story of Akiva and the daughter of Ben Calba Savua in Tractate Ketubot that we have been considering, one may receive the impression that Akiva went off to study Torah immediately after they were married, and they did not live together as husband and wife until after he returned twenty-four years later. Even though one could argue that according to Jewish law this was an acceptable arrangement because the wife consented to it, one might still wonder whether Akiva exceeded any reasonable allowance he might have had to separate from his wife to study Torah. Yonah Fraenkel addresses this issue by pointing out that in writing about the establishment of their relationship, the version in Ketubot states only *iqadesha leih* ("he betrothed her"), not that they were married, before he went away to study Torah. In those days, *qiddushin* (betrothal) took place a considerable period of time before *nissu'in* (marriage), and during the time between the two ritual ceremonies the man and woman did not live together as husband and wife.[22] Therefore, it would seem that Akiva did not, in fact, violate his responsibility as a husband to cohabitate with her when he went to study Torah.

Another version, in Tractate Nedarim, substantially follows the same plot as is found in the version in Ketubot, but it departs from that plot in relating that Akiva and his wife lived together as a married couple for a while before she asked him to go to the study house. This additional scene has been of interest to Israeli readers due to its poignant romantic portrayal of a couple living in poverty but lovingly committed to each other.[23]

> They would sleep in the barn. He would gather straw from her hair. He said to her, "If I could, I would give you [jewelry in the shape of] Jerusalem of gold. Elijah came to them with the appearance of a person and called to them from the doorway. He said to them, "Give me a little straw, because my wife has given birth and I have no place where she can lie down." Rabbi Akiva said to his wife, "Look, here is a man who does not even have straw." She said to him, "Go to the study house." (B. Nedarim 50a)[24]

The devotion of Akiva to his wife in this passage is very moving. Living in poverty due to her being disowned by her father, they slept in a barn on straw, and when Akiva lovingly removed straw from her hair, it reminded him how much he wanted to give her a beautiful gift of a piece of gold jewelry depicting Jerusalem, which he could not afford. In response to the appearance of Elijah, Akiva demonstrated to her an inspiring degree of human empathy when he observed to her that as poor as they were, there were people who were even poorer than they were.[25]

Shamma Friedman and Oded Yisraeli observe that this version gives a more detailed explanation than the version in Ketubot does of what motivated the daughter of Ben Calba Savua to make the rather far-fetched suggestion that he, an ignorant shepherd, should go to study Torah. "[T]he wife's determination to raise him through education," writes Friedman, "[was] inspired by her impoverished husband's noble devotion and tender treatment toward her. The lover's hand extended to remove ... straw from her hair [was] a subtle physical expression, the more powerful through its tenderness and restraint. It [was] enhanced by the verbal expression sustaining her spirit: others do not even have straw."[26] Yisraeli observes that when in response to Akiva's expression of regret that he could not give her an expensive gift she immediately told him that he should go to study Torah, it was as if she were seeking to respond to "the desperate longing of the heart of her beloved who [did] not have in his hand what he want[ed] to give to his beloved. And here [broke] out from the longing of her heart her desire, which [was] not for silver or gold or precious stones or even straw, but rather that he go to the study house."[27] Yisraeli goes on to note how humble a request hers was in keeping with the humility of the little he could offer her: "[Her] request [was] formulated lightly, for she [did] not demand that he become a Torah scholar, not even (although it may be clear that this was her true intention) that he learn Torah, just that he be [in the study house], a modest request that anyone could fulfill."[28]

The Contemporary Significance of the Rabbi Akiva and the Daughter of Ben Calba Savua Story

Much of the appeal of this story to contemporary Israeli readers is due to the portrait of the daughter of Ben Calba Savua as one of the wisest and strongest female characters in any Talmudic story. She saw in Akiva the potential of becoming a great Torah scholar, an insight which no one else, including Akiva, had. In addition, it is impressive to readers that although she was a woman cut off from the central religious engagement in Torah study dominated by men, it was she who convinced Akiva to begin to study Torah, which resulted in his becoming one of the great Jewish sages of all time.

Akiva and his wife appear to contemporary interpreters as very special in the strength that they exhibited in defying social conventions. Interpreters have called attention to voices of normative values that emerge throughout the story and to the ways that this couple rejected those voices. The couple did not allow the father's insistence that they not marry because it is not suitable for a rich daughter to marry a poor shepherd to defeat their love, and they did not allow the fact that her father disowned her to influence their commitment to each other. The daughter of Ben Calba Savua refused to be discouraged by the critical comments of the old man who could not understand why she would spend so much time living apart from Akiva. She later did not rely on the advice of her neighbors to beautify herself for her reunion with Akiva, knowing that their love had a much deeper basis than outward appearances. Furthermore, Akiva rebuked his attendants for assuming that the poverty stricken woman who bowed before him was a worthless nuisance, declaring that she shared in the merit of their Torah study.

It is striking to what extent a range of interpreters have written so positively about the twenty-four year separation between Akiva and his wife, for one would expect contemporary readers to be disturbed by Akiva's apparent neglect of the daughter of Ben Calba Savua. Indeed, Daniel Boyarin raises a serious question about this aspect of the story. He assumes that the story did not reflect marriage practices in the Land of Israel during Akiva's day, but rather was written in Babylonia during a later period. On that basis, he is highly critical of the way the story made use of romantic tropes in an attempt to justify the practice in Babylonia of men separating from their wives to study Torah for long periods of time and to praise wives who gave up their conjugal rights for the higher purpose of their husband's Torah study, a practice that from Boyarin's point of view should be labeled as a form of "female subjugation."[29]

For the most part, however, the contemporary readers we have explored express admiration for the wife's encouragement of this separation. They also very much appreciate the consistency of Akiva's loving devotion to his wife, from the early days when they lived in a barn to his final return as a great Torah scholar. In addition, some write admiringly about how, throughout a period of twenty-four years, this man and woman stayed connected in their souls despite their physical separation, never doubting their mutual devotion.

It is clear, of course, that to a large degree this story does not operate on a realistic level. Is it conceivable that Rabbi Akiva gained one thousand students a year over a period of twenty-four years? Would any real human couple be able to maintain the level of attachment described between Rabbi Akiva and the daughter of Ben Calba Savua throughout such a long separation? The exaggerated elements of this ideal marriage are in fact what have made this story so popular among Israelis, for like most people, they can still be moved by the perfection that is found only in fairy tales.

CHAPTER 7

HUMAN FAILINGS AND NATIONAL DESTRUCTION: KAMTZA AND BAR KAMTZA

According to the master narrative of Zionism that lies at the heart of the national identity of Jewish Israelis, there have been three periods in which the Jewish people lived a sovereign political existence in the Land of Israel, during two of which the spiritual center of the people eventually became the Temple in Jerusalem. The first period of sovereignty, which ended with the destruction of the Temple by the Babylonians in 586 B.C.E., is sometimes referred to by Israelis as the period of "The First Temple" (*habayit harishon*). The second period of sovereignty, which ended with the destruction of the rebuilt Temple by the Romans in 70 C.E., is sometimes referred to by them as the period of "The Second Temple" (*habayit hasheni*). The third period of sovereignty, from the establishment of the State of Israel in 1948 until the present is sometimes referred to by them as the period of "The Third Temple" (*habayit hashelishi*). Although a third Temple has not yet been built, the term *habayit hashelishi* is usable because, like the terms labeling the other periods, it can be understood to mean "the third home," in the sense of the national home of the Jews. The term *habayit* is also sometimes translated as "commonwealth," and the three periods of sovereignty are then referred to as the First, Second, and Third Commonwealths.

The association of modern Zionism with these earlier manifestations of a pattern of establishing sovereignty and experiencing destruction cannot help but arouse in Israelis an underlying sense that there are no historical guarantees that the second part of the pattern, destruction, could not happen again, that in fact just as there was a destruction of the

First Temple/Commonwealth (*ḥurban bayit rishon*) and a destruction of the Second Temple/Commonwealth (*ḥurban bayit sheni*), someday the destruction of the Third Temple/Commonwealth (*ḥurban bayit shelishi*) could occur. In fact, to this day, the dangers facing contemporary Israel are sometimes referred to with this third term.[1]

The most famous reference to the potential danger of the end of Israel's existence as the destruction of the Third Temple was uttered during the Yom Kippur War of 1973. On the morning of October 7, 1973, the second day of the war, when Israel was desperately trying to repel the simultaneous surprise attacks by Egypt in the Sinai Peninsula and by Syria in the Golan Heights, Benny Peled, Commander of the Israeli Air Force, confided to his fellow officers in their underground headquarters that he had received a telephone call from Defense Minister Moshe Dayan in which Dayan declared that under the current military circumstances he considered the very existence of the State of Israel to be in serious danger. "Close the door for a moment," Peled told them. "The situation in the opinion of the Minister of Defense . . . is that we are apparently facing the destruction of the Third Temple (*heres habayit hashelishi*; *heres* is a synonym for *ḥurban*)."[2]

The threat to Israel's existence that it would be conquered by its neighboring enemies, which was operative during Israel's first three major wars in 1948, 1967, and 1973, has been largely eliminated. However, the persistent memory of Jewish vulnerability in the Diaspora culminating in the Holocaust, the threat of nuclear attack by Iran, the ongoing declared commitment of some Palestinians to eliminate Israel, rocket attacks on Israel by Hamas from Gaza and by Hezbollah from Lebanon, and outbreaks of terrorist violence by Palestinians have kept Israelis from enjoying a full sense of security and have raised questions about the future viability of the State.

This fear of the destruction of the Third Temple is focused on it being defeated by its enemies from without. Religious Zionist Rabbi Binyanim Lau has expressed the fear that a third destruction might come from within. He identifies two ways that deficiencies in Israel could endanger the existence of the State: by holding a misguided, arrogant assumption that Israel is destined to continue to exist no matter what, and by failing to realize that only if Israelis fight against the moral failings in their society will there continue to be a State of Israel. He has discussed this fear in the conclusion of a book he wrote on Jeremiah, the biblical prophet of the destruction of the First Temple, and in a statement he made after the book was published. Lau is highly critical of the slogan to which he recalls singing and dancing as a religious Zionist youth: "The Land of Israel belongs to the people of Israel (*erets yisra'el shayyekhet le'am yisra'el*)." "I have never found in any Jewish sources the use of this expression," he writes.[3] He is equally opposed to those religious Zionists to whom he refers as "false prophets [who declare] 'we have a tradition from our ancestors that the Third Temple will never be destroyed (*masoret beyadeinu me'avoteinu—bayit shelishi lo yeḥarev*).'"[4]

In opposition to these slogans, which express the belief that the existence of the State of Israel is unconditionally guaranteed, Lau urges Israeli Jews to recall the central biblical concept embodied in the teachings of Jeremiah and the other prophets of ancient Israel, that the Land of Israel does not belong to the Jewish people, but rather only to God, and that their residence in the Land is always conditional upon their following in God's ways. Lau believes, as he puts it, that "there is no insurance policy for the State of Israel."[5] If we want Israel to continue to exist, he argues, Jews have to earn the approval of the true owner of the Land, God, and just as tradition teaches that He expelled the people for sinning during the last two periods of sovereignty, there is every reason to believe He will do it again if the Jews in Israel do not live up to the moral standards God expects of them. Even with the ongoing success of the State of Israel (as he puts it: "the Third Temple is in the process of being built"), he writes, "holding on to the Land and becoming established in it are dependent on our consciousness and our deeds. Every time we disobey the moral code of humanity. … we lose our hold on the Land."[6] The only hope for Israel's continued existence, Lau believes, is that its citizens will be willing to work hard to keep Israel from being destroyed by the moral corruption from within that leads to social division and discrimination against the weak by the powerful.[7]

A Talmudic story about the events leading up to the destruction of the Second Temple reflects Lau's conviction that a major threat to Jewish sovereignty in the Land of Israel is a morally corrupt society. Another factor that could threaten Jewish sovereignty, according to this story, is the lack of a visionary leadership that would set an example of moral rectitude and operate on the basis of an accurate understanding of historical reality.

Kamtza and Bar Kamtza

On account of Kamtza and Bar Kamtza Jerusalem was destroyed. There was a man whose friend was Kamtza and whose enemy was Bar Kamtza. He made a feast and said to his servant,

"Go bring me Kamtza." He [the servant] went and brought him Bar Kamtza. He [the host] came and saw Bar Kamtza sitting. He [the host] said to him [Bar Kamtza], "You are my enemy. What do you want here? Get up and get out." He [Bar Kamtza] said to him [the host], "Since I have come, let me pay you for what I eat and drink." He [the host] said to him [Bar Kamtza], "No." He said to him, "I will pay for half of the feast." He said to him, "No." He said to him, "I will pay for the entire feast." He said to him, "No." He took his hand, stood him up, and sent him away. He [Bar Kamtza] said [to himself], "Since the rabbis were sitting there and did not protest, I can conclude that this was acceptable to them. I will go and inform on them at the royal palace." He went and said to the emperor, "The Jews have rebelled against you." He said to him, "Who says this? "He said to him, "Send a sacrifice to them and see if they sacrifice it." He went and sent with him a choice calf. When he [Bar Kamtza] was on his way he put a blemish in the lip [of the calf], and some say in the eye, in a place that for us [the Jews] it is a blemish but for them [the Romans] it is not a blemish. The rabbis thought they should sacrifice it to maintain peaceful relations with the government. Rabbi Zechariah ben Avkulus said, "People will say that it is permissible to sacrifice an animal with a blemish." They thought they should kill him [Bar Kamtza], so that he would not tell [the emperor that they did not sacrifice it]. Rabbi Zechariah said, "People will say that a person who puts a blemish in an animal should be put to death." Rabbi Yohanan said, "The humility of Rabbi Zechariah ben Avkulus destroyed our Temple, burned our Sanctuary, and exiled us from our Land. (B. Gittin 55b-56a)

The Mistaken Invitation of Bar Kamtza to the Feast and Bar Kamtza's Revenge

The seemingly improbable assertion by Rabbi Yohanan that an event involving two people with similar names, Kamtza and Bar Kamtza, was the cause of the destruction of Jerusalem prepares readers for the underlying point of the story, that the destruction was not primarily the result of a strategic military failure, but rather of a failure in the way human beings related to each other. In order to understand how, according to the author of the story, human failings contributed to this tragedy, contemporary Israeli readers have made efforts to analyze the significance of the actions of the three central characters of the story: the host to whose feast Bar Kamtza was mistakenly invited, Bar Kamtza, and Rabbi Zechariah ben Avkulus, the sage who determined the national response to the challenge from the Romans orchestrated by Bar Kamtza. In addition, readers have sought to determine the author's assessment of how the spiritual leaders of the time, the rabbis, conducted themselves at the feast and later when they discussed the question of whether they should sacrifice the blemished animal sent to the Temple by the emperor.

It is clear to readers that the author of the story is highly critical of the host of the feast, whose hostility to Bar Kamtza was so great that he refused to consider any of the compromise suggestions made by this mistakenly invited guest that might avoid that guest's humiliation. As Binyamin Kelmanson observes, not only did the host treat a fellow human being in an extremely cruel manner, but he even displayed an extremely spiteful attitude toward the unwanted guest by forfeiting the financial benefit he would have received if he had allowed Bar Kamtza to pay for the entire feast.[8] In fact, notes Kelmanson, once the host and Bar Kamtza began their discussion about whether Bar Kamtza could stay, the only word that the host spoke to Bar Kamtza was "No," and after Bar Kamtza had exhausted his offers of compromise, without saying anything else the host unceremoniously threw him out of his house.[9] Yael Levine Katz comments on how single mindedly the host focused on solving the problem of Bar Kamtza's presence at the feast by casting him out: "There [was] no attempt or inclination on the part of the host to clarify the circumstances of the presence of Bar Kamtza at the feast, while he assume[d] that the guilt [was] that of Bar Kamtza. We do not see him criticizing his servant [who was actually the one responsible for Bar Kamtza's presence at the feast] and if necessary punishing him."[10]

A Morally Rotten Society

The story suggests that underlying the unfortunate events of the story is a society in which ethical interpersonal relations are virtually nonexistent. Yael Levine Katz calls attention to the fact that the host is never mentioned by name.[11] This may suggest that his immoral action is not limited to him, but rather that he represents the ethical failings of the people (perhaps particularly of the wealthy) as a whole. In addition, the story is understood to condemn the rabbis at the feast for not intervening to stop the host's cruel behavior. Aryeh Yoeli speculates that the wealth of the host may have blinded the rabbis' ethical vision. After all, they may have reasoned, if they had stood up to the host, he might have cut off his donations to their Torah institutions.[12] Indeed, it is clear from the reported thoughts of Bar Kamtza that it was the rabbis' lack of action more than the host's cruelty that angered him. Binyamin Kelmanson observes that there may be symbolic significance to the places that Bar Kamtza put the blemishes according to two versions of the story—the mouth and the eyes: "It could be that these two possibilities suggest criticism of the sages—as if the blemish signified the silence of the sages who were present at the feast or [their] 'eyes closed' to the sin that was committed."[13] The unwillingness of the rabbis to intervene and prevent the humiliation of Bar Kamtza, notes Kelmanson, makes clear the tremendous responsibility that the rabbis, the purported spiritual leaders of the people, bore for the destruction of the Temple and of Jerusalem.[14]

In an alternative version of this story found in the midrashic collection Eikhah Rabbah (4:3), Rabbi Zechariah ben Avkulus is specifically named as a rabbi who did not protest against how the host treated Bar Kamtza, although in that version he does not play a role in the decision whether to sacrifice the animal sent by the emperor.[15] Aryeh Yoeli presents a combined reading of the two versions of the stories, placing Rabbi Zechariah both at the feast and at the sacrifice, thereby suggesting a striking contrast between how seriously Rabbi Zechariah took ethical behavior and how seriously he took ritual obligations. "That same rabbi," he writes, "sat at the feast and did not protest against the host. Only afterward, when the fate of the entire people of Israel was in the balance, then he aroused himself and called out, 'How can you go against the Shulhan Arukh?!"[16] By referring anachronistically to the Shulhan Arukh, the medieval code of Jewish law much of which contains rules for ritual practice that is the basis for Orthodox Jewish observance to this day, Yoeli suggests that Rabbi Zechariah's greater preoccupation with ritual than with ethics is a problem that exists in the contemporary rabbinical establishment as well.

Bar Kamtza's response to how he was treated at the feast was very extreme: he attempted to convince the Romans that the Jews had begun to revolt against their rule, and thereby he put his people in grave danger. It is therefore important for readers to try to understand what kind of effect the host's treatment of him had on Bar Kamtza that would lead him to act as he did. Aryeh Yoeli imagines that the humiliation of Bar Kamtza was particularly painful to him because the host was a very important and wealthy person and the feast was more than simply a social gathering of friends but rather a major social event which even rabbis attended.[17] Yael Levine Katz speculates that "[i]t is likely that Bar Kamtza thought that the host invited him out of a desire and intention to reconcile himself with him, but when he arrived at the feast, how great must have been the disappointment he felt," thereby increasing the pain of the experience.[18] Even with these proposed explanations of why Bar Kamtza was so hurt at being expelled from the feast, it is difficult to understand how he could have been driven to take revenge on the Jewish people as a whole by turning the Roman authorities against them. However, it is important to note that the narrator makes clear that what motivates Bar Kamtza to take this extreme step is the silence of the rabbis. A society in which there is no moral voice to protect those who are persecuted, it seems, has produced such alienation that people are willing to work for its destruction.

The Deliberations among the Rabbis

In response to Bar Kamtza's clever arrangement to put a blemish on the animal that would not invalidate a Roman sacrifice but would invalidate a Jewish sacrifice, the rabbis considered three courses of action: (1) obey Jewish ritual law and not offer what they considered to be an invalid sacrifice and thereby anger the Roman emperor, (2) offer the sacrifice in violation of Jewish law, and thereby keep peace with their Roman rulers, or (3) kill Bar Kamtza and thereby keep the emperor from knowing that they did not offer the sacrifice. Although the other rabbis favored the latter two options, Rabbi Zechariah ben Avkulus convinced them to agree to follow the first option, even if it meant potentially undermining relations between the Jews and Rome.

Binyamin Kelmanson sees the silence of the rabbis when Bar Kamtza was expelled from the feast and the misguided decision by Rabbi Zechariah to stick to the letter of the law as identical moral failures. In both cases, he argues, the rabbis and Rabbi Zechariah did not transcend their self-referential perspective and intervene in reality to correctly solve a problem. At the feast, suggests Kelmanson, the rabbis did not intervene to rebuke the host for his immoral behavior either because they were afraid of standing up to an "aggressive host" or because "they thought that they did not know all of the details of the situation so it was not appropriate for them to take a stand."[19] Perhaps, Kelmanson suggests, the rabbis' problem may have been that while they were very good at applying their thoughts to "a theoretical problem" while discussing Jewish law, when it came to a simple moral challenge of preventing "a person [from] hurting another person" they were not oriented to responding and so "they chose to withdraw into inaction."[20] Similarly, argues Kelmanson, all Rabbi Zechariah could think of was his commitment to the law and his fear of what others might say about his decision. He therefore was unable to do what was necessary to preserve the existence of the people: either sacrifice the blemished animal or kill Bar Kamtza.[21] "He who flees the true problem into a preoccupation with the minute details [of ritual law]," writes Kelmanson, "is no different from the one who does not arise and prevent injustice. Both are closing their eyes to the true problem; both are responsible for the destruction that will come down on the head of the people."[22]

The story suggests that the fateful decision not to sacrifice the animal sent by the emperor was not only the responsibility of Zechariah ben Avkulus, but of all the other rabbis. Gil Nativ and Yael Levine Katz point out that the triumph of Rabbi Zechariah over the rabbis was a significant violation of the rabbinic principle that legal decisions are based on majority rule, as captured in the expression "the law is always according to the opinion of the many" (*ein halakhah ella kedivrei hamerubin*, Mishnah Eduyot 1:5) and in the rabbinic understanding that the biblical expression "follow the majority" (*aḥarei rabbim lehattot*, Exodus 23:3) refers to the making of legal decisions (Bava Metzia 59b).[23] Based on this principle, that decisions by the rabbis are arrived at by majority vote, it would seem that the other rabbis had the power and the authority to overrule Rabbi Zechariah. In the end, however, they succumbed to his unfortunate political miscalculation, which led to the Romans' assumption that the Jews were rebelling against them and the subsequent war during which the Temple was destroyed. Pinchas Mandel criticizes the other rabbis not only because they failed to assert their right to majority rule, which would have prevented, at least at that point, a crisis in the relationship between the Jews and Rome, but also for the stark contrast between their initial determination to do what was necessary to maintain the peace between the Jews and their rulers and their refraining from doing anything at the feast to prevent the humiliation Bar Kamtza faced, thereby failing in their responsibility to act as the moral leaders of their people.[24]

The Humility of Rabbi Zechariah ben Avkulus

Many readers of the story have been puzzled by the statement of Rabbi Yohanan at the end of the story that the humility (*anvetanut*) of

Rabbi Zechariah ben Avkulus was what led to the destruction of the Temple. Humility is seen in rabbinic literature as a positive quality.[25] So, how could this quality of Rabbi Zechariah be the cause of the destruction of the Temple? A number of interpreters have compared this story with another passage in rabbinic literature in which Rabbi Zechariah ben Avkulus could not decide between the conflicting opinions of the House of Hillel and the House of Shammai on the manner in which it is permitted to remove leftover bones and shells from a table at which one is eating a meal on the Sabbath. Due to his inability to make a commitment to either approved method of removing the bones and shells from the table, Rabbi Zechariah never put his bones and shells on the table and just threw them behind a couch as he ate. At the end of this story, Rabbi Yossi declared "The humility (*anvetanut*) of Rabbi Zecharia ben Avkulus burned the Temple" (Tosefta Shabbat 17, 4).

It is difficult to understand how Rabbi Zechariah could be characterized as possessing the quality of humility in either the story about removing the bones and shells from the table on the Sabbath or the story about the decision whether to offer the emperor's sacrifice. In the story about removing the bones and shells from the table on the Sabbath, he is portrayed as avoiding deciding which legal school of thought to follow. In the story about whether to offer the emperor's sacrifice, Rabbi Zechariah is portrayed as insisting on strictly obeying the laws of sacrifice despite the potential political consequences of doing so. In neither story is it immediately evident that he is displaying the characteristic of humility.

Daniel Schwartz argues that in the two stories Rabbi Zechariah's actions were motivated by the same feeling, mainly a fear of making a decision that would lead to the violation of Jewish law, and it is to this fear that the term *anvetanut* applies. In the case of the removal of the bones and shells on the Sabbath, he was afraid to choose between the method of the House of Hillel and the method of the House of Shammai, because it was possible that one of the methods was invalid, and so he avoided acting according to either one and just threw the bones behind a couch as he ate. In the case of the decision whether to offer the sacrifice sent by the emperor, he was afraid to adopt either of the alternatives suggested by the other rabbis because he feared that people would get the wrong impression and as a result Jewish law might be broken in the future, and so he refused to sacrifice the animal sent by the emperor, which eventually led to the destruction of the Temple.[26] Gil Nativ supports Schwartz's characterization of Rabbi Zechariah as acting out of fear when confronted with the challenge of whether to offer the emperor's sacrifice. "[From Rabbi Zechariah's point of view] every departure from the letter of the law was a dangerous precedent," he writes, … an opening for reform in the Jewish law, God forbid. …. [Rabbi Zechariah asked himself:] Who are we to break the given laws of sacrifices or the laws of capital punishment to defend ourselves, to guard the interests of the here and now?!"[27]

Pinhas Mandel raises a serious question about Rabbi Zechariah's fear that people would get the wrong impression about how to obey Jewish law if he followed one of the suggestions of the other rabbis. Mandel notes that in other passages in the Talmud when the argument is put forth that one should not act in a certain way because people may get a mistaken impression about how to observe the law, the discussion is about situations related to the everyday life of Jews. No regular Jew would have to deal with the question of whether to sacrifice a blemished animal sent by the emperor or kill a traitor to prevent the emperor from finding out that you did not sacrifice the animal, and therefore it was absurd to argue against offering the sacrifice or killing Bar Kamtza because these would set examples of violations of law that might lead Jews to commit similar violations.[28]

Was the Second Temple Destroyed as a Punishment for Sin?

Another Talmudic passage states that it is clear that the First Temple was destroyed by God in punishment for the sins of that generation, but it is not clear why the Second Temple was destroyed by God, since that generation of Jews were ostensibly piously loyal to God's ways:

> Why was the First Temple destroyed? Because of three [sins]: idolatry, sexual impropriety, and murder. … However, why was the Second Temple destroyed, when people engaged in Torah study, observance of the commandments, and deeds of kindness? Because of baseless hatred (*sinat ḥinnam*), which teaches that baseless hatred is equal in consequence to three sins: idolatry, sexual impropriety, and murder. (B. Yoma 9b)

The point being made in this passage is that one should not assume that the divine punishment of national destruction occurs only because of the commission of what are considered to be grave sins such as idolatry, sexual impropriety, and murder; it can also occur because of failings in the quality of interpersonal relations in a society. This statement about the sin of "baseless hatred" as the cause of the destruction of the Second Temple is often associated with the story of Kamtza and Bar Kamtza, for the treatment of Bar Kamtza by the host provided a prime example of this moral failing when the host humiliated Bar Kamtza for no defensible reason.

Binyamin Kelmanson challenges this reading of the story and declares that in fact the story of Kamtza and Bar Kamtza makes clear that the Second Temple was not destroyed as a direct divine punishment for sin, even the sin of "baseless hatred." Instead, he argues, the story makes the point that the moral state of the people, and particularly of its spiritual leaders, led inevitably to a weakened existence that made them vulnerable to defeat. "In a certain sense," he argues, "active divine intervention was not necessary for the destruction of the Temple; the fact that baseless hatred was rooted in the members of that generation in such a terrible manner is what brought upon them the calamity, and that is certainly why they could not stand up to the army of Rome that arose against Jerusalem."[29]

Yehoshua Grinberg also rejects the notion that the story teaches that the destruction of the Second Temple was a divine punishment for sin. He argues that the real cause of the destruction, according to the story, was the political miscalculation of refusing to sacrifice the blemished animal sent by the emperor. Rabbi Yohanan's statement that the incidents that developed as a result of the confusion between Kamtza and Bar Kamtza caused the destruction of the Temple means that he "blames the destruction on a lack of political understanding and foolishness. If the people really understood before whom they stood [the mighty Roman Empire], they would not have insisted on foolishness [by refusing to sacrifice the animal sent by the emperor]. ... There is here [the notion that redemption will come only by means of] a clear-eyed understanding of reality and acting within it in wisdom."[30]

This rabbinic version of the events leading up to the destruction of the Second Temple makes it seem as if none of the Jews were actually interested in rebelling against the emperor. As Anat Yisraeli-Taran observes, this is far from compatible with the history of the period as we know it, and even with other rabbinic stories about that time.[31] The choice to leave out any indication that at least some Jews advocated the rebellion, of which the rabbis were well aware, appears to be designed to underline the significance of the factor of human moral failure in undermining the inner strength of the people at the time.

Being Afraid and Hardening One's Heart

The story of Kamtza and Bar Kamtza is preceded by a declaration that the story about to be told contributes to an understanding of a biblical verse.

> Rabbi Yohanan said, "What is the meaning of 'Happy is the man who is always afraid, but he who hardens his heart will fall into evil [Proverbs 28:14]?'" (B. Gittin 55b)[32]

In what way does the story of Kamtza and Bar Kamtza illustrate the meaning of the verse from Proverbs quoted by Rabbi Yohanan? Anat Yisraeli-Taran argues that in a certain sense each of the four major characters in the story hardened his heart: "the host, who embarrassed and humiliated Bar Kamtza; the sages, who sat quietly in the face of the insulting of Bar Kamtza; Bar Kamtza himself, who sought revenge out of all proportions to the hurt he suffered; and Rabbi Zechariah, who hardened his heart and did not permit a departure from set procedures when a difficult problem arose."[33] Binyamin Kelmanson offers an understanding of the applicability of the verse's declaration that fear is the positive quality and hardening of the heart is the negative quality: "Fear is preparedness, listening, paying attention, complex critical thinking. The opposite of fear is hardening of the heart. … The one who hardens his heart is sunk into his opinions and does not allow reality to confuse him. … He who cannot change his conceptions, ego considerations, [his preoccupation with] the here and now to wider considerations 'will fall into evil' and will bring down others with him," a characterization that could apply equally to the host, the sages at the feast, Bar Kamtza, and Rabbi Zechariah.[34]

The Contemporary Significance of the Story of Kamtza and Bar Kamtza

For the most part, political analysis of how Israel should deal with its security challenges concentrates on how to accurately perceive the threats presented by Israel's enemies and how to respond to those threats, whether by diplomatic or military means. One can discern in the contemporary readings of the Kamtza and Bar Kamtza story the ways in which, explicitly or implicitly, the rabbis' analysis of the factors that caused the destruction of the Second Temple are seen as relevant to factors to which Israelis should pay attention if they wish to avoid what is sometimes referred to as "the destruction of the Third Temple." A society in which such an event as the cruel public humiliation of a person can occur is one that lacks the moral fiber and sense of personal interconnectedness that is necessary for the viable survival of that society. A society in which arrogant rich people get away with abusing their power, in which the spiritual leaders of that society are too cowed by such people to stand up for those who are vulnerable, and in which a person would slander his own people to the ruling authorities has an inner weakness that can endanger its very existence. Furthermore, a society in which conflicts between people have become so polarized that there is no way to resolve those conflicts can easily become a society in which people turn on each other, in effect aiding the efforts of the enemy to destroy that society.

In addition, one can discern in the contemporary Israeli readings of this story an awareness of what it is saying about the dangers that emerge when leaders think in set and inflexible ways that are based on a fear that existence itself may be threatened by new and creative thinking, when in fact it is that new and creative thinking that might lead the society out of danger. Misperception of the intent of the enemy is also a danger, for if you either underestimate or overestimate the threat the enemy presents, you may cause more damage than if you estimate it correctly. One can also see the danger of a religious leadership excessively preoccupied with the details of ritual observance but ignoring the moral deficiencies of the people it has been designated to lead.

NOTES

Preface

1 Ruth Calderon, "Latalmud nikhnesu yeḥefim" <http://www.alma.org.il>.
2 Ibid.
3 David C. Jacobson, *Modern Midrash: The Retelling of Traditional Jewish Narratives by Twentieth-Century Hebrew Writers* (Albany: State University of New York Press, 1987); David C. Jacobson, *Does David Still Play Before You? Israeli Poetry and the Bible* (Detroit: Wayne State University Press, 1997); David C. Jacobson, *Creator Are You Listening? Israeli Poets on God and Prayer* (Bloomington and Indianapolis: Indiana University Press, 2007); David C. Jacobson: *Beyond Political Messianism: The Poetry of Second-Generation Religious Zionist Settlers* (Boston: Academic Studies Press, 2011).

Introduction

1 Ruth Calderon, Inaugural Knesset Speech, *Divrei hakenesset* 12 February 2013: 33-37, accessible at <https://www.knesset.gov.il>.
2 Unless otherwise noted, the Talmudic story texts in this book are translations of the versions in the classic Vilna edition of the Babylonian Talmud.
3 Calderon, Inaugural Knesset Speech, 36.
4 Ibid.
5 Ibid.
6 Yaakov Blau, "Zeh ha'iyyum haqiyyumi ha'amiti: Ruth Calderon lomedet gemara," <www.kikar.co.il>.
7 Ibid.
8 Ibid.
9 Uri Misgav, "Frayerim ḥilonim rehutim," *Haaretz* 26 February 2013.
10 Ibid.
11 Ibid.
12 Ibid.
13 Ibid.
14 See Zvi Zameret, "Zalman Aran uma'arekhet haḥinnukh," in *He'asor hasheni: 5718-5728*, eds. Zvi Zameret and Hanna Yablonka (Jerusalem, Yad Yitzhak Ben Zvi, 2000), 61-67; Yuval Dror, "Mishelilat hagalut letippuaḥ hatoda'ah hayehudit," *Panim* 24 (2003) <http://www.itu.org.il>; and Yair Sheleg, *Me'ivri yashan leyehudi ḥadash: renesans hayahadut baḥevrah hayisra'elit* (Jerusalem: The Israel Democracy Institute, 2010), 49-63.
15 The most extensive study of the relationship of Ḥug Shedemot to the return to the Jewish bookcase may be found in Gad Ofaz, "Ziqat haqibbuts lemeqorot hayahadut bemaḥshevet 'ḥug shedemot,'" (PhD diss., Hebrew University, 1986). See also Gad Ofaz, *Misiaḥ loḥamim el aron hasefarim hayehudi: dor sheni ushelishi baqibbuts beḥippus hazehut hayehudit* (Jerusalem: The Hebrew University, 2016).
16 Ofaz, *Misiaḥ loḥamim*, 138-139.

17 Alon Gan, "Mitenu'ah shel mesoḥaḥim leḥamamah hamitappaḥat yeḥidim: mifalah shel ḥavurat shedemot," in *Ma'anit halev: minḥat devarim leMuki Tsur*, ed. Avraham Shapira (Tel Aviv: Hakibbutz Hameuchad, 2006), 166. Here, Gan draws on the analysis put forth by Muki Tsur.

18 Ofaz, "Ziqat haqibbuts," Abstract.

19 Ofaz, *Misiaḥ loḥamim*, 50.

20 Ibid., 46.

21 Gad Ofaz, "Hazekhut lidrosh: darkam shel anshei 'ḥug shedemot' el hameqorot," in *Tura: asuppat ma'amarei hagut umeḥqar bemaḥshevet yisra'el muggeshet leProfessor Shlomo (Simon) Greenberg beshenot gevurotav*, ed. Meir Ayali (Tel Aviv: Hakibbutz Hameuchad, 1989), 371.

22 Ibid.

23 Ibid.

24 Ibid., 373.

25 Ibid.

26 Eli Alon, "A Fractured Link," *Shedemot* (English version) 3 (1975): 99.

27 Quoted in Gad Ofaz, "Ziqat haqibbuts," 285.

28 Alon Gan, "Mitenu'ah shel mesoḥaḥim," 165.

29 Ibid., 171.

30 Muki Tsur, "Otsar haruaḥ," in *Shedemot veruaḥ: meḥavat hoqarah veyedidut leAvraham Shapira*, eds. Avihu Zakaki, Paul Mendes-Flohr, Zeev Gries (Jerusalem: Carmel, 2015), 47.

31 Ibid.

32 Ofaz, *Misiaḥ loḥamim*, 20.

33 Ibid., 158

34 Yair Sheleg, "Massekhet avot," *Makor rishon* 31 January 2016. For a study of the engagement of such leading figures with the Jewish tradition, see Zvi Zameret, "Mordim umamshikhim: itsuv hashabbat lefi Y.H. Brenner, A.D. Gordon, B. Katznelson, S. H. Bergman, E. Schweid, veM. Ayali," in *Hayashan yitḥaddesh veheḥadash yitqaddesh: al zehut, tarbut veyahadut: asuppah lezikhro shel Meir Ayali*, eds. Yehuda Friedlander, Uzi Shavit, Avi Sagi (Tel Aviv: Hakibbutz Hameuchad, 2005), 347-373.

35 Quoted in Ofaz, *Misiaḥ loḥamim*, 146.

36 Berl Katznelson, "Ḥurban utelishut," in Berl Katznelson, *Mahpekhah veshorashim: mivḥar devarim*, ed. Avinoam Barshai (Tel Aviv: Yaron Golan, 1996), 211.

37 Berl Katznelson, "Meqorot lo-akhzav," in Katznelson, *Mahpekhah veshorashim*, 216. Emphasis in the original.

38 Ibid.

39 Ibid. Given the engagement of Katznelson and other Second Aliyah thinkers with post-biblical Judaism, it is not surprising that members of Ḥug Shedemot became very interested in exploring the writings of such figures as role models of creative interaction with Jewish sources who could legitimate their own turn to the tradition. A significant example of this phenomenon is the book *Or haḥayyim beyom qetannot: mishnat A. D. Gordon umeqoroteha baqabbalah uvaḥasidut* (Tel Aviv: Tel Aviv University; Am Oved, 1996), in which Avraham Shapira, founding editor of *Shedemot*, studied the kabbalistic and Hasidic sources that inspired the thought of Second Aliyah intellectual A. D. Gordon.

40 Ofaz, "Ziqat haqibbuts, viii.

41 Gad Ofaz, "Terumato shel ḥug shedemot letsemiḥatam shel merkazei torah lo-datiyyim beyisra'el," in Shapira, ed., *Ma'anit halev*, 184.

42 Tsur, "Otsar haruaḥ," 45.

43 Ofaz, "Hazekhut lidrosh," 378, 381. Yariv Ben-Aharon spent time in Jerusalem studying traditional Jewish sources at the Hebrew University and at The Schechter Institute of

Jewish Studies, sponsored by the Conservative Movement. He also engaged in private study with Menachem Froman and David Hartman, religious Zionist rabbis with a less conventional theological orientation than that of mainstream religious Zionist rabbis. Sheleg, "Massekhet avot."

44 Meir Ayali, "Ha'im atidah torah lehishakhaḥ?" in Meir Ayali, *Kirevivim: ḥinnukh yehudi veḥeqer hameqorot: qubbats vekhunnas al yedei talmidim ve'amitim*, ed. Avraham Shapira (Tel Aviv: Hakibbutz Hameuchad, 1996), 115.

45 Ibid.

46 Ibid.

47 Menachem Elon, "Meir Ayali: iḥud veyiḥud," in Friedlander, Shavit, Sagi, eds., *Hayashan yitḥaddesh*, 14.

48 See a list of articles and books by Meir Ayali and edited by him in Ayali, *Kirevivim*, 409-412.

49 The information about Meir Ayali is based on Eliezer Schweid, "Darko shel meḥanekh" and "Qorot ḥayyim," in Ayali, *Kerivim*, 9-18; Ofaz, "Terumato shel ḥug shedemot" and Avi Sagi, "Meir Ayali: bein hayaḥid lakelali" and Menachem Elon, "Meir Ayali: iḥud veyiḥud" and Avraham Shapira, "Im moreshet torat ḥayyav umifalei ḥayyav shel Meir Ayali," in Friedlander, Shavit, and Sagi, eds., *Hayashan yitḥaddesh*, 11-24; Orit Prag, "Metaqqen et haruaḥ," < http://www.kibbutz.org.il>; and on my interview of Anat Yisraeli-Taran, who is on the faculty of Hamidrashah Be'Oranim, in June, 2013. Yisraeli-Taran told me of the tremendous impact Ayali had on her as a participant in his Talmud study group and in the all-night Shavuot study sessions as a high school student, which eventually led to her engagement in doctoral studies in rabbinic literature and her career teaching traditional Jewish texts.

50 Quoted in Prag, "Metaqqen et haruaḥ."

51 Ibid.

52 Ibid.

53 Ibid. See the discussion of the educational work of Meir Ayali in Tsur, "Otsar haruaḥ," 53. Tsur recalls that it was Avraham Shapira who convinced Ayali to share his deep knowledge of Judaism with secular kibbutzniks.

54 See <http://midreshet.org.il>.

55 See <http://www.panim.org.il>. Programs have been presented in Israel to satisfy the thirst for exposure to rabbinic culture among the general public. For example, for several years Beit Avi Chai in Jerusalem has presented a series of talks on aspects of rabbinic literature. In 2013, the National Library presented five evening events under the title "Nifgashim Babavli," in which Talmudic texts (primarily rabbinic legends) were taught, a panel discussion on the relevance of the Talmud to Israeli society was held, and a satirical group poked fun at issues related to the secular return to the study of traditional Jewish texts. For a discussion of attempts in Israel in recent decades to intensify the coverage of areas of Jewish studies, including rabbinic literature, in community centers and the army, see Sheleg, *Me'ivri yashan*, 63-67.

56 Ariel Furstenberg, "Re'ayon im Ruth Calderon," *Zehuyot* 5 (2014): 23. For a discussion of the return to the Jewish bookcase see Sheleg, *Me'ivri yashan*, 27-48. In this book, he analyzes what he sees as two parallel and related contemporary cultural trends in Israel that challenge earlier notions of a dichotomy between religiosity and secularism: individuals and groups of Israelis from a secular background that seek to engage in religious experience and the assertion of the legitimacy of a religious traditionalism characteristic of Jews of Middle Eastern and North African origin that is not as strictly observant of Jewish law as is mainstream Ashkenazic religious Zionist culture.

57 Furstenberg, "Re'ayon im Ruth Calderon," 21.

58 An unpublished essay provided by the author.

59 Ibid.
60 Ruth Calderon, *Alfa beita talmudi: osef perati* (Tel Aviv: Miskal-Yedioth Ahronoth Books and Chemed Books, 2014), 42.
61 Ibid., 43.
62 Ibid.
63 Furstenberg, "Re'ayon im Ruth Calderon," 20.
64 Ibid. Commenting more recently on the persistent interest by secular Israelis in traditional Jewish study, Mordechai Bar-Or, head of the pluralistic study house Kolot, has stated that he believes this stems from their interest in "understanding the meaning of life in Israel, especially in light of the fact that there is no peace on the horizon. People ask themselves why we live and die in this place, and they seek to understand the essence of life here and its meaning and to know if Judaism has something to say about this question." Zohar Almakeis, "20 shanah aḥarei restaḥ Rabin: mah ḥidshah hahitḥadshut hayehudit?," *Haaretz* 15 December 2015.
65 Sheleg, "Massekhet avot."
66 Ibid.
67 Ibid.
68 Muki Tsur, "Otsar haruaḥ," 52.
69 Sara Shadmi-Wortman, "Haqamat hamidrashah 1989-1999: hithavutah shel 'pedagogyah shel zehut,'" in *Massekhet ḥayyim: 20 shanah lamidrashah be'oranim,* ed. Yoram Wearth (Ramat Yishai: Hamidrashah Be'oranim; Hakibbutz Hameuchad, 2010), 13-14.
70 Ayelett Shani, "Berukhim haba'im lameinstrim heḥadash," *Haaretz* 7 December 2012.
71 Ibid.
72 Ibid.
73 Rotem Sela, "Moreh leḥayyim: yisra'el al pi Dr. Mica Goodman," *Maariv nrg* 16 September, 2010.
74 Zohar Almakeis, "20 shanah."
75 Tali Farkish, "Haḥilonim yotsim me'aron hasefarim hayehudi," *Ynet* 20 May 2013. The founders of Bina were inspired by the efforts of the late nineteenth and early twentieth-century Hebrew poet Hayyim Nahman Bialik to bridge the gap between contemporary Jews and the Jewish textual tradition in his day. As Farkish notes, the name Bina, which means "understanding" in Hebrew, is actually an acronym of a line in Bialik's poem "Hamatmid," in which he reflected on whether the traditional study house could really be "a creative home for the Jewish soul" (*beit hayotser lenishmat ha'umah*).
76 These ideas of Mordechai Bar-Or are based on my interview of him at Kolot in Jerusalem in June 2013. This approach is in the spirit of a well-known essay by Hayyim Nahman Bialik, "Halakhah ve'aggadah"(1917) in *Kol kitvei H. N. Bialik* (Tel Aviv: Dvir, 1938), 207-213. See also the discussion of the desirability of an integrated approach to the study of *halakhah* and *aggadah* in Ido Hevroni, *Ḥayyot haqodesh: yetsurei hapere beveit midrasham shel ḥazal* (Tel Aviv: Miskal-Yedioth Ahronoth Books and Chemed Books, 2016), 255-259.
77 Anat Yisraeli and Esther Fisher, eds., *Dorshot tov: perush qevutsati feministi lesugyat issurei yiḥud: qiddushin 80b-82b* (Kiryat Tivon: Hamidrashah Be'Oranim, 2013).
78 Ibid., 4.
79 Feminist readings of rabbinic literature play an important role in the return to the Jewish bookcase. This feminist orientation to rabbinic literature is central to a feminist commentary on the Babylonian Talmud which is in the process of being published in Germany with the participation of some Israeli scholars. See *A Feminist Commentary on the Babylonian Talmud: Introduction and Studies*, eds. Tal Ilan, Tamara Or, Dorothea M. Salzer, Christiane Steuer, and Irina Wandrey (Tübingen: Mohr Siebeck, 2007).
80 See their web site <nigunhalev.org>.

81 See, for example, <https://beitkehila.wordpress.com>, a joint web site including Nigun Halev in Nahalal and six similar communities.

82 See their web site <btfila.org>.

83 See Adina Newberg, "Hitchabrut or Connecting: Liberal Houses of Study in Israel as Political and Spiritual Expression," *Israel Studies Forum* 20, no. 2 (2005): 97-114; Adina Newberg, "New Prayers, Here and Now: Reconnecting to Israel Through Engaging in Prayer, Poetry, and Song," *Israel Studies Forum* 23, no. 2 (2008): 77-98; Adina Newberg, "Elu v'Elu: Towards Integration of Identity and Multiple Narratives in the Jewish Renewal Sector in Israel," *International Journal of Jewish Education Research* 5-6 (2013): 231-278. In my discussion of cultural trends that grew out of the original return to the Jewish bookcase launched by Ḥug Shedemot, I am not considering other new ways that contemporary Israelis have found to connect with aspects of Judaism marginalized by secular Zionism, including the exploration of traditional Jewish spirituality, the study of and adoption of practices central to Hasidism, and the popularity of music drawing on religious themes, especially as composed and performed by Jews of Mizrahi origin. These phenomena are part of a larger cultural context sometimes referred to as a "Renaissance of Judaism," but they are not as directly connected to the resurgence of interest in the study of Talmudic stories as are the phenomena to which I refer in this chapter: pluralistic study houses and communities dedicated to secular prayer and practice and to social action. For a further discussion of the wider picture of the Renaissance of Judaism in Israel, see Sheleg, *Me'ivri yashan*, 109-142.

84 Yair Lorberbaum, *In God's Image: Myth, Theology, and Law in Classical Judaism* (New York: Cambridge University Press, 2015), 63-64.

85 Ibid., 63-64.

86 Ibid., 64-65. For an overview of the problematic relationship of rabbinic scholars to *aggadah* from the period of the Geonim through the Middle Ages, see Marc Saperstein, *Decoding the Rabbis: A Thirteenth-Century Commentary on the Aggadah* (Cambridge, MA and London, England: Harvard University Press, 1980), Chapter 1; Yehoshua Horowitz, "Yaḥas hage'onim la'aggadah, *Maḥanayim* 7 (1994): 122-129; Yaakov Elbaum, "Mavo: ha'aggadah bedivrei ḥakhmei yemei habeinayim," in *Lehavin divrei ḥakhamim: mivḥar divrei mavo la'aggadah velamidrash mishel ḥakhmei yemei habeinayim*, ed. Yaakov Elbaum (Jerusalem: Mosad Bialik, 2000), 13-41; Avinoam Rosenak, "Aggadah vehalakhah: hirhurim al megamot behagut uvemeḥqar hapilosofyah shel hahalakhah," in *Massa el hahalakhah: iyyunim bein-teḥumiyyim be'olam haḥoq hayehudi*, ed. Amichai Berholz (Tel Aviv: Miskal-Yedioth Ahronoth Books and Chemed Books, 2003), 285-312; and Yehoshafat Nevo, "Hayaḥas la'aggadah besifrut hage'onim le'ummat yaḥasam shel ḥakhmei sefarad beyemei habeinayim," *Sha'anan* 13 (2008): 137-151.

87 Micha Yosef Berdyczewski, *Kitvei Micha Yosef Berdyzcewski (Bin-Gorion)* Vol. 1, eds. Avner Holtzman and Yitzhak Kafkafi (Tel Aviv: Hakibbutz Hameuchad, 1996), 82. This passage is cited in Yehudah Mirsky, "An Intellectual and Spiritual Biography of Rabbi Avraham Yitzhaq Ha-Cohen Kook from 1865-1904" (PhD diss. Harvard University, 2007), 226 n26.

88 Avraham Yitzhak Kook, *Shemonah qevatsim* Vol. 2 (Jerusalem, 2004), 53. This entry appears in a section of Rav Kook's diary which he noted was written in St. Gallen, Switzerland during the years 5675-5676 of the Hebrew calendar. Since it is at the beginning of this section, we can safely assume it was written in 5675, which would correspond to 1914-1915.

89 Kook, *Shemonah qevatsim* Vol. 2, 53.

90 Avinoam Rosenak argues that Rav Kook's rehabilitation of *aggadah* as an essential component of Torah study together with *halakhah* is in keeping with views of several important Torah scholars of the medieval and early modern periods, including Rav Shlomo ben

Aderet (Rashba, 1235-1310), Rav Yehuda Lev ben Bezalel (Maharal of Prague, 1520-1609), and Rav Shmuel Eidels (Maharsha, 1555-1631). Avinoam Rosenak, "Aggadah vehalakhah," 285-312. See also Ehud Luz, "Halakhah ve'aggadah bemishnato shel Harav Kook," *AJS Review* 11 (1986): 1-23 (Hebrew section) and Avinoam Rosenak, "Te'oryah upraqsis: terumatam shel ha'aggadah vehasippur haḥazaliyyim lehavanat hahalakhah," in *Karmi shelli: meḥqarim ba'aggadah uveparshanutah muggashim leProfessor Carmi Horovitz*, ed. Nahem Ilan, Avraham Grossman, Arnon Atzmon, Michael Shmidman, Yosef Tabori (New York: Touro College Press, 2012), 193-212.

91 Binyamin Kelmanson, *Al mah avdah ha'arets: iyyunim be'aggadat haḥurban* (Otniel: Yeshivat Otniel, 2009), 7.

92 "Galei masekhta: beit midrash lelimmud aggadah," accessible at <http://eshkolyafo.blogspot.com/p/blog-page_1088.html>.

93 Yehuda Brandes, *Aggadah lema'aseh* Vol. 1 (Jerusalem: The Jewish Agency for Israel-Eliner Library; Beit Morasha, 2005), 11.

94 Ibid.

95 Ibid.

96 Yair Lorberbaum has argued that the academic study of rabbinics should undertake a more integrated approach to the study of *halakhah* and *aggadah*. Lorberbaum, *In God's Image*, 61-88. An example of such an integrated approach as applied to the Talmudic story of Kamtza and Bar Kamtza discussed in Chapter Seven and stories that appear in the Talmud alongside it may be found in Jeffrey L. Rubenstein, "*Bavli Gittin* 55b-56b: An Aggadic Narrative in Its Halakhic Context, *Hebrew Studies* 38 (1997): 21-45.

97 Binyamin Lau, *Ḥakhamim* Vol. 1 (Tel Aviv: Miskal-Yedioth Ahronoth Books and Chemed Books, 2007), 13.

98 Ibid., 14.

Chapter I

The Rediscovery of Talmudic Stories

1 Hayyim Nahman Bialik and Yehoshua Hana Ravnitzky, eds., *Sefer ha'aggadah: mivḥar ha'aggadot shebatalmud uvamidrashim* 3rd edition (Tel Aviv: Dvir, 1960), Introduction.

2 David Stern calls attention to the significance of this paraphrase in the Introduction to Hayim Nahman Bialik and Yehoshua Hana Ravnitzky, eds., *The Book of Legends: Sefer Ha-Aggadah: Legends from the Talmud and Midrash*, trans. William G. Braude (New York: Schocken Books, 1992), xxi. *Sefer ha'aggadah* was not the first modern Hebrew anthology of rabbinic legends. The anthology *Siḥot mini qedem*, by Zeev Yavitz (1887), has been cited as a very influential precursor to *Sefer ha'aggadah*. In composing his anthology, Yavitz was influenced by the work of the Brothers Grimm in that he sought in his work to make use of legendary sources to develop a modern Jewish national identity, just as they made use of such sources to develop a modern German identity. Bialik continued this notion of rabbinic legends as a source of national identity in putting forth his rationale for *Sefer ha'aggadah*. For discussions of *Siḥot mini qedem* and other precursors of *Sefer ha'aggadah* see Yafa Berlovitz, "Siḥot ushemu'ot mini qedem: po'etiqah umetodah betorat ha'ibbud shel Zeev Yavitz," in *Entsiqlopedyah shel hasippur hayehudi: sippur oqev sippur*, eds. Yoav Elstein, Avidov Lipsker, and Rella Kushelevsky (Ramat Gan: Bar-Ilan University Press, 2004), 203-244; Tsafi Sebba-Elran, "Misefer ha'aggadah la'aron hasefarim hayehudi; ha'asuppot ha'aggadiyyot umeqoman be'itsuvah shel hayahudut batarbut ha'ivrit" (PhD diss., Tel Aviv University, 2009); and

Tsafi Sebba-Elran, "Ḥoni hame'agel ve'alpayim shenot shenah," *Iyyunim betequmat yisra'el* 7 (2014): 5-34.

3 Tsafi Sebba-Elran, "From *Sefer Ha'aggadah* to the Jewish Bookcase: Dynamics of a Cultural Change," *Jewish Studies Quarterly* 20 (2013): 276, 293.

4 Bialik and Ravnitzky, *Sefer ha'aggadah*, Introduction.

5 Ibid.

6 Yonah Fraenkel, *Sippur ha'aggadah: aḥdut shel tokhen vetsurah: qovets meḥqarim* (Tel Aviv: Hakibbutz Hameuchad, 2001), 8-9.

7 Meir Ayali, *Kirevivim: ḥinnukh yehudi veḥeqer hameqorot: qubbats vekhunnas al yedei talmidim ve'amitim*, ed. Avraham Shapira (Tel Aviv: Hakibbutz Hameuchad), 1996, 114.

8 Yoram Kaniuk, *Tashaḥ* (Tel Aviv: Miskal-Yedioth Ahronoth and Chemed Books, 2010), 26.

9 Yitzhak Tesler, "Mitlotsets im Rashi: perush Taharlev al hatorah," *Ynet* 23 August 2014.

10 Kaniuk, *Tashaḥ*, 26.

11 Sebba-Elran, "From *Sefer Ha'aggadah* to the Jewish Bookcase," 287-293.

12 Ariel Horowitz, "Sefer ha'aggadah: otsar yashan hotsa'ah meḥuddeshet," <bac.org.il>.

13 Yonah Fraenkel, *Iyyun be'olamo haruḥani shel sippur ha'aggadah* (Tel Aviv: Hakibbutz Hameuchad, 1981), 8. Interest in *Sefer ha'aggadah* may be revived with the publication of a newly revised edition prepared by Avigdor Shinan: Hayyim Nahman Bialik and Yehoshua Hana Ravnitzky, eds., *Sefer ha'aggadah im perush ḥadash me'et Avigdor Shinan* (Jerusalem: Avi Chai; Kinneret, Zmora-Bitan, Dvir, 2015) and a related web site that enables advanced searches in the corpus of legends collected in the book, <agadastories.org.il>. See Horowitz, "Sefer ha'aggadah."

14 See Fraenkel, *Sippur ha'aggadah*, 8-50. See the Introduction by Yehoshua Levinson to *Higgayon leYonah: hebbetim ḥadashim beḥeqer sifrut hamidrash, ha'aggadah vehapiyyut: qovets meḥqarim likhevodo shel Professor Yonah Fraenkel bimelot lo shivim veḥamesh shanim*, eds. Yehoshua Levinson, Yaakov Elbaum, Galit Hasan-Rokem (Jerusalem: Magnes Press, 2006), 28-32. See the posthumously published interview of Yonah Fraenkel in Tamar Kadari, "Hanituaḥ hasifruti nolad bemiqreh, *Makor rishon* 6 September 2012.

15 Amram Tropper, *Keḥomer beyad hayotser: ma'asei ḥakhamim besifrut ḥazal* (Jerusalem: Merkaz Zalman Shazar, 2011), 12-13.

16 Ibid., 13.

17 Fraenkel's approach to Talmudic stories is found in his numerous scholarly articles and in his three major books, *Iyyunim be'olamo shel sippur ha'aggadah* (Tel Aviv: Hakibbutz Hameuchad,1981), *Darkhei ha'aggadah vehamidrash* Vol. 1-2 (Tel Aviv: Massada, 1991), and *Sippur ha'aggadah: aḥdut shel tokhen vetsurah: qovets meḥqarim*. (Tel Aviv: Hakibbutz Hameuchad, 2001).

18 Fraenkel, *Iyyun be'olamo haruḥani, 9.*

19 Books in Hebrew by Israeli scholars include: Azaria Beitner, *Sippurei yavneh: biqqur ḥolim veniḥum avelim* (Ramat Gan: Bar Ilan University, 2011); Nurit Beeri, *Yatsa letarbut ra'ah: Elisha ben Abuyah—Aḥer* (Tel Aviv: Miskal-Yedioth Ahronoth Books and Chemed Books, 2007); Galit Hasan-Rokem, *Riqmat ḥayyim: hayestirah ha'amamit besifrut ḥazal* (Tel Aviv: Am Oved, 1996); Admiel Kosman, *Nashiyyut be'olamo haruḥani shel hasippur hatalmudi* (Tel Aviv: Hakibbutz Hameuchad, 2008); Ofra Meir, *Sugyot bapo'etiqah shel aggadot ḥazal* (Tel Aviv: Sifriat Poalim, 1993); Ofra Meir, *Rabbi Yehudah Hanasi: deyoqno shel manhig bemasorot erets yisra'el ubavel* (Tel Aviv: Hakibbutz Hameuchad,1999); Aharon Oppenheimer, *Rabbi Yehuda hanasi* (Jerusalem: Merkaz Zalman Shazar, 2007); Inbar Raveh, *Me'at meharbeh: aggadot ḥazal mivnim sifrutiyyim utefisot olam* (Or Yehuda: Kinneret, Zmora-Bitan, Dvir, 2008); Amram Tropper, *Keḥomer beyad hayotser: ma'asei ḥakhamim besifrut ḥazal* (Jerusalem: Merkaz Zalman Shazar, 2011); Shulmait Valler,

Nashim venashiyyut basippur hatalmudi (Tel Aviv: Hakibbutz Hameuchad, 1993); Shulamit Valler, *Tsa'ar umetsuqah basippur hatalmudi* (Tel Aviv: Hakibbutz Hameuchad, 2012); Shulamit Valler and Shalom Razabi, *Siḥot ḥulin batalmud habavli* (Tel Aviv: Am Oved, 2007); Ruhama Weiss, *Okhlim lada'at: tafkidan hatarbuti shel hase'udot besifrut ḥazal* (Tel Aviv: Hakibbutz Hameuchad, 2010); Eli Yassif, *Sippur ha'am ha'ivri: toldotav, sugav, umashma'uto* (Jerusalem: Mosad Bialik; Beersheva: Ben-Gurion University,1994); Anat Yisraeli-Taran, *Aggadot haḥurban: mesorot haḥurban basifrut hatlamudit* (Tel Aviv: Hakibbutz Hameuchad,1997); Yaffa Zilkha, *Be'eyn aggadat hayerushalmi: pirqei iyyun be'olamah shel aggadat hatalmud hayerushalmi* (Jerusalem: The Jewish Agency for Israel-Eliner Library; Beit Morasha, 2009). English translations of some of these Hebrew works include Shulamit Valler, *Woman and Womanhood in the Talmud,* trans. Betty Sigler Rozen (Atlanta, Ga.: Scholars Press, 1999); Shulamit Valler, *Sorrow and Distress in the Talmud,* trans. Sharon Blass (Boston: Academic Studies Press, 2011); and Eli Yassif, *The Hebrew Folktale: History, Genre, Meaning,* trans. Jacqueline S. Teitelbaum (Bloomington and Indianapolis: Indiana University Press, 1999). Books published in English by Israeli scholars include: Alon Goshen-Gottstein, *The Sinner and the Amnesiac: The Rabbinic Invention of Elisha Ben Abuya and Eleazar Ben Arach* (Stanford: Stanford University Press, 2000); Tova Hartman and Charlie Buckholtz, *Are You Not a Man of God? Devotion, Betrayal, and Social Criticism in Jewish Tradition* (New York: Oxford University Press, 2014); Galit Hasan-Rokem, *Tales of the Neighborhood: Jewish Narrative Dialogues in Late Antiquity* (Berkeley: University of California Press, 2003); Dalia Hoshen, *Beruria the Tannait: A Theological Reading of a Female Mishnaic Scholar* (Lanham: University Press of America, 2007). Hebrew versions of at least parts of this scholarship by Israeli writers published in English include: Alon Goshen-Gottstein, "Rabbi Elazar ben Arakh: semel umetsi'ut," in *Yehudim veyahadut beyemei bayit sheni, hamishnah vehatalmud: meḥqarim likhevodo shel Shmuel Safrai,* eds. Aharon Oppenheimer, Yeshayahu Gafni, Menahem Stern (Jerusalem: Yad Yitzhak Ben Zvi, 1993), 173-197 and Dalia Hoshen, "Beruria hatana'it: qeriah te'ologit bedemutah shel talmidat ḥakhamim basifrut hatalmudit," *Akdamot* 22 (2009): 168-196.

20 Levinson, Elbaum, Hasan-Rokem, eds., *Higgayon leYonah,* 31. Levinson also notes that the more Fraenkel stimulated interest in legends as literature among the general public the more he worried that people would produce distorted readings of these legends by ignoring or not being aware of the Talmudic context in which they originally appeared.

21 Yonah Fraenkel, *Iyyunim be'olamo haruḥani shel sippur ha'aggadah* (Tel Aviv: Hakibbutz Hameuchad, 1981) and David Zimmerman, *Shemonah sippurei ahavah min hatalmud vehamidrash* (Tel Aviv: Sifriat Poalim, 1981). The publication of these two books with similar purposes in the same year, one by a university scholar and the other by a kibbutz educator, points to a significant convergence of the contribution of the academic study of Talmudic stories and the study of these stories in the context of the return to the Jewish bookcase initiated in the kibbutz movement. This convergence is evident as well in the fact that each book was published by a kibbutz-sponsored publishing house (Fraenkel's by Hakibbutz Hameuchad and Zimmerman's by Sifriat Poalim). In addition, it should be noted, Fraenkel's book was published in a series edited by one of the kibbutz pioneers of the return to the Jewish bookcase, Meir Ayali, mentioned previously in my Introduction.

22 Fraenkel, *Iyyun be'olamo haruḥani,* 9.

23 Zimmerman, *Shemonah sippurei ahavah,* 8.

24 Ibid. Author's emphasis. In the mid-1980s, Yair Barkai (b.1945), an educator who at the time was a graduate student at the Hebrew University studying with Yonah Fraenkel, made use of Fraenkel's approach to Talmudic stories as literature to pilot the teaching of these stories in Israeli secular and religious high schools, the curriculum of which was eventually published in the book *Hasippur hamini'aturi* (Tel

Aviv: David Shun Foundation; Ministry of Education and Culture, 1986). Although at the beginning of the book, Barkai presents an extensive list of schools that participated in efforts to pilot this new curricular unit before the book was published, Talmudic stories did not end up playing a prominent role in the study of literature in Israeli high schools.

25 *Alma di* was eventually published as a book: Ari Elon, *Alma di* (Tel Aviv: Miskal-Yedioth Ahronoth Books and Chemed Books and Bait-Hebrew Creation, 2011). It is divided into four sections: "Sha'ar atsmi ("The Gate of Myself"), which includes a selection from an unfinished autobiographical novel recounting the author's loss of religious faith; "Sha'ar tsiyon" ("The Gate of Zion"), a collection of essays on Jewish identity; "Sha'ar hagay" ("The Gate of the Valley"), which includes a collection of Talmudic stories and other rabbinic legends with a commentary by the author; and "Sha'ar ha'ashpot" ("The Dung Gate"), containing diary selections from the author's army service in the Gaza Strip in 1988, the first year of the first intifada. The section on Talmudic stories and other rabbinic legends had the greatest and most lasting impact on Israeli culture. An English translation of *Alma di* is available: Ari Elon, *From Jerusalem to the Edge of Heaven: Meditations on the Soul of Israel*, trans. Tikva Frymer-Kensky (Philadelphia: Jewish Publication Society, 1996).

26 Elon later published other works drawing primarily on rabbinic texts, most notably *Ba el haqodesh: lamed vav aggadot nistarot* (Tel Aviv: Miskal-Yedioth Ahronoth Books and Chemed Books, 2005), but they did not have the same impact on the Israeli public as *Alma di* did.

27 Elon, *Alma di*, 57.

28 Ibid., 45.

29 Ibid., 59.

30 Like a number of the key authors and teachers who have furthered the process of the return to the Jewish bookcase (including Ari Elon and Ruhama Weiss), in his youth Dov Elbaum abandoned the traditional Jewish lifestyle in which he was raised. Among his contributions to the return to the Jewish bookcase have been: helping to found the Bina-sponsored Secular Yeshiva in Tel Aviv; his autobiography, *Massa baḥalal hapanuy* (Tel Aviv: Am Oved, 2007), which draws heavily on traditional Jewish sources, especially from Kabbalah and Hasidism; and his role as the host of "Meqablim shabbat," a Friday evening television program on the weekly Torah portion. *Massa baḥalal hapanuy* is available in English translation: Dov Elbaum, *Into the Fullness of the Void: A Spiritual Autobiography*, trans. Azzan Yadin (Woodstock, Vermont: Jewish Lights Publishing, 2013). See also his web site, <http://www.dovelbaum.com>. Elon, *Alma di*, 4.

31 Ibid.

32 Ibid.

33 Yariv Ben-Aharon, "Higanukh pumbedita," *Shedemot* 115 (1990): 66. Author's emphasis.

34 Ibid. 68.

35 Yariv Ben-Aharon, *Aggadat pumbedita: shi'ur betalmud* (Oranim: Hamidrashah Be'Oranim, 2000) published in the "Maḥbarot Shedemot" series of Hamidrashah Be'Oranim, in which classic works of traditional Jewish culture and of modern Hebrew literature are presented in a quasi-talmudic format with text and commentary.

36 Yariv Ben-Aharon, "My Encounter with Tradition," *Shedemot* (English edition) 3 (1975): 98.

37 Ben-Aharon, *Aggadat pumbedita*, 4. In the Acknowledgment section of *Aggadat pumbedita*, Ben-Aharon thanks such scholars as Menachem Hirshman, Daniel Boyarin, and Shamma Friedman, as well as Ari Elon, for what they contributed to his knowledge of rabbinics. Ben-Aharon is also the author of two autobiographical novels and the editor of a number of works in the "Maḥbarot Shedemot" series of Hamidrashah Be'Oranim.

38 Ruth Calderon, *Hashuq. habayit. halev: aggadot talmudiyyot* (Jerusalem: Keter, 2001). The work is available in English translation: Ruth Calderon, *A Bride for One Night: Talmud Tales*, trans. Ilana Kurshan (Philadelphia: The Jewish Publication Society, 2014).
39 Ruth Calderon, Inaugural Knesset Speech, *Divrei hakenesset* 12 February 2013: 33.
40 Admiel Kosman, *Massekhet gevarim: Rav vehaqatsav ve'od sippurim al gavriyyut, ahavah ve'otentiyyut besippur ha'aggadah uvasippur haḥasidi* (Jerusalem: Keter, 2002). *Massekhet gevarim* is available in English translation: Admiel Kosman, *Men's World: Reading Masculinity in Jewish Stories in a Spiritual Context*, trans. Edward Levin (Würzburg: Ergon Verlag, 2009). Admiel Kosman, *Massekhet nashim: ḥokhmah, ahavah, ne'emanut, teshuqah, yofi, min, qedushah: qeri'ah besippurim talmudiyym verabbaniyym ushenei midreshei shir* (Keter: Jerusalem, 2007).
41 Ruhama Weiss, *Mitḥayyevet benafshi: qeri'ot meḥuyyavot batalmud* (Tel Aviv: Miskal-Yedioth Ahronoth Books and Chemed Books; 2006); Ruhama Weiss and Avner HaCohen, *Immahot betippul: massa psikhologi-sifruti im gibborot hatalmud* (Tel Aviv: Miskal-Yedioth Ahronoth Books and Chemed Books, 2012).
42 Shmuel Faust, *Aggadeta: sippur haderamah hatlamudit* (Tel Aviv: Kinneret, Zmora-Bitan, Dvir, 2011).
43 Yaara Inbar, *Ḥalom shel bein hashemashot: iyyun uderishah besippurim talmudiyyim* (Tel Aviv: Miskal-Yedioth Ahronoth Books and Chemed Books, 2013).
44 Based on a private communication with the writer.
45 Ido Hevroni, *Ḥayyot haqodesh: yetsurei hapere beveit midrasham shel ḥazal* (Tel Aviv: Miskal-Yedioth Ahronoth Books and Chemed Books, 2016).
46 Calderon, *Hashuq*, 9.
47 Ibid.
48 Ibid.
49 Ibid., 10.
50 Kosman, *Massekhet nashim*, 231-232
51 Ibid., 234.
52 Weiss, *Mitḥayyevet benafshi*, 15.
53 Ibid., 16.
54 Ibid., 14.
55 Ibid., 13.
56 Ibid.
57 Ibid., 17.
58 Faust, *Aggadeta*, 59.
59 Inbar, *Ḥalom shel bein hashemashot*, 11.
60 Ibid., 12.
61 Hevroni, *Ḥayyot haqodesh*, 10.
62 Ibid., 12.
63 Chaim Licht, *Be'avotot hashekhol: iyyunim be'asarah sippurei aggadah al hashekhol be'olamam shel ḥakhamim* (Jerusalem: Carmel, 2007). An English translation of *Be'avotot hashekhol* is available: Chaim Licht, *In the Grip of Bereavement: An Analysis of Ten Aggadic Legends on Bereavement in the World of the Sages*, trans. R. Schwartz (Jerusalem and Lynbrook, NY: Gefen Publishing House, 2009).
64 Ibid., 11. In a previously published book, *Masoret veḥiddush: sugyot besifrut ḥazal* (Givat Haviva: Secular Center for Jewish Creativity, 1989), Licht explored rabbinic texts that deal with the question of how rabbinic Judaism maintained a balance between the authority of the written Torah and the innovative interpretation of the Torah by the rabbis.
65 Benaymin Kelmanson, *Al mah avdah ha'arets: iyyunim be'aggadot haḥurban* (Otniel: Yeshivat Otniel, 2009).

66 In a private communication with the writer.

67 Another manifestation of the interest in relating Talmudic stories to contemporary concerns may be found in works of fiction, drama, and film that have appeared since the 1980s that retell or allude to Talmudic stories. The play *Ma'aseh Beruria* (1982), by the Theatre Company Jerusalem, retells stories about Beruria, to be discussed in Chapter Four of this book. The text of the play and background information about it may be found in Aliza Elion Israeli, *Midrash bamah: qevutsat hate'atron hayerushalmi* (Tel Aviv: Miskal-Yedioth Ahronoth Books and Chemed Books, 2009), 27-70. The film *Beruria* (2008), directed by Avraham Kushnir, makes connections between a contemporary story and stories of Beruria. Two plays retell the story of the relationship of Rabbi Yohanan and Resh Lakish to be discussed in Chapter Three of this book: *Anatomyah shel teshuvah* (2008), by Yosefa Even-Shoshan, and *Da me'ayin bata* (2008), by Gadi Zedaka. The play *Arba'ah nikhnesu lapardes* (1996), by Dani Horovits, tells the story of four sages who engaged in mystical exploration, and his play *Kamtza uBar Kamtza,* alternatively titled *Etz aḥaron beyerushalayim* (2006), tells a story of the time of the destruction of the Second Temple discussed in Chapter Seven of this book. The texts of these two plays may be found in Dani Horovits, *Arba'ah maḥazot,* ed. Shimon Levy (Ramat Aviv: Tel Aviv University, 2007), 103-162. The novel *Bamufla mimenni* (Or Yehuda: Kinneret, Zmora-Bitan, Dvir, 2012), by Emuna Elon, makes connections between a contemporary story and that of Rabbi Yohanan and Resh Lakish discussed in Chapter Three of this book. The novel *Hapardes shel Akiva* (Or Yehuda: Kinneret, Zmora-Bitan, Dvir, 2012), by Yochi Brandes, retells the stories of Rabbi Akiva, including the one to be discussed in Chapter Six of this book.

Chapter 2

Authority, Autonomy, and Interpersonal Relations: The Oven of Akhnai

1 Oded Yisraeli, "'Ḥuts misha'arei ona'ah:' iyyun besippur ha'aggadah 'tanuro shel akhnai,'" in *Al derekh ha'avot: sheloshim shanah lemikhlelet Yaacov Herzog: qovets ma'amarim benosei torah veḥinnukh,* eds. Amnon Bazak, Shmuel Vigoda, Meir Munitz (Alon Shevut: Tevunot, 2001), 269.

2 Ibid. It is safe to assume that passages in this story were written at different times. It appears that the bulk of the story, which is in Hebrew, was composed during the early Tanaitic period, but passages that are in part or completely in Aramaic (Rabbi Yirmiyah's interpretation of "It is not in Heaven," Rabbi Natan's report from Elijah, and the passage in the home of Rabbi Eliezer and Imma Shalom) are likely to be later passages. See Chaim Licht, *Masoret veḥiddush: sugyot besifrut ḥazal* (Givat Haviva: Secular Center for Jewish Creativity, 1989), 18-19. The question of the stages of the composition of the story, however, is not relevant to our discussion, since we are seeking to determine how Israeli interpreters understand the story as a whole literary unit.

3 For an analysis of traditional commentaries on this story, see Yitzhak Englender, "Tanuro shel akhnai: perushehah shel aggadah," *Shenaton hamishpat ha'ivri shel hamakhon leḥeqer hamishpat ha'ivri* 1 (1974): 45-56. For examples of commentaries on the story by traditional and maskilic authors during the sixteenth to nineteenth centuries, see Meir Rafler, "Pilpul, tsenzurah vehaskalah: leqoroteha shel parshanut aḥat lesugyat tanuro shel akhnai," *Meḥqeri yerushalayim besifrut ivrit* 18 (2001): 7-18. For an analysis of the role that this story played in polemical arguments with Christians, Karaites, and philosphers, see Yitzhak Brand, "Tanuro shel akhnai: aggadah belev pulmus," *Tarbiz* 75, no. 3-4 (2006):

437-466. For a comparison of the version of the story from the Babylonian Talmud analyzed in this chapter with the version of the story from the Jerusalem Talmud, see Yoel Raz, "'Lo bashamayim hi'—ha'omnam?! diyyun meḥuddash besugyat 'tanuro shel akhnai' al pi hatalmud habavli vehayerushalmi," *Pittuḥei ḥotam: sefer hama'amarim shel yeshivat hahesder Orot Shaul* (Petah Tikva: Orot Shaul, 2009), 105-126.

4 Yair Schlein, "Tanuro shel akhnai kesug shel tragedyah," *Mo'ed: shenaton lemada'ei hayahadut* 18 (2008): 71.

5 Licht, *Masoret veḥiddush*, 17.

6 Yisraeli, "'Ḥuts misha'arei ona'ah," 276.

7 Ibid., 277.

8 Schlein, "Tanuro shel akhnai," 74.

9 Daniel Statman, "Otonomyah vesamkhut betanuro shel akhnai," *Meḥqerei mishpat* 24 (2008): 641-642.

10 Ibid., 647.

11 Shimshon Ettinger, "Maḥloqet ve'emet: lemashma'ut she'elat ha'emet bahalakhah," *Shenaton hamishpat ha'ivri shel hamakhon leḥeqer hamishpat ha'ivri* 21 (1998): 40.

12 Ibid.

13 Statman, "Otonomyah vesamkhut," 648-649.

14 Yisraeli, "'Ḥuts misha'arei ona'ah,'" 274.

15 Licht, *Masoret veḥiddush*, 17.

16 David Asulin, "Tanuro shel akhnai: bein 'bat qol' le'ro'im et haqolot,'" *Asuppot: bitta'on le'inyenei aggadah* 4 (2013):173.

17 Aliza Shenhar, "Sodo shel Rabbi Eliezer in *Ma'aseh sippur: meḥqarim basipporet hayehudit muggashim leYoav Elstein* Vol. 1, eds. Avidov Lipsker and Rella Kushelevsky (Ramat Gan: Bar Ilan University, 2006), 55.

18 Schlein, "Tanuro shel akhnai," 78.

19 Statman, "Otonomyah vesamkhut," 650.

20 Schlein, "Tanuro shel akhnai," 70-80.

21 Ibid., 72.

22 Ibid., 80. Oded Yisraeli also believes that the positions of the two disputants are presented in the story with equal empathy. See Yisraeli, "'Ḥuts misha'arei ona'ah,'" 280.

23 Binyamin Kelmanson, "Torah shebe'al peh—qonfliqt metukhnan bein Elohim la'adam: iyyun meḥuddash besippur tanuro shel akhnai." *Asuppot: bitta'on le'inyenei aggadah* 4 (2013): 148.

24 Yair Dreyfus, "Kol hashea'arim ninalim? qeri'ah ḥadashah besippur tanuro shel akhnai," *Asuppot: bitta'on le'inyenei aggadah* 4 (2013): 162.

25 Ibid., 164.

26 Ibid., 165.

27 Ibid.

28 Yair Caspi, *Lidrosh Elohim* (Tel Aviv: Miskal-Yediot Ahronoth Books and Chemed Books, 2002), 265.

29 Ibid.

30 Yehuda Brandes, *Aggadah lema'aseh* Vol. 2 (Jerusalem: Eliner Library—The Jewish Agency for Israel; Beit Morsha, 2011), 25.

31 Jeffrey Rubenstein, "Sippur tanuro shel akhnai: nituaḥ sifruti," in *Higgayon leyonah: hebbetim ḥadashim beḥeqer sifrut hamidrash, ha'aggadah, vehapiyyut: qovets meḥqarim likhevodo shel Professor Yonah Fraenkel*, eds. Yehoshua Levinson, Yaakov Elbaum, and Galit Hasan-Rokem (Jerusalem: Magnes Press, 2006), 462-463.

32 Ibid., 464.

33 Tova Hartman and Charlie Buckholtz, *Are You Not a Man of God? Devotion, Betrayal, and Social Criticism in Jewish Tradition* (New York: Oxford University Press, 2014), 70.

34 Ibid.
35 Ibid., 75.
36 Rubenstein, "Sippur tanuro shel akhnai," 463-464.
37 Hartman and Buckholtz, *Are You Not a Man of God?*, 71.
38 Brandes, *Aggadah lema'aseh*, 77.
39 Ibid.
40 Yisraeli, "Ḥuts misha'arei ona'ah," 275.
41 Hartman and Buckholtz, *Are You Not a Man of God?*, 79.
42 Ari Elon, *Ba el haqodesh: lamed vav aggadot nistarot* (Tel Aviv: Miskal-Yedioth Ahronoth Books and Chemed Books, 2005), 188.
43 Rubenstein, "Sippur tanuro shel akhnai," 470.

Chapter 3

When Opposites Attract: Rabbi Yohanan and Resh Lakish

1 Daniel Boyarin, "Rabbanim veḥaverim: ha'im yesh yehudim betoldot haminiyyut?" *Zemanim* 52 (1995): 61, 62.
2 Admiel Kosman makes the observation that by taking the initiative to switch the terms of their interaction from one that is physical to one that is verbal, Rabbi Yohanan succeeded in drawing Resh Lakish into a mode of communication in which he, Rabbi Yohanan, was most capable as a Torah scholar. Admiel Kosman, *Massekhet gevarim: Rav vehaqatsav ve'od sippurim al gavriyyut, ahavah ve'otentinyyut besippur ha'aggadah uvasippur haḥasidi* (Jerusalem: Keter, 2002), 37.
3 Rachel Marani, *Lishmot, sippur ahavah* (Or Yehuda: Kinneret, Zmora-Bitan, Dvir, 2016), 24.
4 There appears to be a consensus among readers of the story, past and present, that when Rabbi Yohanan declared to Resh Lakish, "Your power [should be] for Torah" (*ḥelakh le'orayta*), he meant that the energy of the physical power Resh Lakish demonstrated by jumping into the Jordan could be channeled into the intense study of Torah. When Resh Lakish declared to Rabbi Yohanan, "Your beauty [should be] for women," (*shufrakh lenashei*) his meaning was less clear. The medieval commentator Rashi interprets the meaning to be "your beauty is appropriate for women" (*ra'uy lenashim*), in other words, your beauty is more appropriate for a woman than for a man. Contemporary readers have chosen to interpret the words as suggesting that Resh Lakish's meaning is that it is a shame that such a handsome man as Rabbi Yohanan is not taking advantage of his good looks to live a life of sexual licentiousness. Ari Elon writes that from these words he understands that "it pained Resh Lakish to think of the awesome beauty [of Rabbi Yohanan] as he engaged in Torah study and that [his beauty] was not exploited to conquer all the women in the world." Ari Elon, *Alma di* (Tel Aviv: Miskal-Yedioth Ahronoth Books and Chemed Books and Bait-Hebrew Creation, 2011), 163. Daniel Boyarin reads the meaning of Resh Lakish's words as his saying to Rabbi Yohanan, "This beauty would be wasted in the pursuit of desired objects of a spiritual nature; join me in pursuing women." Boyarin, "Rabbanim veḥaverim," 62. Admiel Kosman understands Resh Lakish's declaration to mean that he is saying to Rabbi Yohanan, "[With your beauty] you could seduce women, if you left the study house." Kosman, *Massekhet gevarim*, 34. My synthesis in this chapter of the contemporary Israeli readings of the story is based on the understanding of the expression by Elon, Boyarin, and Kosman.
5 Elon, *Alma di*, 163.

6 Ibid., 164.
7 Ariel Hirschfeld, "Qafats lanahar, aḥarei ishah," *Haaretz* 23 October 1992.
8 Modi Brodetsky and David Hillel Wiener, *Ve'im tirtseh emor: ḥevruta bemidrash uve'aggadah* (Jerusalem: Rubin Mass, 2007), 39.
9 Ibid.
10 Kosman *Massekhet gevarim*, 47.
11 Elon, *Alma di*, 165-166. Tikva Frymer-Kensky, who translated *Alma di* into English, adds the following observation on this passage: "A narrow womb, of course, is a catastrophe that makes it impossible for a woman to carry a pregnancy. What the Rabbis meant was a tight vagina (colloquially we use a coarser term). However, they either didn't have or didn't record for us a separate word for the vagina. Of course, a tight vagina isn't very good for women, either, but it is a well-known male fantasy." Ari Elon, *From Jerusalem to the Edge of Heaven: Meditations on the Soul of Israel*, trans. Tikva Frymer-Kensky (Philadelphia: Jewish Publication Society, 1996), 53.
12 Elon, *Alma di*, 166.
13 Ibid.
14 Ibid., 163-164.
15 Ibid., 165-166.
16 Yariv Ben-Aharon, *Aggadat pumbedita: shi'ur betalmud* (Oranim: Hamidrashah Be'Oranim, 2000), 23.
17 Yehuda Liebes, "Eros ve'ant-eros al hayarden" in *Haḥayyim kemidrash: iyyun bepsikhologyah yehudit likhevod Professor Mordechai Rotenberg*, eds. Shahar Arzy, Michal Fachler, and Baruch Kahana (Tel Aviv: Miskal- Yedioth Ahronoth Books and Chemed Books, 2004), 153.
18 Daniel Boyarin, *Habasar shebaruaḥ: siaḥ haminiyyut batalmud* (Tel Aviv: Am Oved, 1999), 217. In his article, Liebes also relates the erotic dimension of the story to views of Eros in Hellenistic culture.
19 Ibid.
20 Ibid.
21 Ibid., 282n8; Kosman, *Massekhet gevarim*, 38n12.
22 Brodetsky and Wiener, *Ve'im tirtseh emor*, 40.
23 Elie Holzer, "'Either *Hevruta* Partner or Death:' A Critical View on the Interpersonal Dimensions of *Hevruta* Learning," *Journal of Jewish Education* 75 (2009): 138.
24 Kosman, *Massekhet gevarim*, 38; Ruth Calderon, *Hashuq. habayit. halev: aggadot talmudiyyot* (Jerusalem: Keter, 2001), 39.
25 Ben-Aharon, *Aggadat pumbedita*, 26-27.
26 Holzer, "'Either a *Hevruta* Partner or Death,'"139.
27 Elon, *Alma di*, 166.
28 Ibid.
29 Ibid.
30 Ibid., 168. Emphasis in the original.
31 Ibid., 170.
32 Ibid., 171-172.
33 Kosman, *Massekhet gevarim*, 47-48.
34 Ibid., 43.
35 Ibid., 46-47.
36 Ibid., 42. Kosman bases this interpretation on the words "there was a dispute in the study house," which suggests that this was the first time that Rabbi Yohanan and Resh Lakish had a disagreement.

37 Ibid.
38 Yehudit Bar-Yesha Gershovitz, "Mifgash al hayarden: mi hu sheyakhol laḥazor bo," <http://cms.education.gov.il>; Elon, *Alma di*, 172; Kosman, *Massekehet gevarim*, 41-42.
39 Kosman, *Massekhet gevarim*, 48.
40 Holzer, "'Either a *Hevruta* Partner or Death,'" 140. Emphasis in the original.
41 Ibid., 139.
42 Ibid.
43 Ibid., 141. Emphasis in the original.
44 Rachel Ararat, "Iyyun sifruti be'aggadah 'Rabbi Yohanan veResh Lakish,'" *Bisedei ḥemed* 1-2 (1977): 386; Elon *Alma di*, 167.
45 As Ruth Calderon puts it, "Rabbi Yohanan sought a companion and a monster [*golem*] came into being." Ruth Calderon, *Hashuq*, 39.
46 Ibid., 35.
47 Ibid.
48 Ibid.
49 Ibid.
50 Ibid.
51 Ibid.
52 Ibid., 37.
53 Ibid., 40.
54 Marani, *Lishmot*, 26-27.
55 Ibid., 27.
56 Boyarin, *Habasar shebaruaḥ*, 220.
57 Ibid.
58 Ido Hevroni, "Zonah velistim beveit hamidrash," *Tekhelet* (Spring, 2008): 83.
59 Ibid.
60 Ibid., 84.
61 Ibid., 84-85.
62 Ibid., 85.
63 Ibid., 85-86.
64 Gershovitz, "Mifgash al hayarden," 7.
65 Ararat, "Iyyun sifruti," 385.
66 Gershovitz, "Mifgash al hayarden," 8.
67 Marani, *Lishmot*, 99.
68 Ibid.
69 Holtzer, "'Either a *Hevruta* Partner or Death,'" 144.
70 Ben-Aharon, *Aggadat pumbedita*, 24.
71 Kosman, *Massekhet gevarim*, 45-46.
72 Boyarin, "Rabbanim veḥaverim," 62.
73 Kosman, *Massekhet gevarim*, 43-44;
74 Holzer, "'Either a *Hevruta* Partner or Death,'" 144.
75 Kosman, *Massekhet gevarim*, 50.
76 See Gershovitz, "Mifgash al hayarden."
77 Kosman, *Massekhet gevarim*, 42.
78 Shmuel Faust "Tofa'at habiqqoret bema'asei ḥakhamim min hatalmud habavli" (PhD diss., Bar Ilan University, 2010), 279. See the Jungian interpretation of the story according to which Resh Lakish is the "shadow" figure of Rabbi Yohanan, in Yakir Englender, "Hapersonah vehatsel: perush yungiani lesippur ḥayyehem umotam shel R. Yohanan veResh Lakish, *De'ot* 18 (2004): 32-36.

79 Gershovitz, "Mifgash al hayarden."
80 Ibid.

Chapter 4

Women and Torah Study: Beruria

1 See Eitam Henkin, "Ta'alumat 'ma'aseh deBeruria:' hatsa'at pitaron," *Akdamot* 21 (2008): 141. Henkin points out that the first school established in Israel devoted to the study of all aspects of Torah by women was originally named Midreshet Beruria. Ruhama Weiss was one of the founders of Beruria. Ruhama Weiss and Avner HaCohen, *Immahot betippul: massa psikhologi-sifruti im gibborot hatalmud* (Tel Aviv: Miskal-Yedioth Ahronoth Books and Chemed Books), 216.

2 See David Goodblatt, "The Beruriah Traditions," *Journal of Jewish Studies* 26 (1975): 68-85; Tal Ilan, "The Quest for the Historical Beruriah, Rachel, and Imma Shalom," *AJS Review* 22 (1997): 1-17; Tal Ilan, *Integrating Women into Second Temple History* (Tübingen: Mohr Siebeck, 1999), 175-194; Yifat Monnickendam, "Beruria kedemut analogit-niggudit leRabbi Meir," *Derekh aggadah* 2 (1999): 37-63.

3 The association of the Beruria figure with certain family relations may have been invented. Yifat Monnickendam suggests that the claim that Rabbi Meir was married to Beruria, who was purported to be the daughter of the important sage and martyr Rabbi Hanina ben Tradyon, made up for some of the flaws in the portrait of Rabbi Meir, including the facts that he was a descendant of converts, that his father was never mentioned, and that he insisted on studying with his teacher Elisha ben Abuya, even after the latter became a heretic. Monnickendam, "Beruria kedemut analogit-niggudit, 60-62.

4 The translation is based on the version in M.S. Zuckermandel, *Tosephta Based on the Erfurt and Vienna Codices*, Second Edition (Jerusalem: Bamberger and Wahrmann Publishers, 1937), 573-574.

5 The translation is based on the version in M.S. Zuckermandel, *Tosephta Based on the Erfurt and Vienna Codices*, Second Edition (Jerusalem: Bamberger and Wahrmann Publishers, 1937), 578-579.

6 Although the classic Vilna edition of the Talmud identifies him as a Sadducee (*tseduqi*), there is a wide consensus that the original term was heretic (*mina*), but due to censorship of the Talmud by European Christian authorities, it was changed to *tseduqi*, because *mina* may have referred to the Christian heresy of the time, and any negative portrayal of Christians was offensive to those authorities.

7 This is a translation of the version in Shlomo Buber, ed., *Midrash mishlei* (Vilna: The Widow and Brothers Romm, 1893), 108-109. For a comparison of this story with Jewish folktales with a similar motif, see Aliza Shenhar, "Le'amamiyyutah shel aggadaṭ Beruria eshet Rabbi Meir," *Meḥqerei hamerkaz leḥeqer hafolqlor* 3 (1973): 223-227.

8 Monnickendam, "Beruria kedemut analogit-niggudit, 43.

9 Tova Hartman and Charlie Buckholtz, *Are You Not a Man of God? Devotion, Betrayal, and Social Criticism in Jewish Tradition* (New York: Oxford University Press, 2014), 103.

10 Ibid., 103-104.

11 Monnickendam, "Beruria kedemut analogit-niggudit, 55; Shmuel Faust, "Mot banav shel Rabbi Meir, *Makor rishon* 13 April 2006.

12 Chaim Licht, *Be'avotot shekhol: iyyunim be'asarah sippurei aggadah al hashekhol be'olomam shel ḥakhamim* (Jerusalem: Carmel, 2007), 148.

13 Shulamit Valler, *Tsa'ar umetsuqah besippurei hatalmud* (Tel Aviv: Hakibbutz Hameuchad, 2012), 202.
14 Ibid. 203.
15 Monnickendam, "Beruria kedemut analogit-niggudit," 55.
16 Licht, *Be'avotot shekhol*, 159; Faust, "Mot banav shel Rabbi Meir."
17 Monnickendam, "Beruria kedemut analogit-niggudit," 44.
18 Ibid., 53.
19 Moshe Lavee, "Qabbalat ha'aḥer veha'aḥerut: tahalikhei havlatah vetishtush besippurei ḥazal," *Mishlav* 37 (2002): 92-93.
20 Ibid., 91-92.
21 Ibid, 92n57.
22 Ibid, 92-93.
23 Ibid, 92.
24 Monnickendam, "Beruria kedemut analogit-niggudit," 45.
25 Ibid.
26 Hartman and Buckholtz, *Are You Not a Man of God?*, 93.
27 Ibid.
28 Ibid., 99.
29 Ibid.
30 Dalia Hoshen, *Beruria the Tannait: A Theological Reading of a Female Mishnaic Scholar* (Lanham: University Press of America, 2007), 1.
31 Ibid., 11-12.
32 Ibid., 22. Hoshen's interpretation serves well the approach today of religiously observant women who are not willing to challenge the discrepancy in ritual obligation between men and women but do demand equal access of women to Torah study.
33 Weiss and HaCohen, *Immahot betippul*, 183.
34 Ibid., 185.
35 Ibid.
36 Ibid., 185.
37 Ibid., 188-189.
38 Ibid., 189-191.
39 Ibid., 193.
40 Ibid., 193-194.
41 Ibid., 198-199.
42 Monnickendam, "Beruria kedemut analogit-niggudit," 58.
43 Ibid., 58-59.
44 Weiss and HaCohen, *Immahot betippul*, 212.
45 Ibid., 215.
46 Ibid., 215-217.
47 Ibid., 217.
48 Dalia Hoshen, "Beruria hatanna'it: qeriah te'ologit bedemutah shel talmidat ḥakhamim basifrit hatalmudit," *Akdamot* 22 (2009): 184.
49 Daniel Boyarin, "Diakhronyah mul sinkhronyah: 'ma'aseh deBeruria,'" *Meḥqerei yerushalayim befolqlor yehudi* 11-12 (1990): 8.
50 Hartman and Buckholtz, *Are You Not a Man of God?*, 106.
51 Eitam Henkin, "Ta'alumat 'ma'aseh deBeruria,'" 143.
52 Ibid., 144-145.
53 Tal Ilan, *Integrating Women into Second Temple History* (Tübingen: Mohr Siebeck, 1999), 189-194. Here, Ilan notes that the section of the Talmud in which the Rabbi Meir legend appears actually makes the point that men are just as easily prone to be seduced as women.

54 Hoshen, *Beruria the Tana'it*, 71; Hoshen, "Beruria hatanna'it, 184-185. Eitam Henkin presents a similar interpretation. Henkin, "Ta'alumat 'ma'aseh deBeruria,'" 157.

55 Boyarin, "Diakhronyah mul sinkhronyah," 13.

56 Ibid., 14-15. Ruth Calderon observes that the story has functioned well over the years in discouraging women from studying Torah. Ruth Calderon, *Hashuq, habayit. halev: aggadot talmudiyyot* (Jerusalem: Keter, 2001), 147.

57 Hartman and Buckholtz, *Are You Not a Man of God?*, 112, 114.

58 Ibid., 115.

59 Avraham Grossman, *Ḥasidot umordot: nashim yehudiyyot be'eiropah beyemei habeinayim* (Jerusalem: Merkaz Zalman Shazar, 2003), 266-272.

60 Ibid., 269. Brenda Bacon and Dalia Hoshen cite the version of the Beruria story in *Ḥibbur yafeh min hayeshu'ah* approvingly as providing strong evidence to counter the negative view of Beruria presented in the Rashi story. See Bacon, "Keitsad nesapper et sippur sof ḥayyeha shel Beruria," in *Lehiyot ishah yehudiyyah*, ed. Margalit Shilo (Jerusalem: Kolekh; Urim, 2001), 129-130 and Hoshen, "Beruria hatanna'it," 185.

61 Yoel Bin-Nun: "'Ma'aseh deBeruria': al biryonim, al yeladim metim ve'al ta'alulei hashilton haromi," *Netu'im: bitta'on le'inyenei torah shebe'al peh* 17 (2001): 41-56.

62 This point is particularly emphasized in Hartman and Buckholtz, *Are You Not a Man of God?*, 93-94.

Chapter 5

Eros Repressed and Restored: Rabbi Hiya Bar Ashi and Heruta

1 For a discussion of the association of the evil inclination with sexuality in some rabbinic texts, see Ishay Rosen-Zvi, *Demonic Desires: Yetzer Hara and the Problem of Evil in Late Antiquity* (Philadelphia: University of Pennsylvania Press, 2011), Chapter 6.

2 Yaara Inbar, *Ḥalom shel bein hashemashot: iyyun uderishah besippurim talmudiyyim* (Tel Aviv: Miskal-Yedioth Ahronoth Books and Chemed Books, 2013), 57.

3 Ido Hevroni, "Gera be'eynei desatan: semalim umerḥavei mashma'ut beqovets sippurei pittuy mitalmud bavli qiddushin 81 a-b," (PhD diss., Bar Ilan University, 2005), 180.

4 Yair Barkai, *Hasippur hamini'aturi* (Jerusalem: David Shun Foundation; Ministry of Education and Culture, 1986), 129.

5 In another story that is grouped with the stories about Rabbi Meir, Rabbi Akiva, and Rabbi Hiya, a character named Plimo mocks Satan, and his arrogance is undermined when Satan disguises himself as a disgusting beggar and Plimo relates to him in a most insensitive manner (B. Kiddushin 81a-b).

6 Shlomo Naeh, "Ḥeruta," in *Sugyot bemeḥqar hatalmud: yom iyyun letsiyyun ḥamesh shanim lepetirato shel Ephraim E. Urbach*, eds. Esther Goldberg and Tsofiyah Lasman (Jerusalem: Ha'aqademyah Hale'umit Hayisra'elit Lemada'im, 2001), 12-13.

7 Ibid., 23.

8 Ari Elon observes that Rabbi Hiya's private prostration sets up a situation in which his wife can learn about his concerns without his knowing it. Ari Elon, "Hasimbolizatsyah shel markivei ha'alilah basippur hatalmudi," (masters thesis, Hebrew University, 1982), 42.

9 Admiel Kosman, *Massekhet nashim: ḥokhmah, ahavah, ne'emanut, teshuqah, yofi, min, qedushah: qeri'ah besippurim talmudiyyim verabaniyyim ushenei midreshei shir* (Jerusalem: Keter, 2007), 86.

10 Ruhama Weiss and Avner HaCohen, *Immahot betippul: massa psikhologi-sifruti im gibborot hatalmud* (Tel Aviv: Miskal-Yedioth Ahronoth Books and Chemed Books, 2012), 103-104.

11 Ibid., 87.
12 Kosman, *Massekhet nashim*, 86.
13 Barkai, *Hasippur hamini'aturi*, 130.
14 Elon, "Hasimbolizatsyah shel markivei ha'alilah, 42.
15 Ibid., 43.
16 Ibid.
17 Barkai, *Hasippur hamini'aturi*, 130; Weiss and HaCohen, *Immahot betippul*, 91-92.
18 Hevroni, "Gera be'eynei desatan," 192.
19 Inbar, *Ḥalom shel bein hashemashot*, 66.
20 Elon, "Hasimbolizatsyah shel markivei ha'alilah," 43.
21 Weiss and HaCohen, *Immahot betippul*, 92.
22 Ruth Calderon, *Hashuq. habayit. halev: aggadot talmudiyyot* (Jerusalem: Keter, 2001), 54.
23 Inbar, *Ḥalom shel bein hashemashot*, 65.
24 Weiss and HaCohen, *Immahot betippul*, 95-96.
25 Ibid., 96. See the discussions of possible meanings of the name Heruta in Barkai, *Hasippur hamini'aturi*, 131; Naeh, "Ḥeruta," 14-20; and Hevroni, "Gera be'eynei desatan," 194-202.
26 Ishay Rosen-Zvi, "Yetser hara, miniyyut ve'issurei yiḥud: pereq be'antropologyah talmudit," *Te'oryah uviqoret* 14 (1999): 80. "The verb with the root *q-sh-t* [which describes the physical preparations of Rabbi Hiya's wife]," writes Ido Hevroni, "connotes generally making oneself pretty, and we have not found any place it indicates disguise or camouflage. In most of the places that the term appears it indicates preparation for sexual relations. We would note that this action is the most that a (pious) woman may do when she wants marital relations with her husband, because an explicit request for such relations is considered in the Talmud to be an act of immodesty." Hevroni, "Gera be'eynei desatan," 192.
27 Barkai, *Hasippur haminiaturi*, 131.
28 Inbar, *Ḥalom shel bein hashemashot*, 67.
29 Calderon, *Hashuq. habayit. halev*, 55; Kosman, *Massekhet nashim*, 87.
30 Weiss and HaCohen, *Immahot betippul*, 89-90.
31 Barkai, *Hasippur hamini'aturi*, 130.
32 Ibid., 132-133; Calderon, *Hashuq. habayit. halev*, 55. An example of *tava* as connoting a man demanding sexual satisfaction from his wife may be found in a Talmudic story about Rava who, having been sexually aroused by a woman who was not his wife, went home and demanded his wife have relations with him (B. Ketubot 65a). See the interpretation of this story in Admiel Kosman, *Massekhet nashim*, 94-99.
33 Weiss and HaCohen, *Immahot betippul*, 97-98.
34 Kosman, *Massekhet nashim*, 87.
35 Hananel Mack, "Al gevarim shehitpatu akh ḥata'am lo alah beyadam: ḥamishah sippueri ḥazal al ḥot'im koshlim," in *Higgayon leyonah: hebbetim ḥadashim beḥeqer sifrut hamidrash, ha'aggadah vehapiyyut: qovets meḥqarim likhevodo shel Professor Yonah Fraenkel bimelot lo shivim veḥamesh shanim*, eds. Yehoshua Levinson,Yaakov Elbaum, and Galit Hasan-Rokem (Jerusalem: Magnes Press, 2006), 439.
36 Barkai, *Hasippur hamini'aturi*, 131.
37 Ibid.
38 Ibid., 131-132; Rosen-Zvi, "Yetser hara, 81; Shulamit Valler, *Nashim baḥevrah heyehudit betequfat hamishnah vehatalmud* (Tel Aviv: Hakibbutz Hameuchad, 2000), 50; Naeh, "Ḥeruta," 23; Mack, "Al gevarim shehitpatu," 439-440.
39 I thank Tsafi Sebba-Elran for this point.
40 Inbar, *Ḥalom shel bein hashemashot*, 69.
41 Avigdor Shinan, "Ishah, massekhah vetaḥposet besifrut ha'aggadah shel ḥazal." *Migvan de'ot vehashqafot: al panim, massekhah vehitḥapsut besifriyyot tarbuntenu* 6 (1996): 44.

42 Kosman, *Massekhet nashim*, 87.
43 Hevroni, "Gera be'eynei desatan," 205.
44 Mack, "Al gevarim shehitpatu, 441-442.
45 Barkai, *Hasippur hamini'aturi*, 132. In one Talmudic passage it is stated that if a man engages in sexual relations with his wife while fantasizing that he is having relations with another woman, the children conceived by this sexual act, who are referred to as *benei temurah*, will be born defective. According to Rashi, because the man was thinking of adultery these children are close to having the status of *mamzerim*, children born as the result of a forbidden sexual act such as adultery or incest. (B. Nedarim 20b).
46 Kosman, *Massekhet nashim*, 91. Emphasis in the original.
47 Ibid., 92. Emphasis in the original.
48 Calderon, *Hashuq. habayit. halev*, 56.
49 Ibid.
50 Weiss and HaCohen, *Immahot betippul*, 116-117.
51 Ibid., 117.
52 Rosen-Zvi, "Yetser hara," 81.
53 Ibid.
54 Valler, *Nashim baḥevrah hayehudit*, 51.

Chapter 6

An Ideal Marriage: Rabbi Akiva and the Daughter of Ben Calba Savua

1 Avigdor Shinan, "Shalosh neshotav shel Rabbi Akiva," *Massekhet* 2 (2004): 11.
2 The words were set to music by Moni Amerilio and the song was sung in the festival by Rivka Zohar. For a discussion of how Dalia Ravikovitch drew on rabbinic texts to write her poem, see Shinan, "Shalosh neshotav," 11-25. The appeal of the story has inspired many retold versions by a variety of authors. See Tali Yaniv, "Al ahavatam shel Rabbi Akiva veRachel: legilgulo shel sippur talmudi el hasifrut ha'ivrit bat zemanenu," *Talpiyot* 13-14 (2006): 259-268 and Admiel Kosman, *Nashiyyut be'olamo haruḥani shel hasippur hatalmudi* (Tel Aviv: Hakibbutz Hameuchad, 2008), 111-126. For an overview of the development of the way the story was told throughout history, see Dror Eydar, "Rabbi Akiva veRachel," *Entsiqlopedya shel hasippur hayehudi: sippur oqev sippur* Vol. 2, eds. Yoav Elstein, Avidov Lipsker, Rella Kushelevsky (Ramat Gan: Bar Ilan University, 2009), 145-182.
3 Rabbi Akiva's wife is popularly referred to in Israel as Rachel. However, as Tal Ilan has argued, she is identified as Rachel only in one rabbinic text, in Avot de-Rabbi Natan, which Ilan understands to be the latest rabbinic version of the story of Akiva's origins. Ilan speculates that the assignment of the name Rachel to Akiva's wife in this later text may be based on an expression used to refer to a similarity between Akiva's wife and her mother, "the sheep follows the sheep" in B. Ketubot 63a. As she notes, the Aramaic term for "sheep" (*raḥela*) is from the same root as the name Rachel (*Raḥel*), so perhaps the author of the version in Avot de-Rabbi Natan understood that comment "to hint at the name of the woman by making a deliberate pun on her name." Tal Ilan, *Mine and Yours Are Hers: Retrieving Women's History from Rabbinic Literature* (Leiden, New York, Köln: Brill, 1997), 289-290. Daniel Boyarin suggests that the assignment of the name of Rachel to Akiva's wife fits well with the fact that their story is parallel in certain ways to the romantic biblical story of the relationship of Jacob (whose name in Hebrew, Yaakov, sounds like Akiva) and Rachel. Daniel Boyarin, *Habasar shebaruaḥ: siaḥ haminiyyut batalmud* (Tel Aviv: Am Oved, 1999), 156.

4 From the interpretation of the story by Udi Leon in Yair Barkai, *Hasippur hamini'aturi* (Jerusalem: David Shun Foundation; Israeli Ministry of Education, 1986), 113.

5 Oded Yisraeli, "Qiddushin, nissu'in vetalmud torah besippurei Rabbi Akiva uBat Calba Savua," *Asuppot: bitta'on le'inyenei aggadah* 1 (2010): 100-101.

6 From the interpretation of the story by Udi Leon in Barkai, *Hasippur hamini'aturi*, 114.

7 Ibid., 113.

8 Ibid.

9 Ibid., 115; Kosman, *Nashiyyut be'olamo haruḥani*, 84.

10 Moshe Lavee, "Qabbalat ha'aḥer veha'aḥerut: tahalikhei havlatah vetishtush besippurei ḥazal, *Mishlav* 37 (2002): 104.

11 For a discussion of this series of stories, see Shulamit Valler, "Qovets hasippurim besugyat qetubot 62b-63," *Tura* 1 (1989): 95-108.

12 B. Ketubot 61b-63a. See the discussion of this passage in Yehuda Brandes, *Aggadah lema'aseh* Vol. 1 (Jerusalem: The Jewish Agency for Israel-Eliner Library; Beit Morasha, 2005), 153-181. Brandes's discussion of this passage is in keeping with his approach to Talmudic stories in which he seeks to demonstrate that stories expand upon the legal discussions, providing real life situations to which the law applies. One of the stories in this passage, about Rabbi Rahumi who only came home from his Torah study once a year on the eve of Yom Kippur, was read by Ruth Calderon in her inaugural Knesset speech, as I discussed in my Introduction.

13 Valler, "Qovets hasippurim," 101-102.

14 Yonah Fraenkel, *Iyyun be'olamo haruḥani shel sippur ha'aggadah* (Tel Aviv: Hakibbutz Hameuchad, 1981), 114.

15 Ibid., 115.

16 Ibid.

17 Kosman, *Nashiyyut be'olamo haruḥani*, 95-96.

18 Ibid., 96.

19 Ibid., 92.

20 From the interpretation of the story by Udi Leon in Barkai, *Hasippur haminiaturi*, 117.

21 Kosman, *Nashiyyut be'olamo haruḥani*, 87. Emphasis in the original.

22 Fraenkel, *Iyyun be'olamo haruḥani*, 114.

23 Shama Friedman posits that the version in Nedarim is later than that in Ketubot. Shama Friedman, "A Good Story Deserves Retelling: The Unfolding of the Akiva Legend," *JSIJ* 3 (2004): 62-90.

24 David Zimmerman chose the version in Nedarim for his collection of Talmudic stories. He did so, most likely, because the unifying theme of his collection is "love" and this version has more romantic details than does the version in Ketubot. David Tzimmerman, *Shemonah sippurei ahavah min hatalmud vehamidrash* (Tel Aviv: Sifriat Poalim, 1981), 65-72.

25 In a passage in the Jerusalem Talmud Tractate Shabbat, it is told that even as Akiva was concerned with tidying her hair, she was willing to go so far as to sell her hair to raise money to support him so he could study Torah: "Once Rabbi Akiva made for his wife [jewelry in the shape of] a city of gold. The wife of Rabban Gamliel saw this and was jealous of her. She came and said to her husband [that she wanted such jewelry]. He said to her, "Did you do for me what she did for him? She sold the locks of her hair and gave [the money she received] to him so that he could study Torah" (J. Shabbat Chapter 6, Halakhah 1).

26 Friedman, "A Good Story Deserves Retelling," 75-76.

27 Oded Yisraeli, "Qiddushin, nissu'in," 101.

28 Ibid., 101-102. Contemporary Israeli readers have been less interested in an alternative story about the origins of Rabbi Akiva as a Torah scholar: "What was the beginning of Rabbi Akiva? They said: He was forty years old and had not studied anything. Once he was sitting by the opening of a well. He said, 'Who carved this stone?' They said to him,

'The water that constantly falls on it every day.' They said to him: 'Akiva, don't you know the verse "Water wears down stone [Job 14:19]?"' He immediately concluded a fortiori reasoning that applied to himself: 'If something soft [water] can carve that which is hard [stone], even more so will the words of Torah that are as hard as iron be engraved on my heart which is flesh and blood.' He immediately turned to study Torah. He and his son went to study with a teacher of children. He said to him, 'Rabbi, teach me Torah.' Rabbi Akiva took one end of the tablet and his son took one end of the tablet. He wrote for him [the Hebrew letters] aleph, bet and he learned them, [the Hebrew letters] aleph, tav and he learned them, [the biblical book of] Leviticus (*torat kohanim*) and he learned it. He kept learning until he learned the whole Torah" (Avot de-Rabbi Natan, chapter 6). Although the oft-cited detail that Rabbi Akiva was forty years old when he first studied Torah comes from this source, the rest of the story which makes no reference to a romantic relationship between Akiva and his wife and contains the somewhat pathetic image of Rabbi Akiva going to elementary school with his son, has not attracted contemporary readers as much as the versions of his origins in Ketubot and Nedarim.

29 Boyarin, *Habasar shebaruaḥ*, 154-155.

Chapter 7

Human Failings and National Destruction: Kamtza and Bar Kamtza

1 Note, for example, the following two headlines from the Israeli daily *Haaretz*: "The Reconciliation Between Hamas and Fatah Does Not Portend the Destruction of the Third Temple" (*hapiyyus bein ḥamas lefataḥ eino mevasser et ḥurban bayit shelishi*, 24 April 2014) and "Reactions to the Article by Shlomo Avineri: Between the Destruction of the Third Temple and a Realistic Policy" (*teguvot lema'amaro shel Shlomo Avineri: bein ḥurban bayit shelishi lemediniyyut re'alistit*, 3 October 2015).

2 The conversation from which this quotation is taken was preserved on a recording made that day, which was released to the public by the Ministry of Defense in October, 2013 on the occasion of the fortieth anniversary of the outbreak of the war. For discussions of this conversation see Mordechai Bar-On, *Moshe Dayan: Israel's Controversial Hero* (New Haven and London: Yale University Press, 2012), 171; Mordechai Bar-On, *Moshe Dayan: qorot ḥayyav 1915-1981* (Tel Aviv: Am Oved, Hamikhlalah Ha'aqademit Sapir, 2014), 281-282; and Yair Sheleg, "Hasanegor hagadol," *Makor rishon* 26 December 2014; After the war, Dayan confirmed that he had made that statement to Benny Peled, although in the interview he stated that he had said to Peled, "The Third Temple is in danger (*habayit hashelishi besakkanah*)." In that interview, he claimed that it would be a mistake to interpret his words then as reflecting his feeling at the time that Israel would be defeated. The expression, he insisted, was only meant to have a literary flourish to it (*safah melitsit*). See Yaakov Erez, ed., *Siḥot im Moshe Dayan* (Tel Aviv: Massada, 1981), 85.

3 Binyamin Lau, "Zikkayon al tenai," *Makor rishon* 19 November 2010.

4 Binyamin Lau, *Yirmiyahu: goralo shel ḥozeh* (Tel Aviv: Miskal-Yedioth Ahronoth Books and Chemed Books, 2010), 272-273. This notion has been credited to Yitzhak Herzog, who as Chief Rabbi of the Land of Israel, it is said, asserted it during the period of the Holocaust. See Shmuel Avidor Hacohen, *Yaḥid bedoro: megillat ḥayyav shel haga'on Rabbi Yitzhak Izak Halevi Herzog rosh rabbanei yisra'el* (Jerusalem: Keter, 1980), 163.

5 Lau, *Yirmiyahu*, 273.

6 Lau, "Zikkayon al tenai."
7 Lau, *Yirmiyahu*, 273.
8 Binyamin Kelmanson, *Al mah avdah ha'arets: iyyunim be'aggadot haḥurban* (Otniel: Yeshivat Otniel, 2009), 21.
9 Ibid.
10 Yael Levine Katz, "'Al Kamtza uBar Kamtza ḥarvah yerushalayim: iyyunim bemesorot hasippur," *Derekh aggadah* 3 (2000): 38.
11 Ibid., 35.
12 Aryeh Yoeli, "Lo Kamtza velo Bar Kamtza: mi be'emet ashem baḥurban" <http://www.srugim.co.il/22203>.
13 Kelmanson, *Al mah avdah ha'arets*, 24.
14 Ibid., 23-24.
15 Gil Nativ, "Mi ashem beḥurban yerushalayim? iyyun ba'aggadah 'Al Kamtza uBar Kamtza,'" *Siaḥ mesharim* 22 (1991): 17.
16 Yoeli, "Lo Kamtza velo Bar Kamtza."
17 Ibid.
18 Katz, "Al Kamtza uBar Kamtza," 37.
19 Kelmanson, *Al mah avdah ha'arets*, 26.
20 Ibid.
21 Ibid.
22 Ibid.
23 Nativ, "Mi ashem," 16; Katz, "Al Kamtza uBar Kamtza," 40.
24 Pinchas Mandel, "Aggadot haḥurban: bein erets yisra'el lebavel" in: *Merkaz utefutsot: erets yisra'el vehatefutsot beyemei bayit sheni, hamishnah vehatalmud*, ed. Yeshayahu Gafni (Jerusalem: Merkaz Zalman Shazar, 2004), 153.
25 See Shmuel Lewis, *Velifnei kavod anavah: ide'al ha'anavah keyesod besefatam hamusarit shel ḥazal* (Jerusalem: Magnes Press, 2013).
26 Daniel Schwartz, "Od leshe'elat 'Zechariah ben Avkulas—anvetanut o qana'ut?'" *Zion* 53, no. 3 (1988): 314.
27 Nativ, "Mi ashem," 17.
28 Mandel, "Aggadot haḥurban," 153-154.
29 Kelmanson, *Al mah avdah ha'arets*, 22.
30 Yehoshua Grinberg, "Al mah (be'emet) ḥarav habayit," *Mabua* 41 (2004): 82, 83.
31 Anat Yisraeli-Taran, *Aggadot haḥurban: mesorot haḥurban basifrut hatalmudit* (Tel Aviv: Hakibbutz Hameuchad, 1997), 23. She hypothesizes that this approach may reflect the later perspective of sages in Babylonia who viewed the rebellion negatively.
32 This introduction refers not only to the Kamtza and Bar Kamtza story but also to two other stories that tell of seemingly minor events that caused other acts of destruction by the Romans: "on account of a chicken and a hen Tur Malka was destroyed; on account of a peg of a chariot Betar was destroyed."
33 Yisraeli-Taran, *Aggadot haḥurban*, 20. A similar observation may be found in Katz, "Al Kamtza uBar Kamtza," 49.
34 Kelmanson, *Al mah avdah ha'arets*, 29. Some scholars have sought to connect this story of the refusal by Rabbi Zechariah ben Avkulus to sacrifice the animal sent by the Romans with the account by Josephus of the decision by the High Priest Elazar ben Hananiah to stop making sacrifices donated by Gentiles, which was in effect an act of rebellion against Rome, and some identify Rabbi Zechariah ben Avkulus with the figure of Zechariah ben Amphikaleus, an anti-Roman zealot. See David Rokeah, "Zechariah ben Avkulus: anvetanut o qana'ut?" *Zion* 53, no. 1 (1988): 53-56; Schwartz, "Od leshe'elat 'Zechariah ben Avkulus,'" 313-316; Mandel, "Aggadot haḥurban," 142-143.

BIBLIOGRAPHY

Aderet, Avraham. *Meḥurban letequmah: derekh yavneh beshiqqum ha'umah.* Jerusalem: Magnes Press, 1990.

Almakeis, Zohar. "20 shanah aḥarei restaḥ Rabin: mah ḥidshah hahitḥadshut hayehudit?" *Haaretz* 15 December 2015.

Alon, Eli. "A Fractured Link." *Shedemot* (English version) 3 (1975): 99.

Ararat, Rachel. "Iyyun sifruti ba'aggadah 'Rabbi Yoḥanan veResh Lakish.'" *Bisedei ḥemed* 1-2 (1977): 383-391.

Asulin, David. "Tanuro shel akhnai: bein 'bat qol' le'ro'im et haqolot,'" *Asuppot: bitta'on le'inyenei aggadah* 4 (2013): 169-177.

Avneri, Shmuel. "Biqqoret 'sefer ha'aggadah' userefat kitvei Bialik." *Haaretz* 22 July 2011.

Ayali, Meir. *Kirevivim: ḥinnukh yehudi veḥeqer hameqorot: qubbats vekhunnas al yedei talmidim ve'amitim.* Ed. Avraham Shapira. Tel Aviv: Hakibbutz Hameuchad, 1996.

Bacon, Brenda. "Keitsad nesapper et sippur sof ḥayyeha shel Beruria?" In *Lehiyot ishah yehudiyyah.* Ed. Margalit Shilo. Jerusalem: Kolekh; Urim, 2001, 121-130.

Barkai, Yair. *Hasippur hamini'aturi.* Jerusalem: David Shun Foundation; Ministry of Education and Culture, 1986.

Bar-On, Mordechai. *Moshe Dayan: Israel's Controversial Hero.* New Haven and London: Yale University Press, 2012.

———. *Moshe Dayan: qorot ḥayyav: 1915-1981.* Tel Aviv: Am Oved; Hamikhlalah Ha'aqademit Sapir, 2014.

Bar-Yesha Gershovitz, Yehudit. "Mifgash al hayarden: mi hu sheyakhol laḥazor bo," <http://cms.education.gov.il>.

Beeri, Nurit. *Yatsa letarbut ra'ah: Elisha ben Abuyah—Aḥer.* Tel Aviv: Miskal-Yedioth Ahronoth Books and Chemed Books, 2007.

Beitner, Azaria. *Sippurei yavneh: biqqur ḥolim veniḥum avelim.* Ramat Gan: Bar Ilan University Press, 2011.

Ben-Aharon, Yariv. *Aggadat pumbedita: shi'ur betalmud.* Oranim: Hamidrashah Be'Oranim, 2000.

———. "Higanukh pumbedita." *Shedemot* 115 (1990): 66-70.

———. "My Encounter with Tradition." *Shedemot* (English edition) 3 (1975): 96-98.

Berdyzcewski, Micha Yosef. *Kitvei Micha Yosef Berdyzcewski (Bin-Gorion)* Vol. 1. Eds. Avner Holtzman and Yitzhak Kafkafi. Tel Aviv: Hakibbutz Hameuchad, 1996.

Berlovitz, Yaffa. "'Siḥot ushemu'ot mini qedem:' po'etiqah umetodah betorat ha'ibbud shel Zeev Yavitz." In *Entsiqlopedyah shel hasippur hayehudi: sippur oqev sippur.* Eds. Yoav Elstein, Avidov Lipsker, and Rella Kushelevsky. Ramat Gan: Bar-Ilan University Press, 2004, 203-244.

Bialik, Hayyim Nahman. "Halakhah ve'aggadah." In *Kol Kitvei H. N. Bialik.* Tel Aviv: Dvir, 1938, 207-213.

Bialik, Hayyim Nahman and Yehoshua Hana Ravnitzky, Eds. *The Book of Legends: Sefer Ha-Aggadah.* Trans. William G. Braude. New York: Schocken Books, 1992.

———. *Sefer ha'aggadah im perush ḥadash me'et Avigdor Shinan.* Jerusalem: Avi Chai; Kinneret, Zmora-Bitan, Dvir, 2015.

———. *Sefer ha'aggadah: mivḥar ha'aggadot shebatalmud uvamidrashim.* 3rd edition. Tel Aviv: Dvir, 1960.

Bin-Nun, Yoel. "'Ma'aseh deBeruria:' al biryonim, al yeladim metim ve'al ta'alulei hashilton haromi." *Netu'im: bitta'on le'inyenei torah shebe'al peh* 17 (2001): 41-56.

Blau, Yaakov. "Zeh ha'iyyum haqiyyumi ha'amiti: Ruth Calderon lomedet gemara." <www.kikar.co.il>.

Boyarin, Daniel. *Carnal Israel: Reading Sex in Talmudic Culture.* Berkeley, Los Angeles, London: University of California Press, 1993.

———."Diakhronyah mul sinkhronyah: 'ma'aseh deBeruria.'" *Meḥqerei yerushalayim befolqlor yehudi* 11-12 (1990): 7-17.

———. *Habasar shebaruaḥ: siaḥ haminiyyut batalmud.* Tel Aviv: Am Oved, 1999.

———. "Rabbanim veḥaverim: ha'im yesh yehudim be'toldot haminiyyut?" *Zemanim* 52 (1995): 50-66.

Brand, Yitzhak. "Tanuro shel akhnai: aggadah belev pulmus. *Tarbiz* 75, no. 3-4 (2006): 437-466.

Brandes, Yehuda. *Aggadah lema'aseh* Vol. 1-2. Jerusalem: The Jewish Agency for Israel-Eliner Library; Beit Morasha, 2005; 2011.

Brandes, Yochi. *Hapardes shel Akiva.* Or Yehuda: Kinneret, Zmora-Bitan, Dvir, 2012.

Brodetsky, Modi and David Hillel Wiener. *Ve'im tirtseh emor: ḥevruta bemidrash uve'aggadah.* Jerusalem: Rubin Mass, 2007.

Calderon, Ruth. *Alfa beita talmudi: osef perati.* Tel Aviv: Miskal-Yedioth Ahronoth Books and Chemed Books, 2014.

———. *A Bride for One Night: Talmud Tales.* Trans. Ilana Kurshan. Philadelphia: Jewish Publication Society, 2014.

———. *Hashuq. habayit. halev: aggadot talmudiyyot.* Jerusalem: Keter, 2001.

———. Inaugural Knesset Speech. *Divrei hakenesset* 12 February 2013: 33-37.

———. "Latalmud nikhnesu yeḥefim." <http://www.alma.org.il>.

Caspi, Yair. *Lidrosh Elohim.* Tel Aviv: Miskal-Yedioth Ahronoth Books and Chemed Books, 2002.

———. *Nissayon: psikhologyah veyahadut: massa tiqqun.* Or Yehuda: Kinneret, Zmora-Bitan, Dvir, 2013.

Dreyfus, Yair. "Kol hashea'arim ninalim? qeri'ah ḥadashah besippur tanuro shel akhnai." *Asuppot: bitta'on le'inyenei aggadah* 4 (2013): 157-167.

Dror, Yuval. "Mishelilat hagalut letippuaḥ hatoda'ah hayehudit." *Panim* 24 (2003) <http://www.itu.org.il>.

Elbaum, Dov. *Into the Fullness of the Void: A Spiritual Autobiography.* Trans. Azzan Yadin. Woodstock, Vt.: Jewish Lights, 2013.

———. *Massa baḥalal hapanuy.* Tel Aviv: Am Oved, 2007.

Elbaum, Yaakov, Ed. *Lehavin divrei ḥakhamim: mivḥar divrei mavo la'aggadah velamidrash mishel ḥakhmei yemei habeinayim*. Jerusalem: Mosad Bialik, 2000.

———. "Sefer ha'aggadah: pirqei mavo." *Meḥqerei yerushalayim besifrut ivrit* 10-11 (1987): 375-397.

Elon, Ari. *Alma di*. Tel Aviv: Miskal-Yedioth Ahronoth Books and Chemed Books and Bait-Hebrew Creation, 2011.

———. *Ba el haqodesh: lamed vav aggadot nistarot.* Tel Aviv: Miskal-Yedioth Ahronoth Books and Chemed Books, 2005.

———. *From Jerusalem to the Edge of Heaven: Meditations on the Soul of Israel*. Trans. Tikva Frymer-Kensky. Philadelphia: Jewish Publication Society, 1996.

———. "Hasimbolizatsyah shel markivei ha'alilah basippur hatalmudi." Masters thesis, Hebrew University, 1982.

Elon, Emuna. *Bamufla mimenni.* Or Yehuda: Kinneret, Zmora-Bitan, Dvir, 2012.

Englender, Yakir. "Hapersonah vehatsel: perush yungiani lesippur ḥayyehem umotam shel R. Yohanan veResh Lakish. *De'ot* 18 (2004): 32-36.

Englender, Yitzhak. "Tanuro shel akhnai: perushehah shel aggadah." *Shenaton hamishpat ha'ivri shel hamakhon leḥeqer hamishpat ha'ivri* 1 (1974): 45-56.

Erez, Yaakov, Ed. *Siḥot im Moshe Dayan.* Tel Aviv: Massada, 1981.

Ettinger, Shimshon. "Maḥloqet ve'emet: lemashma'ut she'elat ha'emet bahalakhah." *Shenaton hamishpat ha'ivri shel hamakhon leḥeqer hamishpat ha'ivri* 21 (1998): 37-69.

Eydar, Dror. "Rabbi Akiva veRachel." *Entsiqlopedyah shel hasippur hayehudi: sippur oqev sippur* Vol. 2. Eds. Yoav Elstein, Avidov Lipsker, Rella Kushelevsky. Ramat Gan: Bar Ilan University Press, 2009, 145-182.

Farkish, Tali. "Haḥilonim yotsim me'aron hasefarim hayehudi." *Ynet* 20 May 2013.

Faust, Shmuel. *Aggadeta: sippur haderamah hatalmudit*. Tel Aviv: Kinneret, Zmora-Bitan, Dvir, 2011.

———. "Mot banav shel Rabbi Meir." *Makor rishon* 13 April 2006.

———. "Tofa'at habiqqoret bema'asei ḥakhamim min hatalmud habavli. PhD diss., Bar Ilan University, 2010.

Fraenkel, Yonah. *Darkhei ha'aggadah vehamidrash* Vol. 1-2. Tel Aviv: Massada, 1991.

———. *Iyyun be'olamo haruḥani shel sippur ha'aggadah*. Tel Aviv: Hakibbutz Hameuchad, 1981.

———. *Sippur ha'aggadah: aḥdut shel tokhen vetsurah: qovets meḥqarim*. Tel Aviv: Hakibbutz Hameuchad, 2001.

Friedlander, Yehuda, Uzi Shavit, Avi Sagi, Eds. *Hayashan yitḥaddesh veheḥadash yitqaddesh: al zehut, tarbut veyahadut: asuppah lezikhro shel Meir Ayali.* Tel Aviv: Hakibbutz Hameuchad, 2005.

Friedman, Shama. "A Good Story Deserves Retelling: The Unfolding of the Akiva Legend." *JSIJ* 3 (2004): 55-93.

———. Ed. *Ḥamesh sugyot min hatlamud habavli.* Jerusalem: Ha'iggud Leparshanut Hatalmud, 2002.

Furstenberg, Ariel. "Re'ayon im Ruth Calderon." *Zehuyot* 5 (2014): 20-25.

Gan, Alon. "Mitenu'ah shel mesoḥaḥim leḥamamah hamitappaḥat yeḥidim: mifalah shel ḥavurat shedemot." In *Ma'anit halev: minḥat devarim leMuki Tsur*. Ed. Avraham Shapira. Tel Aviv: Hakibbutz Hameuchad; Yad Tabenkin; Bina, 2006, 165-182.

Goodblatt, David. "The Beruriah Traditions." *Journal of Jewish Studies* 26 (1975): 68-85.

Goshen-Gottstein, Alon. "Rabbi Elazar ben Arakh: semel umetsi'ut." In *Yehudim veyahadut beyemei bayit sheni, hamishnah vehatalmud: meḥqarim lekhevodo shel Shmuel Safrai.* Eds. Aharon Oppenheim, Yeshayau Gafni, Menahem Stern. Jerusalem: Yad Yitzhak Ben Zvi, 1993, 173-197.

———. *The Sinner and the Amnesiac: The Rabbinic Invention of Elisha Ben Abuya and Eleazar Ben Arach.* Stanford: Stanford University Press, 2000.

Grinberg, Yehoshua. "Al mah (be'emet) ḥarav habayit." *Mabua* 41 (2004): 80-84.

Grossman, Avraham. *Ḥasidot umordot: nashim yehudiyyot be'eiropah beyemei habeinayim.* Jerusalem: Merkaz Zalman Shazar, 2003.

Hacohen, Shmuel Avidor. *Yaḥid bedoro: megillat ḥayyav shel haga'on Rabbi Yitzhak Izak Halevi Herzog rosh rabbanei yisra'el.* Jerusalem: Keter, 1980.

Hartman, Tova and Charlie Buckholtz. *Are You Not a Man of God? Devotion, Betrayal, and Social Criticism in Jewish Tradition.* New York: Oxford University Press, 2014.

Hasan-Rokem, Galit. *Riqmat ḥayyim: hayestirah ha'amamit besifrut ḥazal.* Tel Aviv: Am Oved, 1996.

———. *Tales of the Neighborhood: Jewish Narrative Dialogues in Late Antiquity.* Berkeley, Los Angeles, London: University of California Press, 2003.

Henkin, Eitam. "Ta'alumat 'ma'aseh deBeruria:' hatsa'at pitaron." *Akdamot* 21 (2008): 140-159.

Hevroni, Ido. "Gera be'eynei desatan: semalim umerḥavei mashma'ut beqovets sippurei pittuy mitalmud bavli qiddushin 81a-b." PhD diss., Bar Ilan University, 2005.

———. *Ḥayyot haqodesh: yetsurei hapere beveit midrasham shel ḥazal.* Tel Aviv: Miskal-Yedioth Ahronoth Books and Chemed Books, 2016.

———. "Zonah velistim beveit hamidrash." *Tekhelet* 31 (2008): 73-89.

Hirschfeld, Ariel. "Qafats lanahar, aḥarei ishah." *Haaretz* 23 October 1992.

Holzer, Elie. "'Either a *Hevruta* Partner or Death:' A Critical View on the Interpersonal Dimensions of *Hevruta* Learning." *Journal of Jewish Education* 75 (2009): 130-149.

Horovits, Dani. *Arba'ah maḥazot.* Ed. Shimon Levy. Ramat Aviv: Tel Aviv University, 2007.

Horowitz, Ariel. "Sefer ha'aggadah: otsar yashan hotsa'ah meḥuddeshet." <bac.org.il>.

Horowitz, Yehoshua. "Yaḥas hage'onim la'aggadah." *Maḥanayim* 7 (1994): 122-129.

Hoshen, Dalia. "Beruria hatana'it: qeriah te'ologit bedemutah shel talmidat ḥakhamim basifrut hatalmudit." *Akdamot* 22 (2009): 168-196.

———. *Beruria the Tannait: A Theological Reading of a Female Mishnaic Scholar.* Lanham: University Press of America, 2007.

Ilan, Tal. *Integrating Women into Second Temple History.* Tübingen: Mohr Siebeck, 1999.

———. *Mine and Yours Are Hers: Retrieving Women's History from Rabbinic Literature.* Leiden, New York, Köln: Brill, 1997.

———. "The Quest for the Historical Beruriah, Rachel, and Imma Shalom." *AJS Review* 22 (1997): 1-17.

Ilan, Tal, Tamara Or, Dorothea M. Salzer, Christiane Steuer, and Irina Wandrey, Eds. *A Feminist Commentary on the Babylonian Talmud: Introduction and Studies.* Tübingen: Mohr Siebeck, 2007.

Inbar, Yaara. *Ḥalom shel bein hashemashot: iyyun uderishah besippurim talmudiyyim.* Tel Aviv: Miskal-Yedioth Ahronoth Books and Chemed Books, 2013.

Israeli, Aliza Elion. *Midrash bamah: qevutsat hate'atron hayerushalmi.* Tel Aviv: Miskal-Yedioth Ahronoth Books and Chemed Books, 2009.

Jacobson, David C. *Beyond Political Messianism: The Poetry of Second-Generation Religious Zionist Settlers.* Boston: Academic Studies Press, 2011.

———. *Creator Are You Listening? Israeli Poets on God and Prayer.* Bloomington and Indianapolis: Indiana University Press, 2007.

———. *Does David Still Play Before You? Israeli Poetry and the Bible.* Detroit: Wayne State University Press, 1997.

———. *Modern Midrash: The Retelling of Traditional Jewish Narratives by Twentieth-Century Hebrew Writers.* Albany: State University of New York Press, 1987.

Kadari, Tamar. "Hanittuaḥ hasifruti nolad bemiqreh. *Makor rishon* 6 September 2012.

Kaniuk, Yoram. *Tashaḥ.* Tel Aviv: Miskal-Yediot Ahronoth and Chemed Books, 2010.

Katz, Yael Levine. "Al Kamtza uBar Kamtza ḥarvah yerushalayim:' iyyunim bemesorot hasippur. *Derekh aggadah* 3 (2000): 33-58.

Katznelson, Berl. *Mahpekhah veshorashim: mivḥar devarim.* Ed. Avinoam Barshai. Tel Aviv: Yaron Golan, 1996.

Kelmanson, Binyamin. *Al mah avdah ha'arets: iyyunim be'aggadat haḥurban.* Otniel: Yeshivat Otniel, 2009.

———. "Torah shebe'al peh—qonfliqt metukhnan bein Elohim la'adam: iyyun meḥuddash besippur tanuro shel akhnai." *Asuppot: bitta'on le'inyenei aggadah* 4 (2013): 145-156.

Kiel, Mark W. "Sefer Ha'aggadah: Creating a Classic Anthology for the People and by the People." *Prooftexts* 17 (1997): 177-197.

Kook, Avraham Yitzhak. *Shemonah qevatsim* Vol. 2. Jerusalem, 2004.

Kosman, Admiel. *Massekhet gevarim: Rav vehaqatsav ve'od sippurim al gavriyyut, ahavah ve'otentiyyut besippur ha'aggadah uvasippur haḥasidi.* Jerusalem: Keter, 2002.

———. *Massekhet nashim: ḥokhmah, ahavah, ne'emanut, teshuqah, yofi, min, qedushah: qeri'ah besippurim talmudiyyim verabaniyyim ushenei midreshei shir.* Jerusalem: Keter, 2007.

———. *Men's World: Reading Masculinity in Jewish Stories in a Spiritual Context.* Trans. Edward Levin. Würzburg: Ergon Verlag, 2009.

———. *Nashiyyut be'olamo haruḥani shel hasippur hatalmudi.* Tel Aviv: Hakibbutz Hameuchad, 2008.

Lau, Binyamin. *Ḥakhamaim* Vol. 1-4. Tel Aviv: Miskal-Yedioth Ahronoth Books and Chemed Books, 2006; 2007; 2008; 2012.

———. *Yirmiyahu: goralo shel ḥozeh.* Tel Aviv: Miskal-Yedioth Ahronoth Books and Chemed Books, 2010.

———. "Zikkayon al tenai." *Makor rishon* 19 November 2010.

Lavee, Moshe. "Qabbalat ha'aḥer veha'aḥerut: tahalikhei havlatah vetishtush besippurei ḥazal." *Mishlav* 37 (2002): 75-114.

Levinson, Yehoshua, Yaakov Elbaum, and Galit Hasan-Rokem, Eds. *Higgayon leYonah: hebbetim ḥadashim beḥeqer sifrut hamidrash, ha'aggadah vehapiyyut: qovets meḥqarim likhevodo shel Professor Yonah Fraenkel bimelot lo shivim veḥamesh shanim.* Jerusalem: Magnes Press, 2006.

Lewis, Shmuel. *Velifnei kavod anavah: ide'al ha'anavah keyesod besefatam hamusarit shel ḥazal.* Jerusalem: Magnes Press, 2013.

Licht, Chaim. *Be'avotot hashekhol: iyyunim be'asarah sippurei aggadah al hashekhol be'olamam shel ḥakhamim.* Jerusalem: Carmel, 2007.

———. *In the Grip of Bereavement: An Analysis of Ten Aggadic Legends on Bereavement in the World of the Sages.* Trans. R. Schwartz. Jerusalem and Lynbrook, NY: Gefen Publishing House, 2009.

———. *Masoret veḥiddush: sugyot besifrut ḥazal.* Givat Haviva: Secular Center for Jewish Creativity, 1989.

Liebes, Yehuda. "Eros ve'ant-eros al hayarden." In *Haḥayyim kemidrash: iyyun bepsikhologyah yehudit likhevod Professor Mordechai Rotenberg.* Eds. Shahar Arzy, Michal Fachler, and Baruch Kahana. Tel Aviv: Miskal-Yedioth Ahronoth Books and Chemed Books, 2004, 152-167.

Lorberbaum, Yair. *In God's Image: Myth, Theology, and Law in Classical Judaism.* New York: Cambridge University Press, 2015.

Luz, Ehud. "Halakhah ve'aggadah bemishnato shel Harav Kook." *AJS Review* 11 (1986): 1-23 (Hebrew section).

Mandel, Pinchas. "Aggadot haḥurban: bein erets yisra'el lebavel." In *Merkaz utefutsah: erets yisra'el vehatefutsot beyemei bayit sheni, hamishnah vehatalmud.* Ed. Yeshayahu Gafni. Jerusalem: Merkaz Zalman Shazar, 2004.

Marani, Rachel, *Lishmot, sippur ahavah.* Or Yehuda: Kinneret, Zmora-Bitan, Dvir, 2016.

Meir, Ofra. *Rabbi Yehudah Hanasi: deyoqno shel manhig bemasorot erets yisra'el ubavel.* Tel Aviv: Hakibbutz Hameuchad, 1999.

———. *Sugyot bapo'etiqah shel aggadot ḥazal.* Tel Aviv: Sifriat Poalim, 1993.

Mirsky, Yehudah. "An Intellectual and Spiritual Biography of Rabbi Avraham Yitzhaq Ha-Cohen Kook from 1865 to 1904." PhD diss., Harvard University, 2007.

Misgav, Uri. "Frayerim ḥilonim rehutim." *Haaretz* 26 February 2013.

Monnickendam, Yifat. "Beruria kedemut analogit-niggudit leRabbi Meir." *Derekh aggadah* 2 (1999): 37-63.

Naeh, Shlomo. "Ḥeruta." In *Sugyot bemeḥqar hatalmud: yom iyyun letsiyyun ḥamesh shanim lepetirato shel Ephraim E. Urbach*. Eds. Esther Goldberg and Tsofiya Lasman. Jerusalem: Ha'aqademyah Hale'umit Hayisra'elit Lemada'im, 2001.

Nativ, Gil. "Mi ashem beḥurban yerushalayim? iyyun ba'aggadah al Kamtza uBar Kamtza." *Siaḥ mesharim* 22 (1991): 16-18.

Nevo, Yehoshafat. "Hayaḥas la'aggadah besifrut hage'onim le'ummat yaḥasam shel ḥakhmei sefarad beyemei habeinayim." *Sha'anan* 13 (2008): 137-151.

Newberg, Adina. "Elu v'Elu: Towards Integration of Identity and Multiple Narratives in the Jewish Renewal Sector in Israel." *International Journal of Jewish Education Research* 5-6 (2013): 231-278.

———. "*Hitchabrut* or Connecting: Liberal Houses of Study in Israel as Political and Spiritual Expression. *Israel Studies Forum* 20, no. 2 (2005): 97-114.

———. "New Prayers, Here and Now: Reconnecting to Israel Through Engaging in Prayer, Poetry, and Song. *Israel Studies Forum* 23, no. 2 (2008): 77-98.

Ofaz, Gad. "Hazekhut lidrosh: darkam shel anshei 'ḥug shedemot' el hameqorot." In *Tura: asuppat ma'amarei hagut umeḥqar bemaḥshevet yisra'el muggeshet leProfessor Shlomo (Simon) Greenberg beshenot gevurotav*. Ed. Meir Ayali. Tel Aviv: Hakibbutz Hameuchad, 1989, 370-381.

———. *Misiaḥ loḥamim el aron hasefarim hayehudi: dor sheni ushelishi baqibbutz beḥippus hazehut hayehudit*. Jerusalem: The Hebrew University of Jerusalem, 2016.

———. "Terumato shel ḥug shedemot letsemiḥatam shel merkazei torah lo-datiyyim beyisra'el." In *Ma'anit halev: minḥat devarim leMuki Tsur*. Ed. Avraham Shapira. Tel Aviv: Hakibbutz Hameuchad; Yad Tabenkin; Bina, 2006, 183-189.

———. "Ziqat haqibbuts lemeqorot hayahadut bemaḥshevet 'ḥug shedemot.'" PhD diss., Hebrew University, 1986.

Oppenheimer, Aharon. *Rabbi Yehuda hanasi*. Jerusalem: Merkaz Zalman Shazar, 2007.

Prag, Orit. "Metaqqen et haruaḥ." <http://www.kibbutz.org.il>.

Rafler, Meir. "Pilpul, tsenzurah vehaskalah: leqoroteha shel parshanut aḥat lesugyat tanuro shel akhnai." *Meḥqeri yerushalayim besifrut ivrit* 18 (2001): 7-18.

Raveh, Inbar. *Me'at meharbeh: aggadot ḥazal mivnim sifrutiyyim utefisot olam*. Or Yehuda: Kinneret, Zmora-Bitan, Dvir, 2008.

Raz, Yoel. "'Lo bashamayim hi'—ha'omnam?! diyyun meḥuddash besugyat 'tanuro shel akhnai' al pi hatalmud habavli vehayerushalmi." In *Pittuḥei ḥotam: sefer hama'amarim shel yeshivat hahesder Orot Shaul*. Petah Tikva: Orot Shaul, 2009, 105-126.

Rokeah, David. "Zechariah ben Avkulus: anvetanut o qana'ut?" *Zion* 53, no. 1 (1988): 53-56.

Rosenak, Avinoam. "Aggadah vehalakhah: hirhurim al megamot behagut uvemeḥqar hafilosofyah shel hahalakhah." In *Massa el hahalakhah: iyyunm bein-teḥumiyyim be'olam haḥoq hayehudi*. Ed. Amichai Berholz. Tel Aviv: Miskal-Yedioth Ahronoth Books and Chemed Books, 2003, 285-312.

———. "Te'oryah upraqsis: terumatam shel ha'aggadah vehasippur haḥazaliyyim lehavanat hahalakha." In *Karmi shelli: meḥqarim ba'aggadah uveparshanutah muggashim leProfessor Carmi Horovitz*. Eds. Nahem Ilan, Avraham Grossman, Arnon Atzmon, Michael Shmidman, Yosef Tabori. New York: Touro College Press, 2012, 193-212.

Rosen-Zvi, Ishay. *Demonic Desires: Yetzer Hara and the Problem of Evil in Late Antiquity*. Philadelphia: University of Pennsylvania Press, 2011.

———. "Yetser hara, miniyyut ve'issurei yiḥud: pereq be'antropologyah talmudit." *Te'oryah uviqoret* 14 (1999): 55-84.

Rubenstein, Jeffrey L. "*Bavli Gittin* 55b-56b: An Aggadic Narrative in Its Halakhic Context. *Hebrew Studies* 38 (1997): 21-45.

Safrai, Shmuel. *Beyemei habayit hasheni uveyemei hamishnah: meḥqarim betoldot yisra'el*. Jerusalem, Magnes Press, 1994.

Saperstein, Marc. *Decoding the Rabbis: A Thirteenth-Century Commentary on the Aggadah*. Cambridge, MA and London, England: Harvard University Press, 1980.

Schlein, Yair, "Tanuro shel akhnai kesug shel tragedyah." *Mo'ed: shenaton lemada'ei hayahadut* 18: 2008: 70-80.

Schwartz, Daniel. "Od leshe'elat 'Zechariah ben Avkulas—anvetanut o qana'ut?'" *Zion* 53, no. 3 (1988): 313-316.

Sebba-Elran, Tsafi, "From *Sefer Ha'aggadah* to the Jewish Bookcase: Dynamics of a Cultural Change." *Jewish Studies Quarterly* 20 (2013): 272-295.

———. "Ḥoni hame'agel ve'alpayim shenot shenah." *Iyyunim betequmat yisra'el* 7 (2014): 5-34.

———. "Misefer ha'aggadah la'aron hasefarim hayehudi; ha'asuppot ha'aggadiyyot umeqoman be'itsuvah shel hayahudut batarbut ha'ivrit." PhD diss., Tel Aviv University, 2009.

———. "'Sefer ha'aggadah' hemshekh umaphekha." *Panim* 55 (2011): 85-93.

Sela, Rotem. "Moreh leḥayyim: yisra'el al pi Dr. Micah Goodman." *Maariv nrg* 16 September, 2010.

Shadmi-Wortman, Sara. "Haqamat hamidrashah 1989-1999: hithavutah shel 'pedegogyah shel zehut.'" In *Massekhet ḥayyim: 20 shanah lamidrashah be'oranim*. Ed. Yoram Wearth. Ramat Yishai: Hamidrashah Be'oranim; Hakibbutz Hameuchad, 2010, 7-34.

Shani, Ayelett. "Berukhim haba'im lameinstrim heḥadash." *Haaretz* 7 December 2012.

Shapira, Avraham. *Or haḥayyim beyom qetannot: mishnat A. D. Gordon umeqoroteha baqabbalah uvaḥasidut*. Tel Aviv: Tel Aviv University; Am Oved, 1996.

———. Ed. *Siaḥ loḥamim: pirqei haqshavah vehitbonenut*. Tel Aviv: Qevutsat Ḥaverim Tse'irim Mehatenu'ah Haqibbutsit, 1968.

Sheleg, Yair. "Hasanegor hagadol." *Makor rishon* 26 December 2014.

———. "Massekhet avot." *Makor rishon* 31 January 2016.

———. *Me'ivri yashan leyehudi ḥadash: renesans hayahadut baḥevrah hayisra'elit*. Jerusalem: The Israel Democracy Institute, 2010.

Shenhar, Aliza. "Le'amamiyyutah shel aggadat Beruria eshet Rabbi Meir," *Meḥqerei hamerkaz leḥeqer hafolqlor* 3 (1973): 223-227.

———. "Sodo shel Rabbi Eliezer. In *Ma'aseh sippur: meḥqarim basipporet hayehudit muggashim leYoav Elstein* Vol. 1. Eds. Avidov Lipsker, Rella Kushelevksy Ramat Gan: Bar Ilan University, 2006, 51-62.

Shinan, Avigdor. "Ishah, massekhah vetaḥposet besifrut ha'aggadah shel ḥazal." *Migvan de'ot vehashqafot: al panim, massekhah vehitḥapsut besifriyyot tarbuntenu* 6 (1996): 29-52.

———. "Shalosh neshotav shel Rabbi Akiva." *Massekhet* 2 (2004): 11-25.

Statman, Daniel, "Otonomyah vesamkhut betanuro shel akhnai." *Meḥqerei mishpat* 24 (2008): 639-662.

Tesler, Yitzhak. "Mitlotsets im Rashi: perush Taharlev al hatorah." *Ynet* 23 August 2014.

Tropper, Amram. *Keḥomer beyad hayotser: ma'asei ḥakhamim besifrut ḥazal.* Jerusalem: Merkaz Zalman Shazar, 2011.

Tsur, Muki. *Lelo ketonet passim.* Tel Aviv: Am Oved, 1976.

———. "Otsar haruaḥ." In *Shedemot veruaḥ: meḥavat hoqarah veyedidut leAvraham Shapira.* Eds. Avihu Zakaki, Paul Mendes-Flohr, Zeev Gries. Jerusalem: Carmel, 2015, 44-53.

Valler, Shulamit. *Nashim baḥevrah hayehudit betequfat hamishnah vehatalmud.* Tel Aviv: Hakibbutz Hameuchad, 2000.

———. *Nashim venashiyyut basippur hatalmudi.* Tel Aviv: Hakibbutz Hameuchad, 1993.

———. "Qovets hasippurim besugyat qetubot 62b-63. *Tura* 1 (1989): 95-108.

———. *Sorrow and Distress in the Talmud.* Trans. Sharon Blass. Boston: Academic Studies Press, 2011.

———. *Tsa'ar umetsuqah basippur hatalmudi.* Tel Aviv: Hakibbutz Hameuchad, 2012.

———. *Woman and Womanhood in the Talmud.* Trans. Betty Sigler Rozen. Atlanta, Ga: Scholars Press, 1999.

Valler, Shulamit and Shalom Razabi. *Siḥot ḥulin batalmud habavli.* Tel Aviv: Am Oved, 2007.

Weiss, Ruhama. *Mitḥayyevet benafshi: qeri'ot meḥuyyavot batalmud.* Tel Aviv: Miskal-Yedioth Ahronoth Books and Chemed Books, 2006.

———. *Okhlim lada'at: tafkidan hatarbuti shel hase'udot besifrut ḥazal.* Tel Aviv: Hakibbutz Hameuchad, 2010.

Weiss, Ruhama and Avner HaCohen. *Immahot betippul: massa psikhologi-sifruti im gibborot hatalmud.* Tel Aviv: Miskal-Yedioth Ahronoth Books and Chemed Books, 2012.

Yaniv, Tali. "Al ahavatam shel Rabbi Akiva veRachel: legilgulo shel sippur talmudi el hasifrut ha'ivrit bat zemanenu." *Talpiyot* 13-14 (2006): 259-268.

Yassif, Eli. *The Hebrew Folktale: History, Genre, Meaning.* Trans. Jacqueline S. Teitelbaum. Bloomington and Indianapolis: Indiana University Press, 1999.

———. *Sippur ha'am ha'ivri: toldotav, sugav, umashma'uto.* Jerusalem: Mosad Bialik; Beersheva: Ben-Gurion University, 1994.

Yisraeli, Anat and Esther Fisher, Eds. *Dorshot tov: perush qevutsati feministi lesugyat issurei yiḥud: qiddushin 80b-82b.* Kiryat Tivon: Hamidrashah Be'Oranim, 2013.

Yisraeli, Oded. "'Ḥuts misha'arei ona'ah:' iyyun besippur ha'aggadah 'tanuro shel akhnai.'" In *Al derekh ha'avot: sheloshim shanah lemikhlelet Yaacov Herzog: qovets ma'amarim benosei torah vehinnukh.* Eds. Amnon Bazak, Shmuel Vigoda, Meir Munitz. Alon Shevut: Tevunot, 2001.

———. "Qiddushin, nissu'in vetalmud torah besippurei Rabbi Akiva uBat Calba Savua." *Asuppot: bitta'on le'inyenei aggadah* 1 (2010): 94-104.

Yisraeli-Taran, Anat. *Aggadot haḥurban: mesorot haḥurban basifrut hatlamudit.* Tel Aviv: Hakibbutz Hameuchad, 1997.

Yoeli, Aryeh. "Lo Kamtza velo Bar Kamtza: mi be'emet ashem baḥurban." <http://www.srugim.co.il>.

Zameret, Zvi. "Mordim umamshikhim: itsuv hashabbat lefi Y.H. Brenner, A.D. Gordon, B. Katznelson, S.H. Bergman, E. Schweid, veM. Ayali." In *Hayashan yitḥaddesh veheḥadash yitqaddesh: al zehut, tarbut veyahadut: asuppah lezikhro shel Meir Ayali.* Eds. Yehuda Friedlander, Uzi Shavit, Avi Sagi. Tel Aviv: Hakibbutz Hameuchad, 2005, 347-373.

———. "Zalman Aran uma'arekhet haḥinnukh." In *He'asor hasheni: 5718-5728.* Eds. Zvi Zameret and Hanna Yablonka. Jerusalem: Yad Yitzhak Ben Zvi, 2000, 61-78.

Zilkha, Yaffa. *Be'eyn aggadat hayerushalmi: pirqei iyyun be'olamah shel aggadat hatalmud hayerushalmi.* Jerusalem: The Jewish Agency for Israel-Eliner Library; Beit Morasha, 2009.

Zimmerman, David. *Shemonah sippurei ahavah min hatalmud vehamidrash.* Tel Aviv: Sifriat Poalim, 1981.

INDEX

Lightning Source UK Ltd.
Milton Keynes UK
UKHW02f2020240418
321581UK00003B/168/P

9 781618 117885